Bitter Flowers, Sweet Flowers

Asian Voices
Series Editor: Mark Selden

Bitter Flowers, Sweet Flowers

East Timor, Indonesia, and the World Community

Richard Tanter, Mark Selden,
and Stephen R. Shalom

ROWMAN & LITTLEFIELD PUBLISHERS, INC.
Lanham • Boulder • New York • Oxford

ROWMAN & LITTLEFIELD PUBLISHERS, INC.

Published in the United States of America
by Rowman & Littlefield Publishers, Inc.
4720 Boston Way, Lanham, Maryland 20706
http://www.rowmanlittlefield.com

12 Hid's Copse Road
Cumnor Hill, Oxford OX2 9JJ, England

British Library Cataloguing in Publication Information Available

Library of Congress Cataloging-in-Publication Data

Tanter, Richard.
    Bitter flowers, sweet flowers : East Timor, Indonesia, and the world community /
Richard Tanter, Mark Selden, and Stephen R. Shalom.
        p.   cm. — (Asian voices)
    Includes bibliographical references and index.
    ISBN 0-7425-0967-2 (alk. paper) — ISBN 0-7425-0968-0 (pbk. : alk. paper)
        1. Timor Timur (Indonesia)—Politics and government.   I. Selden, Mark.
II. Shalom, Stephen Rosskamm, 1948–   III. Title.   IV. Series.
    DS646.57.T55 T36   2000
    959.8′6—dc21   00-062641

Printed in the United States of America

♾ ™ The paper used in this publication meets the minimum requirements of American
National Standard for Information Sciences—Permanence of Paper for Printed Library
Materials, ANSI/NISO Z39.48–1992.

Sweet Flowers

Sweet is the Flower
That goes on the grave
The food for the souls
Of those departed
Called to climb to the summit
Of Mount Matebian

Sweet it becomes
When prepared by the hands
Of women who chew betel nut
And remember the loved one
Laid to rest

Bitter is the Flower
That goes on the grave
On the seventh day
The sign of sorrow
For those who stay

Sweet is the Flower
That goes on the grave
On the twenty-first day
An offering
Of the final goodbye

Sweet is the Flower
That marks the beginning
Of the time to let go
To hold on to the memory
To let go of the grief

Bitter is the Flower
That becomes sweet
Sweet is the Flower
When the soul is at rest

—Fernando Pires and Emanuel Braz

Contents

Illustrations and Poems

ILLUSTRATIONS

Maps

Figures

Table

Chart

POEMS

Acknowledgments

We would like to thank many individuals who made this book possible. Tom Fenton, the managing editor of the *Bulletin of Concerned Asian Scholars* (now renamed *Critical Asian Studies*), supported the project from its earliest journal incarnation and contributed his sharp editorial pen. (The special double issue of *BCAS*, vol. 32, nos. 1 and 2, January–June 2000, contains additional articles that could not be included in the book.) Geoff Gunn, the late George Kahin, Geoff McKee, Sarah Niner, Charlie Scheiner, Gerry van Klinken, and friends at the East Timor Action Network lent their expert knowledge at many points along the way. Steve Cox and Ross Bird generously provided photographs from their wonderful books: Cox's *Generations of Resistance: East Timor* (1995) and Bird's *Inside Out East Timor* (1999). The East Timor Human Rights Centre in Collingwood, Australia graciously allowed us to use one of Ross Bird's photographs from its *Remember, 2000* calendar, a part of the Centre's documentation activities. John Miller kindly gave us some of the photographs he shot while serving as a ballot observer in East Timor during the summer of 1999. Geoff Gunn made available the reproduction of the Cailaco battle map. Kim Keuk-mi provided invaluable assistance with production of visual materials. James McCaughey and Robin Laurie gathered the poetry. We thank Made Tong Supriatma and Ben Abel of Cornell University for assistance with Indonesian terms in our glossary and José Martins for help with Portuguese. David Bourchier helped us identify military officers in Allan Nairn's congressional testimony. All of the authors responded to frantic deadlines and editorial demands as we raced to produce a volume a step ahead of the cataclysmic events that rocked East Timor and Indonesia in the years 1999–2000. Once again Susan McEachern of Rowman & Littlefield was quick to sense the importance of the project and to provide her professional expertise and support from the outset, and our production editor, Cindy Tursman, efficiently moved our project forward.

Editing and writing a book such as this (and the special issue of the journal that preceded it) against the pressure of rapidly unfolding developments in East Timor, as well as the ordinary pressures of publishing deadlines, placed often impossible demands on those around us. Richard is deeply grateful to Luisa Mac-millan for her love and for her political support for the work on this book; Steve continues to be awed by Evelyn Rosskamm Shalom's remarkable forbearance and love; and Mark thanks Kyoko Selden for being there yet again.

All royalties from this book will be donated to *Feton Foen Sae Timor Lorosae* (the Young Women's Organization of East Timor) and the Sa'he Institute for Liberation (or comparable organizations) working in East Timor to help make the bitter flowers sweet.

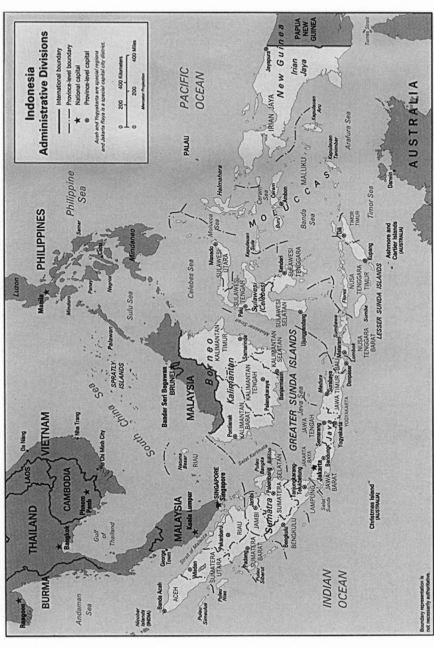

CIA map of Indonesia's administrative divisions, 1998, with East Timor (Timos Timur, lower center) shown as Indonesia's twenty-seventh province.

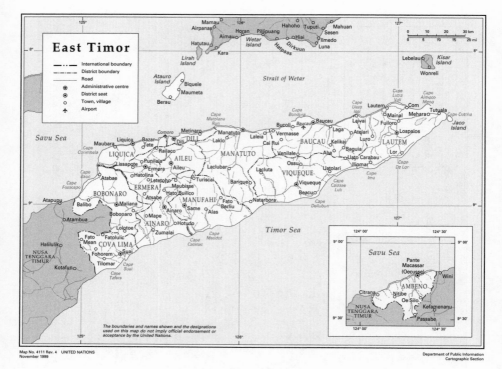

Map of East Timor

Map No. 4111 Rev. 4   UNITED NATIONS
November 1999

Department of Public Information
Cartographic Section

Introduction: East Timor, Indonesia, and the World Community

Richard Tanter, Mark Selden, and Stephen R. Shalom

East Timor is at last, and at terrible human cost, firmly on the road to independence. The significance of its passage to freedom is manifold.

East Timor's independence constitutes one of the final and most poignant moments in the long and bitter history of European colonization and decolonization. Once one of the Spice Islands of European trading lore, Timor under its Portuguese and Dutch masters was a virtual paradigm of the half-millennium of Europe's rise to domination of the world system—and its eventual withdrawal from its colonies.

The struggle for independence did not, however, end with independence from Portugal in 1975. The eight hundred thousand people of East Timor subsequently waged a courageous independence struggle that began with Indonesia's invasion that year and continued over a quarter century of resistance in the face of fierce Indonesian oppression.

East Timor under Indonesian rule was the clearest and most horrific instance of colonialism by a former colony. New Order Indonesia under President Suharto was a state dominated by a military that ran amok both in the wave of anti-Communist killings that took approximately one million Indonesian lives in the years after 1965 and an additional two hundred thousand in East Timor after 1975. For close to a quarter of a century, despite condemnation by successive United Nations' resolutions, Indonesia enjoyed moral and material support from the United States, Japan, Australia, and other powers, facilitating its virtually unconstrained state violence. Indonesia's colonial adventure in East Timor, like most New Order political projects, was decided in secret, carried out for the benefit of the few, burdensome to the Indonesian state politically, diplomatically, and economically, and devastating to the East Timorese.

Indonesia's invasion and occupation of East Timor was a classic product of the Cold War. The United States and its allies supported the Indonesian military dictatorship virtually without question from 1965 to the early 1990s, when, for reasons of strategic and economic interest, these nations began to lose confidence in Suharto. Washington's perennial fear of "communism" and radical national-ism, heightened by military defeat and military withdrawal from Indochina in 1975, led U.S. presidents from Gerald Ford to Bill Clinton to provide the weap-ons, training, money, and international respectability for Jakarta's war on East Timor.

The independence struggle exacted an enormous toll in lives, with the death of more than a quarter of the pre-1975 population in the initial years of conflict. In the paroxysm of Indonesian violence prior to and following the 1999 vote for independence, virtually the entire Timorese population was driven from their homes, with unknown numbers killed. Many were forcibly taken into West Timor or other parts of Indonesia, where a year later, some hundred thousand still re-main, often in desperate circumstances and prevented from returning home. Many thousands are still missing and unaccounted for. Virtually the entire physi-cal infrastructure of the country was deliberately plundered or destroyed by Indo-nesian troops and their militia clients as they withdrew.

The East Timor question is intimately involved in the political turmoil that flowed from the Asian currency and financial crisis which unseated the Suharto dictatorship, gave rise to pro-democracy and nationalist movements throughout Indonesia, and led up to the election of Indonesia's fourth president, Abdurrah-man Wahid. Events in East Timor have strengthened the drive for autonomy or independence in Aceh, West Papua, and other parts of Indonesia.

The struggle for East Timor, both during and after the Cold War, provides a litmus test for issues of international responsibility, posing questions of double standards in unusually clear-cut form. Not only does it reveal the active support by the United States, Japan, Australia, and other powers for the military forces of Indonesia throughout the years of that nation's invasion and repression of East Timor, but also, in the case of the United States, it reveals that some of that sup-port continued in 1999, even as Washington belatedly criticized Indonesian human rights violations and lent its voice to the United Nations–sponsored peace-keeping force.

The protracted independence struggle offers important insight into the role of international solidarity and human rights movements whose determination to support demands for justice over many decades kept the issues alive until such time as the conjuncture of forces at the local and global levels made it possible for the Timorese cause to capture world attention and benefit from a shift in the balance of forces. Today, these same solidarity and human rights groups continue to monitor and support East Timor's passage toward a viable independence.

East Timor will provide an important test of the ability of the international community to contribute to outcomes that will facilitate the efforts of that nation-in-formation, which possesses extraordinary human resources but little else, as a result of the razing of its cities and towns and the plunder and destruction of its economy. For years the people of East Timor have striven to realize their ideals of democracy, community, and development; in the era of transition to independence the extent of international support for these ideals remains to be seen.

The essays in this volume address these themes. Those in Part I, "East Timor: Resistance, Repression, and the Road to Independence," seek to illuminate the dynamics of the long Timorese struggle for independence first from the Portuguese and subsequently from invading Indonesian forces. The focus is on the contribution of two critical institutions in the years since 1975, the National Council of Timorese Resistance (CNRT) and the Catholic Church, while also illuminating the role of youth and students in the resistance.

Part II, "Referendum and Independence," provides four eyewitness accounts of the 1999 ballot and the Indonesian military-supported militia violence before and following the overwhelming vote for independence. The writer-participants were involved with the United Nations Assistance Mission to East Timor (UNAMET) or with independent international monitoring projects. The essays weigh U.N. contributions to independence against the responsibility of the U.N. and leading nations for the massacres. This section includes, too, the voices of East Timorese poets recording the pains of their long struggle and the joys of victory.

The third section on the United States, the world community and East Timor, examines international dimensions of the struggle. Essays explore the role and responsibility of the international community—particularly the United States—and weigh the claims of international law, human rights, and realpolitik. The essays help to clarify and assess the reasons for the turnaround in the position of the powers in 1999, notably those by the United States, Australia, Indonesia, and Japan, as well as the pivotal role played by the United Nations.

The fourth section on Indonesian Politics and East Timor looks at the changing character of the Indonesian state, at the troubled relationship between Indonesia and East Timor, and the sea of changes taking place in Indonesian politics since 1997. The essays explore the impact of Indonesian politics on East Timor and the effect the struggle for independence in East Timor has had on the outlook for the world's fourth most populous country, including the prospects for a society less dominated by the military and more permissive of greater autonomy for the regions that comprise this vast archipelago nation.

The essays in the final section, "The Future of East Timor," consider the prospects for an independent East Timor, charting both the potential and the probable shoals that lie ahead for issues including economic development, security, linguistic and ethnic differences, and social change while analyzing the possible responses of the relevant parties from the resistance forces to the Indonesian government, the United States, and the United Nations.

Our authors are social scientists, writers, poets, journalists, and activists (not mutually exclusive categories), many with lifelong specializations and long experience working on and in Indonesia and East Timor. Many of the contributors have recent, and in quite a few instances long-term, experience in East Timor and

Indonesia. Several witnessed from different parts of East Timor the lead-up to the referendum. Many others among our authors have intimate knowledge of contemporary Indonesian and East Timorese politics, military perspectives, and economics.

Many of the essays in this book were published in earlier form in a special issue of the *Bulletin of Concerned Asian Scholars* (vol. 31, nos. 1 and 2, January–June 2000), written in the eye of the storm in the fall of 1999. In addition to substantial revision and updating of the chapters included here, new essays have been commissioned, strengthening the attention to developments within East Timor.

The struggle for independence by the East Timorese people has been at once inspiring and tragic, presenting important lessons for us all. We dedicate this volume to the hopes for an independent, peaceful, and prosperous East Timor.

Part I

East Timor: Resistance, Repression, and the Road to Independence

The Five-Hundred-Year Timorese *Funu*

Geoffrey C. Gunn

Since Timor was first visited by Portuguese navigators—within years of the passage of the first caravels through the Straits of Malacca in 1511—Portugal has been the dominant external influence on the island, at least on the eastern part. Many Timorese now claim some degree of Portuguese ancestry and many more have adopted the religion of their former colonizer. The exception to Portuguese predominance was the brief but destructive occupation of Timor by Japan (and Australia) during the Pacific War and the near-genocidal impact of the Indonesian military invasion and annexation of the half-island commencing in 1975. Even so, as recent history demonstrates, the Timorese have not easily acquiesced to dominance by outsiders, now or in the past. This chapter sets down the broad contours of that past, investigates how that past has been reclaimed, and reflects on the style of the Timorese resistance or war, loosely labeled *funu* in Timor's Tetum language.

THE SETTING

Timor's location—well-known to American whalers in the nineteenth century—was evoked by the author of *Moby Dick*. Stretching southeastwards "in a continuous line" from the Malay peninsula, Melville wrote, "the long islands of Sumatra, Java, Bally (Bali) and Timor, which, with many others, form a vast mole, or rampart, lengthwise, connecting Asia with Australia, and dividing the long unbroken Indian ocean from the thickly studded oriental archipelagoes."[1] While the deep and narrow straits separating these islands offered passage to the first circumnavigation of the globe, as well as to Melville's migrating whales, the strategic importance of these waterways for U.S. submarines moving from the northern Pacific to the Indian Ocean was also not lost upon Pentagon planners and their Australian counterparts at the time when the Timorese clamored for independence in 1975.

Stretching 470 kilometers along a southwest–northeast axis, 110 kilometers wide at its broadest part, the island of Timor occupies an area of 32,300 square kilometers. Lying about 430 kilometers distant from northern Australia across the Arafura or Timor Sea, the island is situated some eight to ten degrees south of the equator. More than one observer has commented upon the crocodile-like shape of Timor, but the island takes its name from the Malay term for east, reflecting its easternmost location in the archipelago.

Colonial spheres of influence in the eastern archipelago were subject to change, but by the modern period Portuguese administration extended over the eastern part of the island of Timor, including the small enclave of Oecusse on the central north coast, the island of Atauro visible offshore from the capital city of Dili, and Jaco island in the extreme east. With an area of 18,899 square kilometers (official Portuguese source) and a population of 700,000 (1974 figures), Portuguese Timor was considered small. Yet, Timor Loro Sae, as an independent state, would equal in size and population some forty other independent states. In the Southeast Asian region, the territory is four times larger than Brunei Darussalam and forty times larger than Singapore.

The most arid and ecologically precarious of the Lesser Sunda islands, Timor nevertheless bears traces of both the luxuriant rain forests of tropical Indonesia and the arid landscape of northern Australia. Visitors to Timor are surprised to find distinctive eucalyptus and acacia forests along with more typical Southeast Asian flora. As the visiting nineteenth-century English naturalist Alfred Russel Wallace described it, "a vast difference in the natural productions beset the eastern end of the chain from the west, matched by a great contrast in climate, moist in the west with only a short dry season, and dry and parched in the extreme east with only a short wet season."[2] Such ecological vulnerability defined what the modern Dutch geographer F. J. Ormeling called the "Timor problem."[3] Timor, along with the easternmost islands of the Sunda chain, resembles the outer Indonesian islands—where, because of adverse ecological conditions, *ladang* or shifting cultivation predominates—more than it does those areas based upon intensive rice cultivation such as Java and Bali.

From a natural history perspective, Wallace found across the Timor chain a population of bird species derived almost equally from Java and Australia, but quite distinct from both. Of land mammals on Timor, he determined that not one in six was of Australian origin. He found this surprising, especially as the continental shelf of Australia extends to within thirty kilometers of Timor; at the same time it afforded evidence that the two have not been connected in recent geological ages. Timor, he concluded, was a true example of an oceanic island in miniature.[4]

Just as the Timor chain occupies a special niche in natural history, so the island of Timor stands at the crossroads of racial and cultural mixing. Physical anthropologists who have studied Timor all remark upon its racial complexity. Migrations in a past age from both Melanesia and continental Asia have left their mark upon Timor's human ecology. The frizzy-haired Melanesian Antoni or "people of the dry land," now occupying West Timor, are believed to be the original inhabitants of Timor; while the straighter-haired Belu people of the south coast represent a later migration of a Malay type. As Glover observes, generally the later-arriving coastal people have more Malay characteristics and the interior people more resemble the populations of New Guinea and Melanesia. But while the dark-skinned proto-Malay dominate the landscape, language falls into either Malayo-Polynesian or Austronesian, on the one hand, and non-Austronesian, on the other.⁵

In any discussion of indigenous Timorese identity, it should be well understood that colonialism bequeathed its own distinctive *mestiço* or mixed-race culture (more predominant in the towns), including Sino-Timorese, Afro-Timorese, Goan-Timorese, and mixed Portuguese-Timorese. The political importance of all the major ethno-cultural groupings of Timor—from the quintessential Tetum-speaking indigène, styled the "Maubere" by Timor's first independence party, Fretilin, to the so-called mixed race Black Portuguese, *Laran tuqueiros*, or *topasse* of the Oecusse area, to the urbanized Portugalized *mestiço* elite—is central to an understanding of modern Timor history. José Ramos-Horta, cowinner of the 1996 Nobel Peace Prize, has explained this heritage as Melanesian, "which binds us to our brothers and sisters of the South Pacific region; Malay-Polynesian, binding us to Southeast Asia; and the Latin Catholic influence, a legacy of almost five hundred years of Portuguese colonization."⁶

The first Western navigators to touch Timor's shores in the sixteenth century were Portuguese, but their more aggressive commercial and religious rivals, the Dutch, were not far behind. Both, to a degree, were obliged to accommodate to local and regional forms of tributary power. Locally, such power took the form of native coalitions that, surprisingly, endured for a long time. Regionally, neither of the Western powers could survive or prosper without major accommodation from well-entrenched Chinese trading-tributary networks. The role of Timor in the long distance trade in sandalwood gave this otherwise obscure island an unusual prominence, in the view of outsiders.

By setting down the boundary dividing colonial spheres of influence on Timor, however, the two concerned powers, Holland and Portugal, committed a terrible hubris. As with the colonial division of Africa, the powers failed to take into account the ethnic and linguistic heterogeneity of the island's peoples, nor indeed the precolonial political unity—or, at least, cultural bonds—that linked the Tetum-speaking Belu people of central Timor. In 1851, disgraced Governor José Joaquim Lopes de Lima (1851–52), pleading impecunity, sold off to the Dutch the historic Portuguese settlements on Flores and Solor. But the question of colonial boundaries was only settled in 1916 after much complex litigation including numerous complex trade-offs of enclaves.[7] When control over Dutch (West) Timor formally passed to the Republic of Indonesia on November 2, 1949, Portugal, under the Salazar and Caetano dictatorships, delayed the decolonization process in Portugal's territories.

TIMORESE REBELLION

Colonial historiography invariably assigns its military campaigns against rebellious subjects to a benighted pacification or civilization exercise, but national reconstructions of colonial incorporation typically view the doomed stands of rebel chiefs, warriors, and their followers as heroic struggles, wars of independence, and precursors to national liberation. For the colonizer—and the Portuguese in Timor were no exception—the civilizing mission could not proceed without the pacification of rebellious subjects while, ipso facto, the standard colonial agenda of development/exploitation awaited the participation of subjects in metropolitan rituals. As depicted in an eighteenth-century tapestry (see Figure 1.1), the Portuguese (and Dutch) were embroiled in endless rebellions and conflicts for almost the entire duration of their tenure on the island.

Figure 1.1   The Timorese style of war as represented in the Cailaco map (1727), one of the first European images of Timor. Original: Artur Basilio De Sa, A Planta De Cailaco, 1727 (Lisbon: Agencia Geral Das Colonias, divisao de Publicacoes E Biblioteca, 1949). Courtesy: Geoffrey Gunn.

As was also typical in colonial settings, the missionization of erstwhile pagan masses was the test of colonial success. On Timor, the matter was more complex, as state–church relations were always testy and, following the expulsion of the pioneering religious order of Dominicans in 1834, and, in their wake, the Jesuits, the Roman Catholic Church really only made headway late in the century, complaining all the while of a profoundly traditional and animist culture and barbarous beliefs and practices (a particular reference to blood oaths and headcutting).

As the debate surrounding the quincentenary of Columbus's discovery of America reiterated, incorporation was not achieved without extremes of violence, acts of high plunder, and massive deracination if not genocide of the victims, given the unequal exchanges in naval and military technology. Yet, the characterization of anticolonial rebellions that typically confronted outside intruders and erstwhile "civilizers" alike is not so straightforward and, in any case, is the subject of much theorizing as well as hyperbole. First, as was the case in Timor, such rebellions were not of a piece. Second, not all rebellions were anticolonial; they could equally be understood as revolts against this or that traditional power (*liurai,* little kings) or as internecine revolts that pitted one clan or ethnic group against another.

Another phenomenon, widely described in the literature on incorporation, is the proclivity to revolt by devotees of some messianic belief, a practice that predates and postdates the colonial encounter. On Timor, the irrational or "mad" features of certain revolts were widely noted. Messianic forms of rebellion recurred in the *makdok* movement in the context of the Indonesian pogrom against "communists" in West Timor in 1966.[8]

Monocausal accounts such as these often downplay the destabilizing impact of the colonial encounter, especially as colonial agents and their local collaborators were called upon to lean ever more heavily upon the subject people to supply military details, corvées, and, in a later stage, taxes and dues redeemable in money form. On Timor, we find that a trend away from collecting tribute in kind (*fintas*) and toward tax redeemed in money (in the late nineteenth century) signaled the eruption of major revolts by the Manufaistas in the central–western districts especially against Governors Celestino da Silva (1894–1908) and Filomeno da Camara (1911–17).

Besides taking into consideration the degree of incorporation or, in other language, the differential impact of colonial capitalism upon an erstwhile precapitalist setting, it is also important to consider the changing balance of military technology. Whereas in the seventeenth, eighteenth, and late nineteenth centuries, the Portuguese basically only survived on the island through the cultivation of loyal allies and a loyal militia (*leal moradores*), the advent of the steam gunboat—the deployment of the *Patria* was crucial to Portugal's success in defeating the rebellions of 1912—turned the tide irreversibly against the Manufaistas and their leader Boaventura, the last of the great rebel chiefs.

Portuguese Timor, then, stands out in the Southeast Asian context, not so much for the level of violence used to neutralize rebellion, but for the longevity and even the intergenerational character of the rebellions down to modern times. Indeed, the exceptional and ritualized character of warfare in Timor, the Timorese *funu,* was recognized by such Portuguese officials as Governor Affonso de Castro (1859–63): "Rebellion in Timor continues successively, leading us to conclude that revolt is a normal state and that peace is exceptional."[9] Better than his predecessors, Governor Castro also understood the ritualized character of the Timorese *funu*: the collecting of heads, the macabre *tabedai,* or war dance, and retribution. From Castro until the advent of the Portuguese Republic in 1911, all governors in Timor incorporated displays of severed heads of Timorese rebels in official pacification ceremonials.

RECLAIMING TIMORESE HISTORY

From a Westernizing perspective, or at least a perspective that engages the colonial incorporation of Timor as a dependent tributary within a broader modern world-system, several discrete stages are identifiable in Timorese history, albeit within a five-hundred-year framework. I argue here that the problem of periodization of Timorese history is not just academic, but is at the heart of attempts to reclaim history.[10]

The first stage commences in 1515 with the formation of Christian communities on the islands of Solor and Timor; Timor, however, was not yet a seat of religious and temporal power but was controlled from the nearby island of Flores. This period also coincides with Timor's incorporation into long-distance maritime trading networks, part of a global European-dominated system of capital accumulation.

The second stage commences in 1695 with the advent of rule by the Portuguese Crown from its seat of power in Lifau in the enclave of Oecusse. This period was characterized by fierce rivalry between church and state and desperate efforts to survive the repeated challenges mounted by both the Dutch and the mixed race *Larantuqueiros* or *topasse,* who, at the time of the visit in 1600 by English privateer William Dampier, were observed to be running the show.

The third period coincides with the eastward shift of the capital from Lifau to Dili in 1769 by a rescue party sent from Macau. Within the first few decades of arriving in the east, the Portuguese set down the first permanent government structures, in the form of *fortaleza* or fortresses and customs houses, at strategic intervals along the northern coast.

The fourth period starts in 1836 with various administrative rationalizations linking Timor with, respectively, Goa and Macau, or after 1896, as a direct colonial dependency of Portugal. For almost one hundred years Macau supported Timor's budget through an annual subvention. Chinese arriving from Macau also brought valuable skills and otherwise formed an important element of colonial society. Populated, variously, by African slaves and soldiers, Indian clerks and soldiers, a core of metropolitans, and deportees from Portugal's empire, Dili earned a notorious reputation as graveyard for governors and visitors alike.[11]

To degrees, the modern period also represented a transition from indirect rule based upon the extraction of goods in kind to experimentation with precapitalist and even capitalist forms of accumulation, especially in the plantation sector, exemplified by the development of the highly successful coffee industry pioneered by Governor Castro.[12]

Politically, the success of this project would not have been possible without the pacification of the territory and the implantation of colonial structures and infrastructure, embryonically accomplished during the opening years of the Portuguese Republic and further developed under the Novo Estado of Portuguese Premier António Salazar in the late 1920s.

Already proceeding at an abysmally low level of production and extraction, the colony's development was set back massively by the preemptive Australian-Dutch invasion of neutral Portuguese Timor, and, in turn, by the large-scale Japanese invasion and occupation of 1941–45. Timor was left devastated as a result of these intraimperialist struggles. Some sixty thousand Timorese were killed and the Timorese *funu* was rekindled, a reference to the tribal and ethnic animosities aroused by the Japanese, especially in their introducing murderous elements from West Timor called the *colunas negras* or "black columns." Reminiscent of today's deadly Indonesian army-encadred militias, the black columns, recruited by the Japanese from among disgruntled elements in West Timor, did not stand back from killing Portuguese missionaries and administrators, as took place in the siege of Aileu on August 31, 1942.[13]

With the connivance of the Allied powers after the war, Portugal eased its way back into power in Dili, as if the war were but an interruption to its empire-building. As I have argued elsewhere, the essential pact between the postwar Salazar state and the United States turned on a restoration of the colonial status quo in Africa, Macau, and Timor alike in return for U.S. access to Lajes airfield in the Azores, key to Washington's mid-Atlantic nuclear strategy.[14]

Essentially, Portuguese Timor remained a political anachronism in a largely postcolonial world until the collapse of the Caetano-Salazar dictatorship in 1974. This is not to say, as numerous critics of Portuguese colonialism have averred, that no development occurred in Timor. In some spheres, Portuguese Timor was more advanced or more modern than West Timor (Indonesian Timor), at least until the oil boom of the 1970s. In any case, Timor to the end was dependent upon metropolitan subventions, with most people still living outside a monetized economy. Political preparation under the Salazarist order was also retarded, and the reformist Portuguese administration that arrived in the wake of the "flower revolution" in 1974 was clearly no match for the predatory generals in Jakarta and their dark propagandists and agents who sought, by striking an alliance with the moderate, albeit elitist, UDT (União Democrática Timorense, or Timorese Democratic Union) to discredit, then eliminate, the left-leaning, populist-majority Fretilin Party.

The question as to whether the short-lived Fretilin administration, which emerged out of the brief but bloody Indonesian-fomented civil war of October 1975 that ended with the full-scale Indonesian invasion of December that year—could have sustained a viable economy is academic,[15] but the alternative to international support for Fretilin's unilateral declaration of independence—and acquiescence (including by some Timorese) in Indonesia's annexation of the territory—has been, as the world now recognizes, genocide.[16]

Needless to say, the Indonesian state created its own historiographical view of the annexation of East Timor as the twenty-seventh province of Indonesia. Key to this project was the dissemination and exultation of the widely ballyhooed "Balibo Treaty," the alleged instrument of incorporation.[17] In a general sense Indonesian historiography characterized anticolonialism in Portuguese Timor as somehow consonant with the broader archipelagic-wide Republican struggle against the Dutch.[18] Accordingly, Indonesian historiography places great store on the 1959 or Viqueque rebellion, essentially a localized rebellion in the district of the same name, inflamed (with the evident blessing of the Indonesian consul in Dili) by Indonesian exiles from the failed Pemesta or eastern islands rebellion against Jakarta. Ruthlessly crushed by the Salazarist state, this little-studied event received major media attention in Indonesia in the late 1990s when certain of the exiled families returned from Portugal to Jakarta.[19]

Can the five-hundred-year-history thesis, as defended by Wallerstein,[20] be sustained against the argument developed by Frank and Gills,[21] namely, that much of the periphery was home to world-systems of its own long before the Columbian revolution, stretching back at least five thousand years? In the case of Timor, archaeology (naturally), myth and legend (albeit more tenuously), but also Timorese pride in their Melanesian roots would tend to support the latter view. So would Timor's seminal importance as the eastern terminus of a Hinduized trading-tributary network, and, far better documented, as the southernmost outpost of Chinese trading tributary networks in the South Seas, a reference to the island's famed sandalwood trade. Such a perspective would loosely fit with the thesis of Japanese scholar Takeshi Hamashita,[22] which supports an integrated East Asian tributary trade system to which Western interlopers were forced to accommodate, but never came to dominate. While Indonesia did not base its legal claims to occupied Timor upon such tributary considerations (as China did with Macau), it is also easy to see how Sino/Islamic/Indo and other civilizational alternatives to Eurocentric history can be turned to national advantage. After all, the Portuguese and their Western successors were mere five-hundred-year interlopers in these waters. Or were they?

Typically, nationalist historiography ascribes hero status to rebels against colonial authority. The Boaventura rebellion in Timor (ending only in 1912) is a case in point, although it has significant preludes and certain sequels. To take another Melanesian example, the Kanak insurrection of 1878, although crushed, is seen by modern nationalists in New Caledonia as a major historical event in the drive for self-determination and for control over land otherwise dispossessed by the colonial invader.[23]

The question also arises in nationalist historiography: was the revolt led by men and women with a national vision, one that subordinated primordial loyalties into a quest for national independence and statehood, or was it backward or regressive in character? While there have been notable exceptions—the slaves' revolt in Haiti was one such—*national* struggles awaited the great decolonization struggles of the last half of the twentieth century, led by scions of the colonial education system, nationalist intellectuals whose world view, sophistication, and military prowess were such as to turn colonial rhetoric of liberty, equality, and democracy back upon the erstwhile colonial masters.

But in Portuguese Timor no such nationalist/independence movement was spawned by the Japanese, such as transpired in Indonesia under Sukarno, Burma under Aung San, Malaya under Ibrahim Yacuub, and so on. Alone in colonial Southeast Asia, Portuguese Timor had no underground communist movement, in either the prewar or the postwar period. In part this was due to the successes of Salazar's secret police, but also to the failure of the state in Timor to even succor an educated class such as was developed in the neighboring Dutch, British, and French colonies.

From a nationalist East Timorese perspective, however—as expressed by Abilio Araujo (also known as Abilio d'Araujo), the expelled Fretilin leader turned pro-Jakarta businessman—can the former colony's history be glossed as simply a two-part movement: first, the period comprising *guerras independentistas*, wars waged from 1642 to 1912, and the second phase (1912 to 1975), characterized as *resistência passiva*, punctuated by the rise of Japanese-backed anti-Portuguese *colunas negras* during World War II and the revolt of 1959, out of which emerged a national liberation movement at the vanguard of a struggle leading to the proclamation of the Democratic Republic of East Timor? This schema is seductive and therefore merits our attention as an authentically East Timorese interpretation. But while refuting Portuguese (although not necessarily Indonesian) historiography, this is, after all, a reductionist view of history, one that diminishes the complexities of Timor's world incorporation, the building of elite coalitions, the whole question of collaboration, not to mention the broadband question of elite nationalism of which Araujo was evidently such a product.[24]

Modern Timor thus presented itself to the world as a paradigm of underdevelopment, an exemplar of a backward, dependent colonial periphery where precolonial and even tributary modes of production coexisted with an embryonic plantation economy and where noneconomic motives of imperialism appeared to be primordial. But as with Mozambique, Angola, and other African colonies of Portugal, Timor—or at least the zones of primary colonial and church contact—entered the modern world as a Latinized-creolized society par excellence. The fragility of this legacy under the twenty-four-year Indonesian military domination suggests that Portugal erred, not by being there, but by not doing enough.

It is tempting to apply to the Timor case certain of the ideas of the center–periphery school of thought in the context of the expansion and penetration of European capitalism. But if, by the nineteenth century, the major centers of development in the colonial peripheries were centered on Java and Singapore, and later extended to the estate zones of Sumatra and Borneo, then backward zones like Dutch New Guinea, Dutch Timor, and Portuguese Timor may be seen, in the words of one modern historian, "as extremely unimportant backwater reserve(s) or, like American Indian reservations or South African homelands," deliberately left dormant as outposts and borderlands, that confirm the importance of the centers and semiperipheries and true peripheries.[25]

To some extent, the Indonesian incorporation of East Timor was a culmination of the unfulfilled social engineering of Dutch imperialism in the East Indies. But such a mechanistic or reductionist reading of colonial logic does little service to the Timorese as actors or as victims. While we should not neglect to trace the world-incorporation of Timor into Eurocentric networks of accumulation, it is also important to acknowledge that, unlike American Indian or other aboriginal societies, the Timorese did not collapse under the weight of Portuguese colonialism. The long history of Timorese rebellion suggests that from the earliest colonial times until the first decades of the twentieth century, the Portuguese were bound to accommodate themselves to local forms of tributary power. Unlike colonizers in parts of aboriginal Australia or post-Columbian America, exterminism was not on the Portuguese's agenda. While the technological means to exterminate had certainly arrived by the early twentieth century and while the principle was severely tested in the crushing of the Boaventura rebellion and even the 1959 rebellion, the fact of the matter is that the genocide of the Timorese was not a crime committed by Latin conquistadors but by their postcolonial successors—a reference to the Norwegian Nobel Peace Prize Committee's 1996 description of the systematic oppression of the people of East Timor by Indonesia (post-1975), which led to an estimated one-third of the population of East Timor losing their lives due to starvation, epidemics, war, and terror.[26]

NOTES

This article is adapted from the author's recently published book *Timor Loro Sae: 500 Years* (Macau: Livros do Oriente, 1999).

1. Herman Melville, *Moby Dick, or The Whale* (1851; reprint, New York: Bantam, 1981), 351.

2. Alfred Russel Wallace, *The Malay Archipelago: The Land of the Orangutan and the Bird of Paradise* (London: Dover, 1964), 155–62.

3. F. J. Ormeling, *The Timor Problem: A Geographical Interpretation of an Underdeveloped Island* (Djakarta and Groningen: J. B. Wolters, 1957), 25.

4. Wallace, *The Malay Archipelago*, 155–62.

5. Ian Glover, *Archaeology in Eastern Timor, 1966–67* (Department of Prehistory, Research School of Pacific Studies, Australian National University, 1986).

6. José Ramos-Horta, Address to the Royal Institute of International Affairs at Chatham House, London, 23 April 1996.

7. *Portuguese Timor*, Foreign Office (London: H.M. Stationery Office, 1920), 7–9.

8. R. A. F. Paul Webb, "The Sickle and the Cross: Christians and Communists in Bali, Flores, Sumba and Timor, 1965–67," *Journal of Southeast Asian Studies* 17, no. 1 (March 1986): 94–112.

9. Affonso de Castro, *As possessões Portuguesas na oceania* (Lisbon: Imprensa Nacional, 1867), 101.

10. See, for example, J. Ferraro Vaz, *Moeda de Timor* (Lisbon: BNU, 1964). Other key Portuguese texts treating Timor history are these: Luna de Oliveira, *Timor na historia de Portugal*, 3 vols. (Lisbon: Agencia Geral das Colonias, 1949–1952); Humberto Leitão, *Os Portuguêses em Solor e Timor de 1515 a 1702* (Lisbon: Tip. LCGG, 1948); Artur Teodoro de Matos, *Timor Português: 1515–1769: Contribuição para a sua historia* (Lisbon: Instituto Historico Infante Dom Henrique, Faculdade de Letras da Universidade de Lisboa, 1974); and writings of F. R. Thomaz.

11. The single published text treating this period in great detail is René Pélissier, *Timor en Guerre: Le Crocodile et les Portugais, 1847–1913* (Orgeval, France: Pélissier, 1996). See author's review in *Journal of Contemporary Asia* (Manila) 28, no. 1 (1998): 127–29.

12. See W. G. Clarence-Smith, "Planters and Smallholders in Portuguese Timor," *Indonesia Circle* (London), no. 57 (March 1992): 15–27, which offers the best analysis of the foundation of a European plantation system in Timor, the development of an export economy based largely on coffee production, and the differential role of Timorese producers within this system.

13. The voluminous Australian and Portuguese wartime literature on Timor has been expertly reviewed by Kevin Sherlock, "Timor during World Wars I and II: Some Notes on Sources," *Kabar Seberang* (Townsville, Queensland), nos. 19–20 (1988): 41–56.

Somewhat more revisionist approaches, at least as to international motives behind the interventions, are found in the author's "Wartime Portuguese Timor: The Azores Connection" (Clayton, Victoria: Centre of Southeast Asian Studies, Monash University, 1988), Working Paper no. 50 (reprinted in author's *New World Hegemony in the Malay World* [Trenton, N.J.: Red Sea Press, 1999]); Carlos Bessa, *A Libertação de Timor na Guerra Mundial: Importância dos Açores para os Interesse dos Estados Unidos* (Lisbon: Academia Portuguesa da Historia, Subsidios para a Historia Portuguesa, vol. 25, 1992); and Henry Frei, *Japan's Southward Advance and Australia: From the Sixteenth Century to World War II* (Honolulu: University of Hawaii Press, 1991). For a recent Japanese perspective (in Japanese), see chapter 4 of Ken'ichi Goto, *Modern Japan and Southeast Asia* (Tokyo: Iwanami, 1997).

14. Gunn, "Wartime Portuguese Timor."

15. See Grant Evans, "Portuguese Timor," *New Left Review*, no. 91 (May–June 1975):

67–79. Evans observed much resistance to Fretilin's embryonic co-operativization program generally hampered by a "lack of political clarity." Fretilin, he observed, would have had little choice but to work with the World Bank, an institution unlikely to have accepted Fretilin's radical economic policies.

16. Key English language texts relating the closely packed events of 1974 to 1976 are the following: Bill Nicol, *Timor: The Stillborn Nation* (Melbourne: Visa, 1978); Jill Jolliffe, *East Timor: Nationalism and Colonialism* (Brisbane, Queensland: University of Queensland Press, 1978); James Dunn, *Timor: A People Betrayed* (Milton, Queensland: The Jacaranda Press, 1983). From the perspective of Timor's last Portuguese governor, see Mario Lemos Pires, *Descolonização de Timor: Missão Impossivel?* (Lisbon: Publicações Dom Quixote, 1991). Key Indonesian texts are the following: E. M. Tomodok, *Harihari Akhir Timor Portugis* (Jakarta: Pustaka Baru, 1994), written by a former Indonesian consul in Dili; Julius Pour, *Benny Moerdani: Profile of a Soldier Statesman* (Jakarta: Yayasan Sudirman, 1993); and Hendro Subroto, *Saksi Mata Perjuangan Integrasi Timor Timur* (Jakarta: Sinar Harapan, 1998).

17. Akihisa Matsuno, "The Balibo Declaration: Between Text and Fact," in *The East Timor Problem and the Role of Europe*, ed. Pedro Pinto Leite, International Platform of Jurists for East Timor (IPJET) (Lisbon: Publiçaes Universitaria e Cientifica, 1998), 159–94.

18. Indonesia's archipelagic concept (*wawasan nusantara*) with reference to East Timor is well unmasked in Akihisa Matsuno, "Reading the Unwritten: An Anatomy of Indonesian Discourse on East Timor," in Leite, *The East Timor Problem*, 195–210.

19. For example, "Jeremias Pello, Pejuang Timtim yang Kesepian," *Kompas* (Jakarta), 21 May 1999, tellingly recounts that certain of the Indonesia infiltrators involved in this rebellion were treated as heroes of Indonesia's independence struggle and incorporated into the TNI (army). Jeremias Pello, part of a group captured and exiled by the Portuguese to Angola, returned to Indonesia in 1962. Pello, along with forty-six other Timorese participants, was granted an audience with former President-General Suharto on November 10, 1996. Nevertheless, as the title of this article implies, government promises of support for Pello have long since evaporated.

20. Immanuel Wallerstein, *The Modern World-System III: The Second Era of Great Expansion of the Capitalist World-Economy, 1730–1840s* (San Diego: Academic Press, 1989).

21. Andre Gunder Frank and Barry K. Gills, *The World-System: Five Hundred Years or Five Thousand?* (London: Routledge, 1993).

22. Takeshi Hamashita, "The Future of Northeast Asia-Southeast Asia," in *Rediscovering Russia in Asia: Siberia and the Russian Far East,* ed. Stephen Kotkin and David Wolff (New York: M. E. Sharpe, 1995), 312–22.

23. Wilfred G. Burchett, *Pacific Treasure Island: New Caledonia* (Melbourne: F. W. Chesire, 1942); Martin Lyons, *The Totem and the Tricolour: A Short History of New Caledonia since 1774* (Kensington: New South Wales University Press, 1986).

24. Abilio d'Araujo, *Timor Leste: Os Loricos Voltaram a Cantar: Das Guerras Independendistas a Revolução do Povo Maubere* (Lisbon, 1977).

25. Gerard J. Telkamp, "The Economic Structure of an Outpost in the Outer Islands in the Indonesian Archipelago: Portuguese Timor, 1850–1975," in *Between Peoples and Statistics: Essays on Modern Indonesian History,* ed. P. Creutzberg (The Hague: Martinus Nijhoff, 1979), 82–83.

26. Statement by Norwegian Nobel Committee on Friday, 11 October 1996.

2

A Long Journey of Resistance: The Origins and Struggle of CNRT

Sarah Niner

A National Timorese Convention held in Peniche, Portugal, in April 1998 announced the creation of the National Council of Timorese Resistance, CNRT, with Xanana Gusmão as president. The creation of CNRT was the culmination of a tortuous political journey by the East Timorese people beginning in 1974 at the conclusion of over four hundred years of Portuguese colonialism and spanning the subsequent quarter century of brutal Indonesian occupation. The crisis of Indonesian invasion and occupation forged Xanana Gusmão's leadership and the evolution of the Timorese resistance to its status as a "government in waiting" and Xanana Gusmão as the most obvious, if reluctant, presidential candidate.

RESISTANCE ORIGINS

Until the 1970s the Portuguese colony of Timor was in a colonial time warp in the midst of newly independent Southeast Asian neighbors. But on May 5, 1974, the new Portuguese regime authorized the establishment of political parties as part of the long overdue process of decolonization.[1] The two largest parties were UDT (*União Democrática Timorense*—Timorese Democratic Union) and ASDT (*Associação Social Democrática Timorense*—Timorese Social Democratic Association).[2] UDT was the first to form. Its most important leaders were a prosperous farmer and university graduate, Mario Carrascalão, and his brother João, a land surveyor. Their Portuguese father, an anarchist, had been exiled to Timor. Calling for progressive autonomy oriented toward a federation with Portugal with an intermediary preparatory stage of ten to twenty years leading to independence, UDT enjoyed the support of many *liurai*, the regional elite.

ASDT was the fruit of a clandestine anticolonial movement of members of the young urban elite inspired by nationalism. Many of them were officials and teachers who had been meeting regularly on Dili's esplanade prior to the Portuguese revolution. Francisco Xavier do Amaral, a respected older intellectual and graduate of the Jesuit seminary in Macau who worked in the Dili Customs House, became the founding ASDT president at the suggestion of José Ramos-Horta. Ramos-Horta, a journalist, was a founder of the initial clandestine anticolonial group who had also participated in the founding of UDT and had even suggested the UDT name.[3] Ramos-Horta, a moderate who was impatient with the radical ideological debates then taking place within the emerging Timorese nationalist movement, drafted ASDT's manifesto.

At its inception ASDT was a broad-based, anticolonial association with a nationalist ideology calling for independence following a ten-year preparatory period and demanding an end to racial discrimination and corruption. In September 1974, ASDT was transformed into *Frente Revolucionária do Timor Leste Independente*, the Revolutionary Front for an Independent East Timor, commonly known as Fretilin, the new name reflecting the influence of the African liberation movements, especially Frelimo. Like its predecessor, ASDT, Fretilin continued to call for socialist democracy. The formation of Fretilin marked a shift to the demand for immediate independence and a metamorphosis from an association to a "front" presenting itself as the sole representative of the Timorese people. A group of Timorese students from Portugal, influenced by Maoist and Marxist thought then current in Europe, returned on the eve of Fretilin's formation and radicalized the group.[4] Ramos-Horta observed that the young radicals "were our best cadres; much was owed to their enthusiasm and ideas"; he also noted their lack of a power base within Fretilin. The more moderate Xavier do Amaral and Nicolau dos Reis Lobato led the group and enjoyed the strongest support.[5]

By December 1974 the movement had developed social and political programs, including educational and literacy programs based on the teachings of Paulo Freire, agricultural co-operatives, basic health care, political consciousness-raising, and the promotion of indigenous culture and religion. In his 1994 autobiography, Xanana recalls his skepticism about this new political process that was creating tensions and divisions in Timorese society: "I struggled between getting involved and keeping to the sidelines. It was not that I did not want to join in, but I could see that the situation could get completely out of hand." But months later he says he realized that "if I wanted to fight for my Homeland there was only one way to do so," and during Fretilin's first year anniversary celebrations on May 20, 1975, he joined them.[6]

In January 1975 a coalition for independence between UDT (which abandoned its strong pro-Portuguese stance) and Fretilin (which accepted a longer period of transition to independence) was formed. Following internal disagreements UDT

Figure 2.1   November 12, 1991. Courtesy: Steve Cox.

withdrew from the coalition on May 26, 1975. Between March and July 1975 the Portuguese Decolonization Commission organized local elections to select *liurais* to form an executive council that would prepare for general elections for a Constitutional Assembly to convene in October 1976. In these elections—in which villagers threw a pebble into the basket of their chosen candidate—most of the victors were apparently Fretilin members or supporters.[7] Following several anti-Fretilin and anti-Communist rallies in Dili on August 9 and 10, UDT mounted a full-scale *coup* on the eleventh.[8] For several days fighting raged in the streets of Dili. Credible estimates of the death toll in the civil war range from 1,500 to 3,000.[9] When Fretilin gained the upper hand, numerous UDT supporters were beaten and jailed.[10]

During the three-week civil war Fretilin formed an armed wing, Falintil (*Forças Armadas de Libertação Nacional de Timor-Leste*—Armed Forces for the National Liberation of East Timor). Having gained control of the territory, Fretilin transformed itself from a loose political group into a de facto government bent on achieving political stability and economic recovery. Dunn notes that the civil war led to a "perceptible decline in the influence of the radical wing with the incorporation in Fretilin of conservative soldiers who had served in the Portuguese army." The ascendancy of Nicolau Lobato at this time increased the influence of his blend of "revolutionary African nationalism, pragmatism and conservative self-reliance."[11] A growing tension between Marxism and nationalism within the Timorese resistance movement from this time would become acute after the Indonesian invasion.

The Indonesian government and military had been directing a destabilization campaign called *Operasi Komodo (Dragon)* against Portuguese Timor since October 1974, broadcasting anti-Communist messages into the territory from Kupang and infiltrating Apodeti and later UDT. In early 1975 *Komodo* was transformed into a military operation and training of Apodeti supporters in West Timor began. After being "invited" by UDT leader Lopes da Cruz to intervene militarily in September, Indonesian forces took the western town of Batugade on October 8, and on October 16 five foreign journalists filming these battles were killed at Balibo. Atabe fell on November 28.

On November 28, 1975, Fretilin declared East Timor independent at a formal ceremony outside the palace in Dili and named Xavier do Amaral the first president of the "Democratic Republic of East Timor" and Nicolau Lobato prime minister. Xanana, who was then working for the new Department of Information as a journalist and newspaper editor, was nominated to the Central Committee, Fretilin's fifty-member policy making council.

Nine days later, on December 7, 1975, the Indonesian military invaded Dili. Two thousand citizens, including seven hundred Chinese, were killed in Dili in the first few days of the invasion. Tens of thousands of East Timorese, including entire villages, fled to the mountains behind Fretilin lines as Indonesian troops advanced. By the end of 1975 twenty thousand Indonesian troops were stationed in East Timor and by the following April this figure had risen to thirty-five thousand.[12]

Armed with an arsenal of modern NATO weapons taken from Portuguese stocks, twenty thousand Fretilin troops put up substantial resistance for the next three years. Behind Fretilin lines life was easier than in occupied areas: food was adequate and people were united. Xanana, previously trained during a three-year period of national service in the Portuguese army, became a Falintil fighter and commander.

The Supreme Council of the Resistance, a Fretilin structure created in response to the crisis, met in Soibada from May 20 to June 2, 1976. The agenda included changes in military strategy toward more guerrilla warfare, the tightening of political organization, and increasing food production. In sum, the council created the basis for an organized resistance.[13] East Timor was divided into six sectors, each supervised by a commander, then subdivided into smaller political and military units. Falintil troops were further divided into intervention forces and smaller units or shock brigades. A political commissar took charge of social and political activities in Fretilin-controlled areas. Each region had its own regional commander and a regional secretary who was responsible for organization of food production, housing, education, health care, and political education.[14] Within two years Fretilin had grown from a broad political front to a de facto government to a resistance army confronting a full scale invasion by vastly superior forces.

At the council meeting, ex-Portuguese colonial army soldiers, many of whom came from strong Catholic and politically conservative backgrounds, were frequently at odds with the politicians. Differences centered on Fretilin's social and political programs calling for the overthrow of colonial and traditional power structures. Professional soldiers, committed to classical fixed-position warfare, also clashed with proponents of mass mobilization in a guerrilla-style military resistance.[15] The Council appointed many professional soldiers to the Fretilin Central Committee in a bid for unity.[16]

At a national conference in Laline in 1977, sharp debate centered on a proposal to declare Fretilin a Marxist movement. In the end, stepped-up Indonesian military operations prevented ratification of this proposal. Xanana recalls of that period that "we were still dazzled by a vision of a miraculous process of human redemption" through Marxism.[17] As the Indonesian offensive isolated Fretilin bases, internal conflicts grew and opponents of a single revolutionary front were denounced as "counterrevolutionary" and "reactionary."[18] The revolutionary ideology that the Fretilin Central Committee had embraced provided the rationale for arrests and executions of "counterrevolutionaries."[19] Cadres were tried. Some were tortured and killed. One such trial eventually drove Xanana to question and disobey his superior, Sera Key, who in late 1977 was conducting an investigation into a group of supposed counterrevolutionaries. Xanana announced to the Fretilin Central Committee members present that he would no longer tolerate violence and torture in his region. In his autobiography, he would emphasize that his commitment to "persuasion and conciliation" grew out of the civil war and this early period in the mountains.

One particularly poignant episode concerns Xavier do Amaral, the founding president of ASDT–Fretilin who was arrested by Fretilin in September 1977 after failing to attend the council meeting. In circumstances that are still far from clear, he had apparently sought to arrange a compromise with the occupying forces. He was deposed as president, charged with treason, and arrested for planning unauthorized negotiations with the enemy, plotting to seize personal power, creating divisions between the military and civilian sectors of the resistance, paying insufficient attention to the war, and behaving like a traditional lord.[20] Xavier's closest associates were expelled from the Central Committee and some were beaten in a subsequent purge.

In early November 1977, Vice President Nicolau Lobato replaced Xavier as president only to be killed by Indonesian troops a year later. In November 1978 the last resistance base at Mt. Matebian fell. Together with the death of Nicolau Lobato and many other resistance leaders, this brought an end to this initial phase of resistance. An estimated one hundred thousand East Timorese died during the first three years of the invasion and occupation. Most Timorese who had survived in the mountains with the guerrillas surrendered and were forced to live in concentration camps where famine was rife.[21]

Xanana and a number of other resistance fighters escaped Matebian. Throughout 1979 and 1980 he walked from village to village through enemy strongholds to consult with the people about whether to continue or end the war and to contact remnant resistance forces. This period of grassroots consultation became the basis for his decision to reorganize the battered resistance.[22]

In March 1981, the First National Conference for the Reorganization of the Country was held near Lacluta. The conference overhauled organizational and political structures. Falintil units would be fully mobile, unsupported by fixed or "support" bases as in the first three years of occupation. For the first time, clandestine grassroots organizations were set up inside the camps and population centers of the Indonesian occupied zones to support the armed resistance in the bush. (Earlier, revolutionary supporters were required to remain within Fretilin-controlled zones.) At the highest level, the resistance was now to be led by the *Conselho Revolucionária de Resistência Nacional*, the National Council for Revolutionary Resistance, CRRN, a Marxist-Leninist movement.[23] Xanana was elected National Political Commissar, president of CRRN, and commander in chief of Falintil, thereby assuming the top leadership positions in all three spheres of activity.

Xanana has explained that he retained the previously mandated Marxist-Leninist ideology out of loyalty to his martyred comrades. Moreover, he did not feel it within his mandate to prescribe political ideology and none of the leaders left on the inside felt they possessed the theoretical background necessary to define the struggle in any other way. The Fretilin ideological agenda was thus set by leaders in the diaspora, principally by President Abilio Araujo. In his October 1982 messages, Xanana asserted that Fretilin was the sole representative of the Maubere people and sought to overcome the lack of unity that bedeviled the movement.[24]

In 1983, having negotiated a six-month cease-fire, while appearing to consider Indonesian offers of amnesty, Xanana rethought resistance strategy. The cease-fire freed him to move about the territory without restriction by enemy forces for the first time since the invasion seven years earlier. Xanana recalls that he began to talk at this time about pluralism and a multi-party system and to envisage Fretilin once again as a broad national movement that could encompass differing ideologies. Xanana's overriding message was "National Unity."[25] At the same time, Fretilin dropped its claim to be the sole representative of the people of East Timor.[26] Xanana's midyear 1984 message "What Is National Unity?" offered nationalists two choices, either to join Fretilin, "a liberation movement bringing together all nationalists without discrimination on grounds of color, sex, age, political belief, religious faith, or social condition," or to "establish a common platform for national independence with other nationalist movements." He added, "Fretilin also knows that there are people unwilling to belong to a movement or party. What is important, however, is that everyone is moved by a common feeling—that of national identity." Xanana recognized earlier sectarian errors: "Fretilin in the past had an extremist policy indeed; but from what it has learnt, a new political opening will allow the participation of other nationalist move-

Chart 2.1   The Origins of CNRT

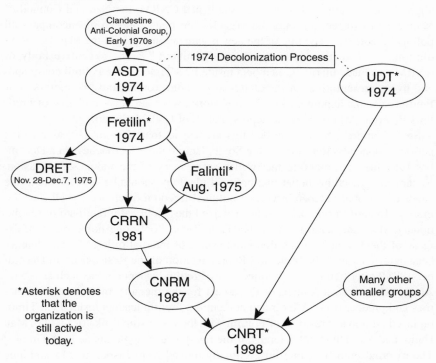

ASDT—Timorese Social Democratic Association [PRIVATE]
Fretilin—Revolutionary Front for an Independent East Timor
UDT—Union of Democratic Timorese
DRET—Democratic Republic of East Timor
Falintil—Armed Forces for the National Ligeration of East Timor
CRRN—National Council of Revolutionary Resistance
CNRM—National Council of Maubere Resistance
CNRT—National Council of Timorese Resistance

ments."[27] He declared that all atrocities committed during the civil war and in the early resistance period would be punished and guaranteed that Fretilin would respect freedom of expression, conscience, and association. Xanana explicitly rejected the use of force to impose a government, calling instead for free and democratic elections in an independent East Timor.

In March 1986, a "National Convergence" agreement was signed in Lisbon between UDT and Fretilin resulting in some cooperative efforts both within East Timor and in diaspora communities.[28] Yet unity proved fragile in the face of old suspicions and Indonesian military offensives.

Increasingly disenchanted by the inability of political parties to forge unity, in

December 1987 Xanana resigned from Fretilin[29] and declared that Falintil was aligned with no political party. He established CNRM, the National Council of Maubere Resistance, an umbrella organization that proposed to encompass all political ideologies. The title of the new organization replaced the Marxist "Revolutionary" with the nationalist term "Maubere."[30] The executive body of CNRM was made up of ten members inside East Timor: three Falintil commanders, five representatives of the clandestine underground, and two members of Fretilin. Xanana appointed José Ramos-Horta, who had been in charge of Fretilin's External Affairs, Special Representative of CNRM abroad.

Some Timorese have described this process as their *Perestroika*, akin to the period of openness to reform in the Soviet Union under Gorbachev. In a December 1987 message marking the twelfth anniversary of the Indonesian invasion, Xanana elucidated his belief that political ideology should be subordinate to the cause of national independence and political freedom of choice for all East Timorese. In hard-hitting phrases, he criticized the "political infantilism of revolutionary Marxism" and declared that Falintil had "only one noble mission, defense of the Motherland and the maintenance of internal order." These changes became official in "The Structural Reorganization of the Resistance" in December 1988[32] after being initially rejected by Fretilin leaders abroad such as Abilio Araujo who accused Xanana of disrespect for the memory of their national heroes and predecessors. After much contention, Fretilin leaders inside East Timor replaced Araujo as president of Fretilin with the leadership troika of Lu Olo, Mau Hudo, and Ma' Huno, all veterans of the resistance struggle inside East Timor.[33] The external branch of Fretilin eventually moved from Lisbon to Mozambique under the direction of José Guterres. Its leftist ideology was subsequently diluted.

In November 1988, President Suharto visited East Timor and announced that as of January 1989 for the first time since the 1975 invasion, eight of East Timor's thirteen districts would be open to entry by Indonesians and foreigners. Communication with resistance forces inside and outside increased and Ramos-Horta tirelessly promoted the Timorese cause in the international arena. Support from foreign governments, aid groups, and human rights organizations increased, spurred in part by international press coverage. Beginning with the Pope's visit to Dili in September 1989, the urban-based clandestine youth movement began organizing public demonstrations, signaling its "coming of age."[34] The November 1991 Santa Cruz massacre of several hundred peaceful East Timorese by Indonesian forces, recorded on film and broadcast internationally, provided a turning point for the resistance as Indonesian violence in East Timor was firmly fixed in the international public gaze.[35]

Shortly before the first anniversary of the Santa Cruz massacre, in November 1992, Xanana was captured in Dili. To nullify anything he might say under duress, Ramos-Horta announced that Xanana was no longer leader. Xanana was sentenced to life imprisonment, but by March 1993 he again took up leadership of the movement from his prison cell.[36] Imprisonment actually increased Xanana's international visibility and some hailed him as the Mandela of Southeast Asia. In prison, for the first time he became accessible to representatives of the United Nations, foreign governments, and human rights organizations. He also made invaluable links with Indonesian political prisoners, many of them important members of the prodemocracy movement.

THE NATIONAL COUNCIL OF TIMORESE RESISTANCE

The nonpartisan nationalist strategy pioneered with the formation of CNRM developed further in 1998 with the creation of CNRT. "Maubere" was removed from the title and replaced with "Timorese" as many Timorese objected to the term "Maubere," either because of the derogatory connotations remembered from Portuguese days or for its Fretilin association. For Xanana, "CNRT's establishment represented a refinement of this process of uniting the Timorese."[37] UDT was now integrated in the resistance structure and the many Timorese who had served the Indonesian occupiers or been compromised by the Indonesian regime were welcomed. CNRT offered voting rights to all major political parties as well as to nationalist, cultural, and religious groups both inside and outside East Timor. The imprisoned Xanana was unanimously elected president of CNRT.

Following the May 1998 ousting of Suharto, the new Indonesian leader, President B. J. Habibie, offered the East Timorese wide-ranging autonomy and announced troop reductions in the territory.[38] With options of autonomy and independence being negotiated throughout 1998, Xanana expressed a willingness to accept three years or more of autonomy under Indonesian rule as a transitional stage toward independence. Such a process had been spelled out by CNRM as early as 1989. The Timorese resistance, flexible and open to negotiation, had become sophisticated and adept at appealing to international and Indonesian opinion.

The mood in Dili, East Timor's capital, initially euphoric following Suharto's fall, had become bleak by October 1998 as early promises of change failed to materialize. The fourth meeting of the All-Inclusive, Intra-Timorese Dialogue in Austria in November 1998 produced little agreement. Proautonomy militia violence increased in Timor, and the Indonesian government began to explain the conflict in East Timor as one between proautonomy militias and proindependence groups, portraying its own military as a neutral and benign force. However, with Indonesian-directed atrocities receiving wide international publicity, Jakarta faced mounting diplomatic pressures to resolve the East Timor situation. Indonesia's heavy dependence on international financial aid following the 1997 financial collapse increased its vulnerability to international pressure at a time when the government was also facing demands from rising democratic forces inside Indonesia.

An important diplomatic break occurred in January 1999 when Australia suddenly changed its policy to one of "self-determination" for East Timor. Shortly thereafter, President Habibie announced that if the majority of East Timorese rejected autonomy in favor of independence in a "process of consultation," Indonesia would grant independence. Xanana responded by calling for a cease-fire, disarmament, and real troop reductions. In February he was moved from jail to house arrest, facilitating his participation in negotiations and heightening his international visibility.

Recognizing the necessity of framing a development plan for the future, CNRT convened a conference in April in Melbourne, Australia.[39] Conference participants, spanning the spectrum of political ideology and allegiances, built upon the new dynamic of inclusiveness in Timorese politics that was born with CNRM and reached maturity with the creation of CNRT. The conference projected a vision "based on the fundamental principle of a free, independent, peaceful, and democratic East Timor." The conference report outlined a broad social program detailing long-term goals and strategies for development across major sectors (public administration and infrastructure, economy, agriculture and environment, health, education, governance, judicial and legal systems, and mass communication) and the establishment of the necessary institutions and programs that would be required to achieve these results.

THE CONSULTATIVE BALLOT

In the lead up to the ballot and as part of the Dare[40] peace and reconciliation process, Xanana offered proautonomy and militia leaders a place in future planning for an independent East Timor. The goal of Dare II, held on June 25, 1999, in Jakarta, was a comprehensive and peaceful solution for East Timor. Delegates from prointegration and proindependence groups refined a statement of basic ideas but could find little common ground for the joint committee proposed by Xanana to implement these ideas. Their efforts were soon bypassed by increasing militia violence as the referendum approached.

In the wake of the devastation wrought by the Indonesian military-backed militias after 78.5 percent of voters chose independence, this reconciliation strategy appears to have been unduly optimistic, and the May 5 signatories, who had placed security in the hands of the Indonesians during the election period, naive in the extreme. International pressure applied earlier, instead of after the atrocities, could have diverted, or at least reduced the magnitude of, the tragedy. Yet Xanana, while sharply criticizing the Indonesian military-sponsored reign of terror, defended the secretary general's decision to proceed with the referendum despite warnings of violence. "For twenty-three years, the people of East Timor had lived in danger and suffered a huge death toll to gain the right to self-determination. The risk was taken by them. . . . Now, with media attention, the world was witnessing the barbarous actions and questioning the secretary general's decision. But for twenty-five years no one had known what was happening—we were taking the risks on our own."[41]

Both before and after the voting, CNRT and Falintil maintained the moral high ground by abstaining from violence, pledging tolerance, and sounding a note of compromise with Indonesia and with East Timorese rivals. In the lead-up to the ballot, Xanana stated that the only way the world could be made aware that it was the Indonesian military and its subordinate militias that were perpetrating the violence was if Falintil forces were clearly in cantonment. Falintil forces entered containment areas and refrained from attacking Indonesian soldiers, even when thousands of Timorese were terrorized and killed. Xanana warned that the Indonesian military, which far outnumbered Falintil, would take advantage of any attack to launch a massive offensive and delay their withdrawal.[42] "We did not want to be drawn into their game and their orchestration of violence in a civil war. We were ready to accept and receive victims to save our country. We never expected such a dimension in the rampage that followed."[43]

In September 1999 the Indonesian government released Xanana from house arrest amid the extensive military and militia slayings in East Timor that followed

Figure 2.2   Poster of Xanana Gusmão, leader of the National Council of Timorese Resistance (CNRT). Courtesy: John M. Miller.

the announcement of the proindependence vote. Initially taking refuge in the British embassy in Jakarta, Xanana fled to Darwin in Northern Australia after receiving death threats. On September 15, 1999, following massive violence, the United States at last pressured Indonesia into accepting a peacekeeping force, and the U.N. Security Council authorized an Australian-led multinational force (InterFET) to restore peace and security in East Timor. On October 22, 1999, Xanana returned to a devastated East Timor and made emotional pleas for all Timorese to return home, to forgive, and to rebuild.

CNRT AND THE FUTURE TIMOR LORO SAE

Under the U.N. Transition Administration in East Timor (UNTAET), CNRT would experience yet another major change: a transformation from a resistance group, brought together by opposition to the Indonesian occupation, with the primary task of fighting for independence, to a group dedicated to developing and unifying a new nation after a national holocaust. CNRT and Xanana can be expected to play central roles in charting that future.

NOTES

1. Decolonization followed a leftist coup in Lisbon, the April 1974 Carnation Revolution that deposed the fascist regime that had held power since the thirties.

2. José Ramos-Horta, *Funu. The Unfinished Saga of East Timor* (Lawrenceville, N.J.: Red Sea Press, 1996), 29–39. Three other parties were: Apodeti (*Associação Popular Democrática Timorense,* Timorese Popular Democratic Association, first called the "Association for the Integration of Timor into Indonesia") which called for integration with Indonesia but with local autonomy; the short-lived Trabalhista or "Labor Party"; and KOTA, *Kilbur Oan Timur Aswain,* literally Sons of the Mountain Warrior Dogs, a royalist party promoting a return to the traditional *liurai* system.

3. Ramos-Horta, who had been exiled to Mozambique for his anticolonial activities from 1970 to 1972, became party secretary of Fretilin. Mandated in 1974 to 1975 to represent East Timor abroad, he left the island three days before the Indonesian invasion. Four of his eleven brothers and sisters were killed by the Indonesian military. Ramos-Horta, *Funu,* 34–35.

4. Ramos-Horta, *Funu,* 38. The students included Abilio and Guilherma Araujo, Antonio Carvarino (Mau Lear), and Vincente dos Reis (Sahe).

5. Ramos-Horta, *Funu,* 53. Lobato, eldest son of a schoolteacher from Soibada, was one of the founders of ASDT. A graduate of the *Milician* Sergeant's School, he had served in the Portuguese army for two years before entering the Public Service and studying economics. He set up agricultural co-operatives in his home in Bazatete, twenty miles from Dili. As vice president of Fretilin, he shaped agricultural and economic policy. Helen Hill, "Fretilin: The Origins, Ideologies and Strategies of a Nationalist Movement in East Timor" (master's thesis, Monash University, 1978), 75.

6. Xanana Gusmão, *To Resist Is to Win: The Autobiography of Xanana Gusmão with Selected Letters and Speeches,* ed. Sarah Niner (Victoria, Australia: Aurora Books, 2000), 21 (cf. the Portuguese version of the autobiography, *Timor Leste: Um Povo, Uma Patria* (Lisbon: Editora Colibri, 1994).

7. The outcome of the elections remains controversial. Hill states that 90 percent of *liurais* elected were Fretilin supporters, while Dunn quotes a figure of 55 percent. Taylor, based on an interview with Portuguese administrator Jonatas, claims that the results were even. Most commentators state that support for Fretilin was higher in the rural areas. Hill, "Fretilin," 122–23; James Dunn, *Timor: A People Betrayed* (Sydney: ABC Books, 1996), 88; John Taylor, *Indonesia's Forgotten War* (London: Pluto Press, 1991), 45.

8. Dunn, *Timor: A People Betrayed,* 150–51. In a signed statement, João Carrascalão, the coup leader, acknowledged his responsibility for the civil war (189).

9. Carmel Budiardjo and Liem Soei Liong, *War Against East Timor* (London: Zed Books, 1984), 50; Jannisa Gudmund, "The Crocodile's Tears: East Timor in the Making," *Lund Dissertations in Sociology* 14, Lund University, 1997, 211.

10. Ramos-Horta, *Funu,* 55.

11. Jill Jolliffe, *East Timor: Nationalism and Colonialism* (St. Lucia: University of Queensland Press, 1978), 153–54.

12. Dunn, *Timor: A People Betrayed,* 259.

13. Gusmão, *To Resist,* 42.

14. Yvette Lawson, *East Timor: Roots Continue to Grow* (Amsterdam: University of Amsterdam, 1989), 53–54.

15. Lawson, *East Timor,* 53.

16. Gusmão, *To Resist,* 42.

17. Gusmão, "Ideological Turnaround" (1987), in *To Resist,* 133.

18. Gudmund, "Crocodile's Tears," 231–32; Lawson, *East Timor,* 66–73; and Constâncio Pinto and Matthew Jardine, *East Timor's Unfinished Struggle: Inside the Timorese Resistance* (Boston: South End Press, 1997), 72.

19. Gusmão, *To Resist,* 45–51.

20. Dunn, *Timor: A People Betrayed,* 278. After being held in captivity by Fretilin, Xavier was captured or surrendered to the Indonesians during the battle for Remexio on August 30, 1978. Living in Indonesia under close government scrutiny for the next twenty-two years, he was associated with a proautonomy faction.

21. As early as February 1976 UDT leader Lopes da Cruz, the Indonesia-appointed vice-chairman of the Provisional Government of East Timor, stated that sixty thousand East Timorese had died in six months of "civil war" (*New York Times,* 15 February 1976, cited in Gudmund, "Crocodile's Tears," 231). Portuguese priests in East Timor estimated that the numbers might be as high as one hundred thousand (Dunn, *Timor: A People Betrayed,* 274). One year later, Adam Malik, Indonesian foreign minister, was quoted as saying that fifty to eighty thousand Timorese had been killed in the war (*Sydney Morning Herald,* 4 May 1977, cited in Budiardjo and Liong, *War Against East Timor,* 49). Five years later the figure had reached two hundred thousand. Since the early eighties, the latter figure has been widely accepted as the death toll, worked out on population projections based on Indonesian census figures (Budiardjo and Liong, *War Against East Timor,* 50).

22. Gusmão, "Letter to Father Jaime Coelho" (18 May 1992), in *To Resist,* 166.

23. CRRN included members of the Fretilin Central Committee (including members of

the Delegation of Fretilin in Overseas Service), commanders of Falintil units and representatives of people living in Indonesian-controlled areas. The structure included Regional Committees for the Resistance, below these Centers of National Resistance and, at the lowest level, Cells of Popular Resistance. Lawson, *East Timor*, 137.

24. Xanana Gusmão, "Presidential Message to the Nation: 1983 The Year of National Unity" (13 October 13, 1982), *Nacroma*, March–April 1983, Delegacão da Fretilin em Servico no Exterior, Maputo, Mozambique. English translation with author.

25. Xanana Gusmão, interview by the author, Salemba, Jakarta, July 1999.

26. Editorial, *East Timor Maubere News* 1, no. 1, May/June 1996, Sydney; Agio Pereira, "1987: Structural Readjustment of the Struggle and the Creation of the National Council of Maubere Resistance (CNRM)" (paper presented to a solidarity gathering in Sydney, August 1994).

27. Xanana Gusmão, "What Is National Unity?" *East Timor News* (Darwin), Winter 1985.

28. The greatest change in diaspora communities did not come until after the Santa Cruz massacre of 1991.

29. Gusmão, "O Publico Interview" (June 1991), in *To Resist*, 149.

30. José Ramos-Horta explained the use of the term "Maubere" to signal a distinctive Fretilin approach to social democracy, "coining the word Mauberism—from Maubere, a common name among the Mambai people that had become a derogatory expression meaning poor, ignorant. Though vaguely defined without any serious theoretical basis, Maubere and Mauberism proved to be the single most successful political symbol of our campaign. Within weeks, Maubere became the symbol of a cultural identity, of pride, of belonging." Ramos-Horta, *Funu*, 37.

31. Pinto and Jardine, *East Timor's Unfinished Struggle*, 123.

32. Pereira, "1987: Structural Readjustment." The document itself is included in Xanana Gusmão, *Timor Leste: Um Povo, Uma Patria*.

33. Gusmão, interview by the author, Salemba, Jakarta, July 1999. Abilio Araujo, who has lived in Lisbon since the invasion, has since the early nineties been a proponent of the Portuguese-Indonesia Friendship Society supporting integration. He also entered into business dealings with Suharto's eldest daughter.

34. For details on the clandestine movement, see the interview with Constâncio Pinto in this volume.

35. One result of the wide publicity given Indonesian atrocities was the award of the 1996 Nobel Peace Prize to José Ramos-Horta and Bishop Carlos Filipe Ximenes Belo for their efforts on behalf of the people of East Timor.

36. Ma' Huno headed the resistance inside East Timor until his own capture six months later. Taur Matan Ruak, chief of staff of Falintil, Ramos-Horta, and Konis Santana led the struggle in the military, the diplomatic sphere, and the clandestine movement respectively, until Xanana's powers were fully reinstated. Agio Pereira, "Obituary for Konis Santana," *Timor Link,* no. 43, (June 1998).

37. Xanana Gusmão, "New Year's Message for 1999," in *To Resist*, 230–31.

38. Habibie ordered one thousand soldiers sent home in widely publicized withdrawals. Timorese leaders disputed the claim that any significant troop reduction had taken place.

39. The conference was planned by a coordinating committee in Melbourne made up of East Timorese and Australian supporters and academics including the author. Funding

was principally provided by the Portuguese and Australian Ministries of Foreign Affairs, Catholic groups, and aid agencies (notably Oxfam United Kingdom, Community Aid Abroad, the Overseas Services Bureau, and the Fred Hollows Foundation). Some forty East Timorese participants from East Timor and Indonesia took part in sector workshops, joined by Timorese from the diaspora. In addition, participants included non-Timorese from international organizations as well as development experts. Observers from the governments of Australia, Portugal, Norway, and Sweden and the World Bank attended. The conference was interrupted by news of slayings in East Timor on April 5 and 6. One conference delegate from East Timor lost four family members.

40. Dare, the small town twelve miles south of Dili, is the location of a seminary that a number of East Timorese leaders attended, including Xanana Gusmão and Nicolau Lobato. The first meeting of the Dare peace and reconciliation process took place in Baucau, East Timor, in 1998 at the initiative of Bishop Belo.

41. U.N. Press Briefing, Press Conference on East Timor by Xanana Gusmão and José Ramos-Horta, 28 September 1999.

42. Sander Thoenes, "Gusmão Moves to Darwin Ready for Return Home," *Financial Times,* 20 September 1999, 5.

43. Nora Boustany, "Riding the Tide of History," *Washington Post,* 1 October 1999, 28(A).

3

The Student Movement and the Independence Struggle in East Timor: An Interview

Constâncio Pinto

Constâncio Pinto was head of the underground movement in East Timor until 1992, when he was forced to flee the country. He now serves as the representative of the National Council of Timorese Resistance (CNRT) to the United States and Canada. He was interviewed by Mark Selden and Stephen R. Shalom at Columbia University in New York on January 22, 2000.

THE ORIGINS OF THE EAST TIMORESE STUDENT MOVEMENT

Q: What can you tell us about the origins of the student movement in East Timor?

Constâncio Pinto: The student movement in East Timor began to organize in 1974–75, after the Carnation Revolution in Portugal. When we talk about the student movement in East Timor we're talking about high school students, since there were no universities in East Timor at the time. And we're talking about a small number of people, not like in the United States; perhaps one to two thousand students in the mid-1970s. And only a few of them were politically aware about the movement's role, about Portuguese colonialism, and so on. They were the ones who were somehow critical of the government and curious to read some extracurricular books. But the rest of the students at the time were very closed minded, sometimes not even knowing what politics meant, or what colonialism was.

As three main political parties emerged in 1974–75—UDT, Fretilin, and Apodeti—the students too split into different groups. Most of the young people were part of Fretilin's student organization, Unetim, which stands for *União Nacional de Estudantes Timorense* (National Union of Timorese Students).

Fretilin was very serious in using the students to reach a wide audience throughout East Timor. They were very effective. They could go anywhere, and they could live with people in the villages and try to teach and politicize them— political education, the education system, health care, and literacy. This was the Fretilin program and the students promoted it very successfully. And that's why Fretilin was able to get the support of the majority of the people of East Timor in 1975. Otherwise things would have been very difficult for Fretilin because UDT was then working closely with the local leaders, the *liurai*, who at that time had a very strong influence on the population. But Fretilin was able to break this influence because of the students' contribution.

Beginning in 1975, some Unetim members were involved in the armed struggle. Even in the jungle Unetim played a role in the movement, as part of the Fretilin structure. Some Unetim members joined Falintil, others became members of the Fretilin Central Committee, or its national and regional structures. Unetim was replaced in 1976 or 1977 by the Popular Organization of Timorese Youth (OPJT), a Fretilin youth organization of both students and nonstudents.

Q: What was the impact of Indonesia's education policies on East Timor?

Pinto: The number of East Timorese students grew enormously. In 1975, when Portugal left East Timor, the literacy rate was extremely low. But between 1975 and 1999 the number of students tremendously increased and we have many more educated people now than we had in 1975. The increase of students was due to the compulsory primary education imposed by Indonesia, the greater opportunity for students to study in Jakarta, and the opening of a university and technical institutes in East Timor. But if there were more opportunities for East Timorese students to study than under Portuguese rule, these opportunities were still inadequate. If we compare student enrollment in East Timor with that in other parts of Indonesia, East Timor was way behind.

In instituting these educational policies, Indonesia's motives were hardly benevolent. Indonesia hoped that if they could educate young people, they would be able to change the political conditions in East Timor in favor of integration. The education basically tried to Indonesianize the East Timorese. They were forced to learn the Indonesian language, Indonesian culture, Indonesian history, and Indonesian heroes—everything on Indonesia and not East Timor. It was essentially a brainwashing process. But to do this, Indonesia expanded the schools, from the primary through the college level.

THE REEMERGENCE OF THE STUDENT MOVEMENT IN THE 1980s

Q: Could you describe the reemergence of the student movement in the 1980s?

Pinto: Starting in the early 1980s a different kind of student movement emerged in East Timor. Students began to get involved in the underground movement mainly through their parents or through their friends at school. In the beginning they organized in cells—with three, four, or five people in a cell—and these spread all over East Timor. Each cell had direct connection with Falintil and Fretilin in the mountains. But cells could not contact one another for security reasons.

In early 1983, I was a student at Externato de Sâo Jose in Dili. I was able to reconnect my link with the resistance movement through a group of students at the same school. We then decided to try to link all the student cells in the underground. So we started with Externato and linked with other schools. Externato was not a state school, but a private school run by the Catholic church; it was independent of the Indonesian government. There was a kind of flexibility in Externato de Sâo Jose. You could talk politics with your friends, while in the state-run schools you were not even allowed to mention the name of the resistance leaders.

So this environment allowed us to debate and to know each other and we began to connect. And because almost everyone who went to Externato de Sâo Jose had friends in government schools, we were able to connect to those people too.

Q: What about the East Timorese students studying in Indonesia?

Pinto: The environment for students in Indonesian schools in East Timor and for those in Indonesian schools in Indonesia was different. The former had very limited access to resources and no freedom to discuss political issues. But those who studied in Indonesia, in Bali, in Jakarta, and so on, had some freedom to discuss the issues. They were even able to mobilize, and that's why Renetil—an underground student organization—was formed in Bali and then later spread throughout Indonesia. Renetil played an important role in educating the Indonesian people about East Timor.

Q: But within East Timor you were not very successful in mobilizing students who went to Indonesian schools?

Pinto: We recruited mainly from the Catholic schools. There were some from Indonesian schools in East Timor, but not many. However, we began to attract more participation from students in all schools after the 1989 protest during the Pope's visit.

1989: A BREAKTHROUGH YEAR

Pinto: Indonesia decided to "open" East Timor in 1989. The Indonesians wanted the Pope to come to East Timor as a way to confer legitimacy on Indonesian rule and they were determined to prevent any protest happening at that time. But we saw this as the best opportunity—a unique opportunity for us to show the international community that we still existed and that we still suffered under Indonesian oppression. Pope John Paul II's visit was the first protest organized by East Timorese youth, and it was extremely successful.

The year 1989 marked the beginning of nonviolent actions in the cities and villages. Before that, although people were organized in small groups, their awareness was very much limited to their own cells. Sometimes they felt: "Are we the only ones who struggle for these things? What about the others?" When the protest movement started, people suddenly opened their minds and their vision: "We are not the only ones who are fighting for self-determination! There are others!" So it was easy for us after that. When we began to approach them, we could say we are the ones who did this, so let's get together.

Q: How did the resistance movement as a whole respond to this new protest activity?

Pinto: Because of the 1989 actions during the Pope's visit to Dili, CNRM (National Council of Maubere Resistance) decided to form an executive committee of the underground movement. In 1990, I was elected head of the executive committee. I had finished high school in 1986. In 1990 I was head of the Catholic Boy Scouts, as well as the head of one of the underground movement's most active cells, called 007, that had been able to unite all the groups. So I was still involved in the student movement.

Starting from 1989, we saw increased participation. In 1989 only a very small number protested. But in 1990 when we held another protest in front of the Hotel Turismo when U.S. Ambassador John Monjo was in East Timor, the number was greater. And then later in 1990, when we had another protest in Licidere, a neighborhood in Dili, many people joined. And that's why, building on these experiences, in 1991 we had some five thousand students—and not only students, but others, too—at our November 12 protest at Santa Cruz. That protest resulted in the massacre. The participants in the 1989–91 protests were not only students, but students led the protests and organized the network.

What makes the turnout at the Santa Cruz protest so surprising and impressive is how it was organized. I issued the instructions for that event, contacting the main local leaders on the evening of November 10. The message to the students was not issued until November 11, directing them to go to the protest the next day. The turnout was incredible: five thousand people in such a short time, just twenty-four hours.

THE SANTA CRUZ MASSACRE

Q: Could you describe your strategy for the November 12 protest?

Pinto: First, we tried to avoid anything that would provoke violence against us from the Indonesian army. The students were instructed not even to use strong language. They were not allowed to use words that would anger the Indonesian army. Nor were they to provoke the police—because we wanted to help them maintain order. Above all, we would do nothing violent. We would simply call for our rights.

Second, we decided that the churches were the safest places to gather in, which is why we began the November 12, 1991, protest at the church.

Third, all protests in East Timor were organized to ensure the presence of the international community—foreign journalists, foreign members of parliament, and so on. In October, the Indonesians had shot to death a young boy. In November, many journalists came to East Timor to cover a visit by a Portuguese parliamentary delegation. The delegation canceled its visit, but the journalists had already arrived: British TV journalist Max Stahl, the Italian press, the Japanese, the Australians, all were there. We decided that we had to do something since we had all these foreigners. If we didn't act, the Indonesians would just continue to kill us. The best way to tell the world how we suffered was to rock the boat, and that's why we decided to protest. The night before the protest, I met with U.S. journalists Allan Nairn and Amy Goodman, and I asked them to invite all the journalists there.

Q: So what happened?

Pinto: We had a Mass at the church for the student who was killed by the Indonesians. Then people marched from the church to the cemetery. Our banners called for a referendum, for dialogue—"Long live East Timor!" "Long live Xanana Gusmão!"—that's all; there was no confrontation. People prayed and sang in the streets. The majority of the demonstrators were students. What we didn't know was that the Indonesians planned to kill the protesters when they reached the cemetery. When the protesters arrived at the cemetery, the Indonesian troops let them file in. The cemetery was surrounded by a wall. Then the troops began to shoot. Allan Nairn and Amy Goodman were there and tried to prevent the Indonesian troops from firing, but the soldiers just continued shooting, killing 271 people. Because the Indonesians had recently tried to kill me, I was not in the march, but was in hiding nearby.

The massacre turned out to be a big mistake for Indonesia. They were able to confiscate Allan's and Amy's film, but they didn't get Max Stahl's. He was able to smuggle his film out and put it on TV from London. For the first time we were able to break the silence and attack the complicity of the international community toward the invasion of East Timor.

Q: This was a real turning point. How did it affect the resistance?

Pinto: From 1991 up to 1998–99 we focused not on underground actions but on public protests. On the diplomatic front, we also became more persistent, because now we had strong evidence with which to fight Indonesia.

LEARNING FROM THE *INTIFADA*

Pinto: In some respects we tried to imitate tactics of the Palestinian *intifada* (the unarmed popular uprising). We'd raise a Falintil flag somewhere, or we'd leaflet. We tried to educate people to say words that would make the Indonesian troops uncomfortable. For example, "*kapan pulang,* when are you going back to your country?" and even children would say, "Hello, *kapan pulang.*" Like the *intifada*, too, the underground movement was unarmed. We could have obtained weapons—we had some people in the Indonesian armed forces, we had access to Falintil, and we could buy weapons from Indonesia. But we thought it would be a mistake. For example, after the Santa Cruz massacre people were very angry about the massacre and wanted to revolt in response, but we thought it would be a big mistake. If we did that they would just go from house to house and wipe out everyone. We knew how the enemy behaved toward the population, and because of this, unlike the *intifada*, where people threw rocks at Israeli troops, there was no single incident in East Timor of youths confronting the military with rocks.

Q: How would you characterize the different forms of resistance between 1975 and 1999?

Pinto: By 1980 the armed struggle had collapsed. In 1981 Xanana was able to reorganize Falintil, but the armed resistance basically changed its strategy from offensive to defensive. So they existed in the mountains as a symbol, not as an important tool to directly challenge Indonesian forces and win the war. In short, the underground movement became much more important to the whole resistance from 1981 to 1999. And, it became especially important after 1991.

From 1991, the diplomatic front became equally important to the resistance. This enabled us to begin getting some support from Western countries, like the United States. The grassroots movement also began to emerge throughout the world to support East Timor. From 1991 to 1999, the activities of the underground and the diplomatic front were complementary. The underground continued its peaceful activities and at the same time the diplomatic front made great advances, helping to build support for the struggle worldwide.

But Falintil was also important. Their presence in the mountains forced the international community to recognize that the resistance would not be extinguished for many years and that the situation could only be resolved by negotiation, which meant coming to terms with Falintil.

INTERNATIONAL SUPPORT NETWORKS

Q: What role did students play in enabling the resistance inside East Timor to communicate internationally?

Figure 3.1   Young man writing placards for an expected Portuguese delegation visit, November 4, 1991. Courtesy: Steve Cox.

Pinto: Without students it would have been difficult for the movement to channel information abroad. The information flow was mainly through East Timorese students in Jakarta or Bali. In the beginning we did it through individuals, students who were in Indonesia, but still individuals—usually students whose parents were involved in the underground movement in East Timor. There was no problem traveling from Dili to Indonesia. The only problem was that police or customs might search everything and find a letter. But we had some people—customs and police—at the airport in Dili, so every sensitive document would be channeled to these people and then it was easy for us to smuggle information from East Timor to Indonesia, and from Indonesia abroad. In the beginning these communications went through individuals, but then through Renetil, the organization of the Timorese student movement in Indonesia.

A second channel we used was our network with tourists, from Australia and elsewhere. Even here students were crucial. Many of those who came to East Timor in 1989 and 1990 were not real tourists, but disguised tourists, including journalists who were very receptive to the East Timorese. But the problem was that only someone who had enough courage was able to approach them—not because the journalists didn't want to talk to the Timorese, but because the Timorese feared arrest if they talked to white guys from Australia or the United States. Students were the ones who had the courage and determination to accept the consequences and some also had the language skills.

Students also facilitated contacts between foreigners and resistance leaders. For example, in September 1990 the Australian lawyer Robert Domm became the first foreigner to visit Xanana Gusmão in the Falintil camp in the mountains, and it was Domingos Sarmento, a Timorese student who studied in Indonesia, and I, as well as some others, who took him to meet Xanana.

Q: Could you tell us about the student role in the 1999 independence referendum campaign?

Pinto: Students did most of the work in the campaign. Because we were so confident in the students, we made no attempt to have an open electoral campaign with mass public rallies. The Indonesians had rallies, but we didn't need to; we could organize people one-on-one.

We were confident because the Indonesians made a mistake right from the beginning, starting in 1975, by killing almost a third of the population, so that almost everyone in East Timor had lost family. Despite all the repression to stop the resistance, we were able to carry on. The idea of the right to self-determination and independence had been inculcated for many years. So when we spoke about the referendum in East Timor, the immediate reaction among Timorese was against Indonesia and for independence. The repression explains everything.

The day before the vote I was interviewed by public television newscaster Jim Lehrer, who asked my opinion about the outcome. I said it was difficult to say, but I'd say the majority would vote against the Indonesian proposal. But he continued to ask what majority, how many? And I said, well, between 75 and 80 percent, and it turned out to be 78.5 percent.

I was so confident because the students were doing a great job. They were the ones who were going from house to house explaining to people about the process of the vote. The vote itself was very complicated and you needed to explain it carefully to people or else they could vote wrong by mistake. I think the 21 percent who voted against independence were confused and checked the wrong box! (laughs)

STUDENTS IN AN INDEPENDENT EAST TIMOR

Q: Turning to the situation in the new East Timor, what are the relations between East Timorese students and the Renetil students returning from Indonesia?

Pinto: There are some difficulties because of their different educational backgrounds and different approaches to the struggle. There were other student organizations in East Timor: for example, the East Timorese Youth and Student Organization (OJETIL), LORIKO, FITUN, and the Students Solidarity Movement, all of which were part of the CNRT underground. Those in East Timor think they made the most important contributions. They were inside East Timor and they did the most dangerous work on the ground. They say, "You were abroad in Indonesia, having a good time, while we put our bodies on the line." So these are problems that have to be worked out, but I think they will work out once those in East Timor become aware that the students in Indonesia were part of the struggle.

Q: How do students fit into the broader politics of East Timor today?

Pinto: Renetil, which used to be part of CNRT, is now distancing itself from the organization. That's mainly because of the current confused political structure. There is a strong sense that students should be independent from the parties and from any political institution. That will allow them to mobilize against wrongdoing whether by the parties or the state. Renetil just had its congress and decided to withdraw from CNRT. But they are just one organization, one of many.

There is now an effort to create an umbrella student organization. There will be a CNRT congress in August 2000 and during that week there will be a separate meeting for students to see if an umbrella organization can be set up.

Q: Looking ahead, what are the most critical challenges for the student movement?

Pinto: Now that we have gotten our freedom, we are free, but of course we are not yet really free. The struggle will continue: for development, for reconstruction, for social justice, and so on. This will be more difficult than the twenty-four year struggle for independence. The major opponent that kept us together, that

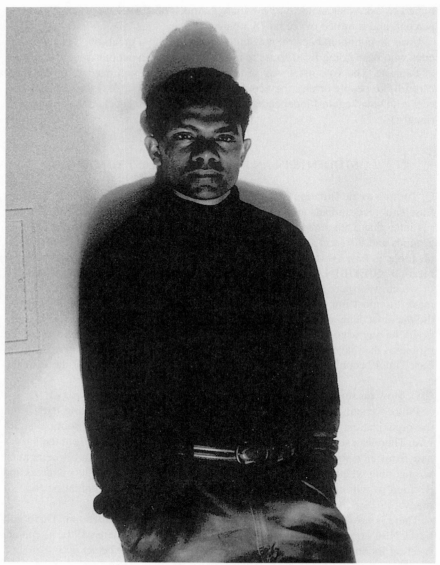

Figure 3.2   Constâncio Da Conceicao Pinto, Sydney, 1996. "In 1989, Pope John Paul II arrived in Timor—the first major international visitor since the invasion. As he conducted Mass for 100,000 people, a group of the Catholic Boy and Girl Scouts unfurled protest banners hidden in the girls' clothing. It was like a bomb blast. People thought the Indonesians were going to start shooting and began to flee. But the Pope was there and it was difficult for them to open fire. They hurried him away but the media were present and for five minutes or so watched the whole thing. It was the first time we put East Timor on the international map." Courtesy: Ross Bird.

maintained our unity—Indonesia—is now gone, or at least no longer rules our country. So there is a risk of selfishness and divisiveness. And in fact this is happening now. The unity we had in East Timor is beginning to unravel.

So the role of the students will continue to be important. They are the ones who will promote peace, unity, and development in East Timor.

4

The Catholic Church and the Independence of East Timor

Arnold S. Kohen

When elite *Kopassus* forces spearheaded the now infamous attack on the residential compound of Bishop Carlos Ximenes Belo in Dili on September 6, 1999, destroying his home and chapel and routing thousands of refugees from the area, they knew exactly who and what they were targeting. For years, Belo's home had represented the ultimate in safety, at least in comparison with most other places in East Timor. For the most part, it was considered inviolate. But that fateful day, the bishop's residential compound was viciously attacked by local militias (apparently forced to do so by Indonesian Special Forces), who attacked the bishop's home in order to drive out those who had taken sanctuary there. The house was set on fire, and Bishop Belo himself was forced to take refuge in the town of Baucau with his brother bishop, Basilio do Nascimento. After Belo left, eyewitnesses say, more than ten people were killed.

The assault on the bishop's residence, in addition to operations aimed at other religious houses, was "clearly designed to attack two of the last symbols of sanity, shelter and protection," in the words of a well-placed international official. As another observer put it, the worldwide reputation of the bishop had cast a shadow on the Indonesian regime, especially army elements who were most identified with the drive to subdue East Timor and who were seen to be behind the violent campaign of the so-called militias. Belo and the church he represents, quite simply, had long been a major impediment to the military rulers of Indonesia, who were bent on winning international recognition of their sovereignty over East Timor. In particular, the Nobel Peace Prize awarded Bishop Belo and José Ramos-Horta in 1996 was a severe blow against this effort; the bishop himself has stated that the attack on his home was to some extent an act of revenge because of the Nobel award.

A curious combination of respect and rage on the part of the Indonesian authorities was on display when the bishop was taken to a police station on September 6 before being evacuated from Dili by helicopter. On the one hand, he was not physically harmed; on the other, Indonesian authorities did not disguise their base motivations. Indeed, according to the bishop, a top police official told Belo that the attack was carried out to teach the people a lesson. "Bishop, every time there are demonstrations, people flock to the Church for protection," the official told him, with the inference that such activity must somehow be punished. Belo also said that he heard the police reporting to superiors in Jakarta that the people at the bishop's compound had been successfully removed from the area.

The attack, then, can be regarded as a final outburst against an institution that, despite much effort over more than two decades, the Indonesian military could never really control. But this was only the latest of a series of increasingly aggressive actions against a body that had managed, through nonviolent resistance, to defy the army of the world's fourth most populous nation. On April 6, 1999, for instance, dozens of people taking refuge at a church in the coastal town of Liquiça were brutally murdered by militiamen; Indonesian security forces either assisted the killers or simply stood by. The Liquiça massacre was a signal of what elements of the Indonesian military were prepared to do to maintain control of East Timor.

In no small measure, the August 30 U.N.–sponsored referendum, in which 78.5 percent of registered voters opted for independence from Indonesia, could be traced to Bishop Belo's 1989 letter to then U.N. Secretary General Javier Perez de Cuellar. In that letter, written in an office in the bishop's now-gutted home, the Timorese prelate, who at the time had been regarded in some quarters as open to the prospect of integration with Indonesia, stated: "We are dying as a people and a nation." He pleaded that the East Timorese must "decide their own destiny, freely, consciously, and responsibly."

Bishop Belo's action was broadly representative of the stance taken by many leaders of East Timor's Catholic Church throughout the past twenty-four years of Indonesian occupation. But other key elements of the history of the Catholic Church in East Timor since the early colonial period also should not be overlooked. Though in many ways the Catholic Church was a central instrument in Portugal's so-called civilizing mission in its colonies, East Timor included, it was also true that the Church, its faults notwithstanding, was an institution that demonstrated a closer connection with the people than any other organization from the early colonial period on.

LINKS WITH THE PEOPLE

Dominican missionaries first landed on Timor in 1515, and over the next four centuries the Catholic Church was a central vehicle in transmitting Portuguese

Figure 4.1   Girl and man outside church in Letefoho. Since the 1940s the Catholic Church has been using the indigenous Tetum language, so its liturgy is an important expression of national identity. Since 1976, when the Vatican entrusted a Timor-born priest, Martinho da Costa Lopes, to administer the Dili Diocese, the Church has also provided a physical and spiritual sanctuary for the East Timorese. Courtesy: Ross Bird.

culture to local people. The Church, in fact, had a far more widespread presence in the villages of East Timor, and in many instances greater credibility, than the Portuguese authorities, who until the twentieth century were virtually absent from the interior of the territory. As later, the Church was the main nonstate institution in East Timor and a principal source of education and community life. Literacy levels were quite low throughout the colonial era, but the Church provided much of what education was available. Although only about 20 percent of East Timor's 1974 population of 688,000 were Catholic, many of the leaders of the parties that emerged in East Timor after the fall of the Portuguese dictatorship in 1974 were graduates of the Jesuit-run seminary in the town of Dare in the hills overlooking the capital, Dili, as was Bishop Belo. Despite the Church's identification with the Portuguese state, some elements of the Church were critical of colonial injustices and defended the people against abuses, even if only in a minor way. But the key factor was that members of the clergy had closer links with the people of East Timor than any other colonial-era institution. It was perhaps fitting that in the critical weeks after the August 30, 1999, ballot, tens of thousands of East Timorese gathered in Dare after fleeing the violent anti-independence campaign orchestrated by the Indonesian military. In Dare they were ministered to by several priests, some of whom were former teachers at the seminary. The connection between the Catholic Church and the East Timorese people was on vivid display during those weeks in September 1999, as televised images of the celebration of the Mass in Dare under these arduous circumstances were broadcast throughout the world.

Bishop Belo's 1989 letter to the United Nations, and numerous statements on human rights since Belo took office in 1983, were in some sense an expansion of earlier efforts by clergy to defend the people against abuse. Belo's statements also came to symbolize the role the Church had played as a thorn in the side of Jakarta's effort to conquer the territory. It is indisputable that the failure to co-opt East Timor's most important nongovernmental institution had a profound impact on the course of events in the territory. Indeed, anecdotal evidence gathered in East Timor in October 1999 suggests that many members of the clergy played an indispensable role in providing people with the moral courage to vote their conscience on August 30, reminding them that if they wanted to free themselves of the military occupation they had endured since 1975, they should register with the United Nations and vote for independence. It is worth noting that Indonesia had tried to move the referendum day from Sunday, August 8 to Monday, August 9 because Jakarta feared that on a big church-going day people would receive strength from the clergy and from gathering with fellow East Timorese in church settings to defy intimidation by the Indonesian military and their local allies. Those fears were probably correct, but they only underscored the utter absence of moral legitimacy on the part of Indonesian authorities and their cohorts. In the end, the date was moved because the United Nations needed additional time to organize the ballot, and a Monday was chosen.

In late 1998, Indonesian forces and paramilitary groups under their control stepped up a wave of increasingly violent attacks on East Timorese villagers. According to Church sources who gathered information at the local level, an estimated three thousand to five thousand proindependence people were killed in the six to eight months preceding the August 30 vote in an effort by military elements to produce a result in favor of continued Indonesian rule. In years past, Bishop Belo had taken the position that the people must be allowed to freely decide their future and that their bishop had no right to choose for them. But the murderous campaign designed to derail a free vote convinced Belo that there was no future for the East Timorese under Indonesian rule. Under these conditions, Belo ordered the local Church to increase its efforts to defend the people from attack and to help enable voters to make a free choice. During those months and in the period following the ballot, many tens of thousands of East Timorese took refuge on Church properties throughout the territory, often spending the night in such places to avoid attacks on their homes.

The Church paid a fearsome price for standing by the East Timorese population under these trying circumstances. For example, in the south coast town of Suai in early September, three priests were killed during a massacre of hundreds of people taking shelter at the local church. Near the town of Laga in the far eastern part of the territory, nine Church workers, including two nuns and three seminarians, were butchered by a militia gang. On a different level, the diocesan offices, called the Camara Ecclesiastica, the center of the local Church and the repository of its history, were destroyed; archives dating to the sixteenth century, when Dominican missionaries first landed on Timor, were put to the torch. During the army's assault on the diocesan offices in September 1999, some people hiding there were killed.

But it was the people at large who suffered the most, with untold deaths and as many as 90 percent displaced by Indonesian forces. Countless homes were set ablaze. When he returned in early October, after being forced to leave in the midst of the September violence, Belo emphasized that under such conditions, "a bishop has no special status."

EMBODIMENT OF THE ASPIRATIONS OF THE PEOPLE

Sentiments such as this one, manifested not only by Bishop Belo but also by many in East Timor's Catholic Church as a whole, help explain how an institution once regarded by critics as a colonial anachronism had become an embodiment of the aspirations of the people. And while the Church's role in East Timor's referendum and subsequent siege of terror are clearly of pivotal importance, they are only the latest examples of the Church's staunch defense of the East Timorese throughout the Indonesian occupation.

This defense began in the earliest hours of Indonesia's assault on Dili in 1975,

Figure 4.2   Unmarked graves, Mount Matebian. After the invasion, many people fled to Mount Matebian. Located in the east, the mountain came to symbolize the will of the East Timorese to survive. Xanana called Mount Matebian "our big home" when it became the last resistance stronghold in 1978. Courtesy: Ross Bird.

as people flocked to the bishop's waterfront home, then inhabited by a Portuguese prelate, Dom José Joaquim, for protection. As one priest recently put it, "In the first twenty-four hours of the invasion, Indonesia lost both the Catholic Church and the people." Belo's predecessor, Martinho da Costa Lopes, also a native East Timorese, was revered for fearless statements and actions that highlighted the plight of his beleaguered compatriots. Monsignor Lopes and a number of members of the clergy did what they could to defend the people from attack. Some clergy suffered alongside the hundreds of thousands who lived in the mountains from 1975 through 1978 when these areas were still largely under the control of the Falintil, the military wing of East Timor's independence movement. These clergy were important eyewitnesses to the terrible bombing conducted by the Indonesian air force with U.S.–supplied OV10 Bronco counterinsurgency planes, which destroyed crops and otherwise made farming impossible and ultimately led to a catastrophic famine in the countryside that claimed many tens of thousands of lives by 1980. Thousands more were forced to surrender to Indonesian forces during this period, and in various ways clergy helped save the lives of many people and offered comfort to countless others. When East Timorese later were required under Indonesian law to choose a religion, they naturally chose the Catholic Church, which had become a rallying point and was, throughout most of the Indonesian occupation, the only legal indigenous institution that could provide some measure of protection to the population. By 1999, more than 90 percent of East Timor's 750,000 to 800,000 people had become Catholic. The fact that relations between the Catholic Church and indigenous religious groups had been historically friendly facilitated the large-scale conversions to Catholicism.

DELICATE AND DIFFICULT ROLE

The Church played an extremely delicate and difficult role throughout the years of the Indonesian occupation. For years, Catholic clergy were the only ones to have regular access to the prisons where many East Timorese were held under appalling conditions. Until recently the Church had a degree of immunity in its dealings with the Indonesian state, but it was also the object of coercion. Thus, Monsignor Lopes was removed by the Vatican in 1983 after years of pressure by influential Indonesian military leaders, who resented his statements as well as his moral support for East Timor's resistance movement.

Military authorities believed that Bishop Belo might be a more pliable figure than his predecessor. They were proved wrong. For example, Belo continued the policy first proposed by Monsignor Lopes that established Tetum, the East Timorese lingua franca, as the language in which Mass was celebrated throughout the territory, rather than Indonesian, as the authorities had wanted. The importance of this linguistic decision should not be underestimated, for it helped reinforce the role of the local Catholic Church as a place of cultural and spiritual resistance to Indonesian rule. This was part of a complex stance by the Church and the bishop himself. Although Belo generally made a point of discouraging active Church support for the organized resistance movement, believing as he did that such support could lead to harsh reprisals by the Indonesian military, he also did what he could to mediate between the two sides and defend his fellow East Timorese from attack. More to the point, while some in the resistance and in the international solidarity movement saw him as being too accommodating, Belo refused to endorse any position, whether that of the Indonesian state or of the resistance, that he did not see as having immediate and concrete benefits for the people as a whole.

Church events and church buildings and facilities became an important locus of the struggle between Indonesian authorities and the East Timorese independence movement. In the first major public demonstration in East Timor to gain international attention since the 1975 invasion, dozens of young people waved banners and shouted slogans following a Mass celebrated by Pope John Paul II in October 1989. Dozens were arrested and tortured, while scores of others took refuge in Bishop Belo's residence. In November 1991, thousands of young people marched from the church of St. Anthony of Motael to commemorate the death of Sebastiao Gomes, a young activist who had been killed on the grounds of that church two weeks earlier. When the assemblage reached the Santa Cruz cemetery, Indonesian forces opened fire on the group, killing dozens; many more "disappeared" in subsequent days. The Indonesian military brutally interrogated priests suspected of assisting the young demonstrators. Some priests were forced to leave East Timor; others were severely threatened. Coexistence became the watchword, even among members of the clergy who were staunch supporters of the resistance, as I saw myself during a visit to the territory in 1995. Some in the clergy supported the resistance; others collaborated to some extent with Indonesian authorities; most worked in a kind of delicate limbo in which life on a day-to-day basis depended upon reasonable relations with all sides.

On the international stage, however, the position of the Church helped derail Jakarta's drive to gain legitimacy for its takeover of East Timor. At no time did the Vatican extend official recognition to Indonesia's claim of sovereignty over East Timor, despite numerous attempts by the Suharto regime to coax Rome in that direction. The Church's stance was simply in accordance with the position of the United Nations as a whole, but it denied Jakarta important diplomatic backing that would have made it much easier to gain wider support for recognition of its claim. Beyond the elite levels of Rome, numerous church organizations throughout the world, Protestant as well as Catholic, played an indispensable role in international solidarity efforts with regard to East Timor. Without this kind of support from church sources, in terms of political backing as well as human links, it would have been impossible to sustain a movement of such solidarity over the years. Without such international support, the situation of the people of East Timor might have been even worse than it was.

As he had in the past, Bishop Belo played a critical role in 1999 in bringing the full horror of what was taking place to world notice. In the face of the attacks of September 6 and the likelihood that they would not cease without international intervention, Bishop Belo needed to leave East Timor as soon as possible. Thus he began the long journey to Italy to meet with Pope John Paul II at his summer residence outside Rome to give an account of the latest shocking developments in a conflict that two decades ago had already claimed a third of East Timor's population. The Pope responded to the plight of East Timor with several sharply worded statements in September 1999. These helped to galvanize international public opinion. The Vatican, known for its caution on matters regarding East Timor because of the delicate role of Catholics in Indonesia, had clearly changed its position. On the critical question of armed peacekeepers in the face of the slaughter of 1999, Archbishop Jean-Louis Tauran, Secretary for Relations with States, in early September was the first Vatican official to call for an international force to be sent to East Timor. Looking back in an interview in New York on

October 24, 1999, Tauran stressed that international troops had to be sent to East Timor "in order to avoid a full-scale massacre."

As East Timor moves toward independence, the Catholic Church in East Timor will play a crucial role in the bereavement and recovery of a long-suffering people, even as the Catholic Church internationally provides diplomatic, moral, and material support to help ensure the survival of this new nation.

Part II

Referendum
and Independence

5

With UNAMET in East Timor—
An Historian's Personal View

Geoffrey Robinson

For ten days in September, armed militia gangs and their Indonesian army patrons laid siege to the U.N. compound in Dili, East Timor. Inside were some five hundred U.N. staff and more than 1,500 local people who had sought refuge there. I had been working with the United Nations since June and was one of those trapped in the compound during those days. Like others there, I slept on a bit of cardboard, ate appalling French army rations, grew accustomed to the constant sound of automatic weapons fire just outside the wall, and breathed in the acrid smoke that filled the air from the city burning around us. Like others, I worried that the militia might come over the wall at any time, unimpeded by the Indonesian army soldiers who were ostensibly protecting us.

Despite these natural fears, many of us who worked with the United Nations were actually less worried about the militia than about being party to a failed and perhaps a shameful process—failed for the people of East Timor and shameful for the United Nations. Most of us knew from what we had heard of other U.N. missions, in Rwanda for example, and from our own experience in East Timor, that such an outcome was not impossible. Even during the worst of the violence, and in the midst of the terrible siege of early September, we often asked ourselves what the legacy of our mission would be, and whether we would be party to another United Nations fiasco.

I do not have any simple answers to those questions, but I can offer some insights based on my own experience as a member of the U.N. team on the ground in East Timor.

SOME HISTORY

Claiming to be threatened by communist insurrection in its neighborhood, and supported by the United States government, in early December 1975 Indonesia launched a combined land, sea, and air invasion of East Timor, which was until then a Portuguese colony. The following year, Indonesia formalized its forced annexation of the territory, declaring East Timor its twenty-seventh province. Though the move was never recognized by the United Nations, and the people of East Timor and their international supporters resisted it tenaciously, Indonesia continued to occupy the territory for the next twenty-four years.

During those years, Indonesian forces were responsible for human rights violations on a staggering scale, leading to the death of an estimated two hundred thousand people, more than one quarter of the preinvasion population. Throughout this period, neither the United Nations nor any individual state had the inclination to challenge so important a political and economic player as Indonesia over a small half island the size of New Jersey. On the contrary, those best placed to help, such as the United States, declined to do so. For its part, Indonesia refused categorically to contemplate any challenge to its claimed sovereignty.

The apparent impasse changed dramatically in January 1999, when Indonesia's new president, B.J. Habibie—who had surfed to power in May 1998 on the popular wave that swept President Suharto away after thirty-two years—suddenly proposed that the people of East Timor should be given a chance to vote on whether they wished to remain a part of Indonesia or not. This stunning about-face shocked many Indonesians, and in particular the armed forces, the TNI.

Despite TNI dissent, Habibie's proposal led to a set of accords between Indonesia, Portugal, and the United Nations—known as the May 5 Agreements—under which East Timorese would be given an opportunity to vote on their political future. More precisely, they were to be asked, in a referendum or "Popular Consultation," to accept or reject an offer of special autonomy under Indonesian rule. The rejection of special autonomy, the agreements made clear, would set East Timor on the path toward independence.

If that part of the May 5 Agreements appeared too good to be true, there was another element that from the outset was fundamentally, indeed dangerously, flawed. That was the agreement on security that placed sole responsibility for maintaining law and order during the Popular Consultation in the hands of Indonesian security forces—the same forces that had been responsible for twenty-four years of systematic human rights abuse and that were known to oppose the very idea of a Popular Consultation. Notwithstanding this flaw, the U.N. Assistance Mission in East Timor (UNAMET) began to deploy personnel in late May 1999, with the almost impossible aim of holding the Popular Consultation in August, less than three months away.

POPULAR CONSULTATION: THE DECISION TO PROCEED

UNAMET's Political Affairs office, of which I was a part, had the job of assessing whether the conditions existed for a free and fair ballot, and advising both the head of the mission, Ian Martin, and the U.N. secretary general, on this matter.

In practice, the advice we gave was mediated, and occasionally contradicted, by an array of bureaucratic and political actors in the U.N. system in New York. The lead agency within the U.N. secretariat was the Department of Political Affairs (DPA), but the Department of Peace Keeping Operations (DPKO) was closely involved in strategy discussions. At the political level, the United Nations' East Timor policy was informed and guided by a group of five countries—the United States, United Kingdom, Australia, New Zealand and Japan—together known as the Core Group. During the summer, the Core Group met with DPA and DPKO officials roughly every week and, when the situation grew critical in early September, they met on a daily basis.

To those of us on the ground in East Timor, it was immediately apparent that the conditions did not exist for a free and fair ballot, and that message was reported consistently to the Core Group in New York. Of particular concern was the presence of armed pro-Indonesian militia gangs that roamed with impunity throughout the territory, engaging in acts of violence and terror against ordinary people. These militia groups were armed, trained, and fully backed by the Indonesian armed forces, the TNI, and in many cases TNI soldiers were themselves militia members. The TNI's reasons for supporting the militia were in one sense rather simple: they wished to terrorize the population into accepting continued Indonesian rule, while distancing themselves from any responsibility for the violence.

Faced with this situation, the question naturally arose: Should we proceed with the ballot despite the violence and terror that characterized the pre-election security environment? The advice we put to the head of mission, and to the U.N. authorities in New York, in July was that we should *not* proceed and that we should use the threat of postponement to pressure the Indonesian government into fulfilling its commitments under the May 5 Agreements. In the end, that argument did not prevail. Although there were two minor postponements, and strong declarations from the UNAMET head of mission and the U.N. secretary general that Indonesia would need to do more to guarantee security, the process continued without significant interruption.

Though initially we took a stand against them, it must be said that the arguments in favor of proceeding with the vote had merit. DPA and DPKO officials, and the Core Group, wished to proceed according to schedule because they feared that delay might lead to a decline in international support for the mission, especially within the Security Council. There was also concern at U.N. headquarters that any serious delay might derail the process altogether—for example, by providing Indonesia with an excuse to back out of the agreement—and thereby throw away a unique historical opportunity to resolve the East Timor issue.

That was certainly how many East Timorese saw it, particularly those—as it turned out, the vast majority—who wanted a chance to change the political status quo. They pointed out that any serious delay would only benefit the pro-Indonesian side, the side responsible for the violence, and the side that did not wish to see a free expression of popular will. East Timorese from all walks of life urged UNAMET to proceed in spite of the violence and the militia threats.

Based on these considerations, voter registration proceeded with only a minor delay. And as the registration process got underway in July, we witnessed something quite remarkable. East Timorese defied the militias and the TNI. They walked or rode for miles, stood in long lines in the hot sun—and braved militia threats and outright assault—all for the chance to register. After twenty-two days, roughly 450,000 had registered, about 100,000 more than the most optimistic estimates of U.N. electoral officials.

Nobody who was there to witness it will forget August 30, the day of the vote. East Timorese—many dressed in their Sunday best, and some having left home in the middle of the night to reach the polling station by dawn—once again defied the militias for the chance to vote on their future. When the figures were tallied at the end of the day, an extraordinary 98.6 percent of registered voters had cast their ballots. And when the results were announced a few days later, an overwhelming majority—78.5 percent—had rejected special autonomy under Indonesian rule and chosen independence.

BACKLASH AND SIEGE: THE DECISION TO EVACUATE

While it had not been what we Political Affairs officers had advised, the decision to proceed with the registration and with the vote appeared to have been vindicated. Almost immediately, however, the wisdom of that decision was thrown into question. Within hours of the end of voting, pro-Indonesian militia groups began a rampage of violence against those perceived as enemies. Among the first victims was a local UNAMET staff member, a school teacher, stabbed to death by militia men as he helped to load the ballot boxes into U.N. vehicles for transport to the counting center, just after the polls had closed.

The situation grew even more volatile after the announcement of the result on the morning of September 4. Within an hour or so, the militias and the TNI began an unprecedented campaign of violence, burning, and looting in all the major towns in the territory, including Dili where the United Nations had its headquarters. Within days, hundreds of thousands of people had been forced to flee their homes, UNAMET had evacuated all of its regional offices, and the militias, who had overwhelmingly *lost* the vote, effectively controlled the territory. In Dili, UNAMET personnel who ventured out on September 4 and 5 came under direct,

Longing

How I long, how I long
For the pillows of my dreams
How I long for the cushion where I'll sleep
How I long, how I long
for the place where I'll dream

I will sleep, I will dream
I will fly, fly up high
I will reach, I will go
Climb Ramelau* I will try

I will climb, I will climb
I will reach the peak up high
I will see I will shout
I will scream oh so loud

I will look at the sky
stare the makikit** fly
See such might so high
Look up and wish I could fly

Flying high, flying high

I will ask for a word I will whisper
Please teach me how to fly
I want to go, I want to leave
Leave all this behind

I can't stand it anymore
I can hear the screams close by
Too much pain too much sorrow
Too much grief, too much

I can feel the walls closing in all around
Squeezing, draining, sucking all that is me
How easy it would be to drop, to fall from this peak
Fall from up high, let myself go . . . simply just die

—Emanuel Braz

*Mount Ramelau, East Timor
**makikit = eagle

armed attack by the militia, with the result that movement outside the compound was stopped, and the United Nations compound was effectively under siege.

In this context, the question arose: Would the United Nations evacuate its international staff, leaving behind roughly four hundred local staff, and more than 1,500 East Timorese who had taken refuge in the compound? From the perspective of those responsible for security both in Dili and New York, the answer was clear. The security situation was untenable, and the standard U.N. procedure under such circumstances was to evacuate international staff, and only international staff, as soon as possible. There was relief when the unusual decision was taken, after strong representations from UNAMET, to evacuate all local staff first. But relief was followed quickly by shock when, on the evening of September 8, a decision was taken to evacuate all international staff, leaving the 1,500 refugees to their fate.

Three of us in the Political Affairs office were given the task of conveying that terrible news to the community leaders within the compound, to people like the courageous Canossian nun, Sister Esmeralda, and others whom we had come to know and respect. Sitting on wooden chairs in that drab office, surrounded by friends whom we were about to betray, we could scarcely find the strength to speak. And as we spoke we wept. But we also resolved to fight this decision. Immediately after the meeting, we approached the head of mission and conveyed our view that the decision to evacuate was wrong, politically and morally. He did not disagree.

Meanwhile, a sense of outrage had begun to grip other U.N. staff and the journalists and observers who had taken refuge in the compound. Those feelings fueled a rebellion of sorts. By about 9:00 p.m. there was near unanimity that international U.N. staff would not leave before the 1,500 refugees had been taken to safety. Surprised, but I believe also heartened, by this show of resolve, the head of mission contacted U.N. officials in New York by telephone. By the end of the evening the decision to evacuate had been reversed. UNAMET staff would not be leaving until the 1,500 had been taken to safety. What happened in the next few days was almost as remarkable. After weighing all of the possibilities, it was decided that the refugees would be airlifted to Darwin together with UNAMET staff. Facing intense international pressure—including direct representations from the U.N. secretary general and the Security Council—the government of Indonesia had agreed to let them go.

THE DECISION TO SEND IN TROOPS

The decision to airlift East Timorese refugees was unprecedented in the United Nations' experience. The crisis had highlighted one of the major weaknesses of the UNAMET mandate: Throughout the consultation process and the siege, both U.N. staff and refugees were without real protection.

Figure 5.1 UNAMET poster, August 1999. (In Tetum: "No matter what the outcome on August 30th, UNAMET will NOT leave after the consultation. UNAMET is here to: Conduct the popular consultation, transport the ballot papers, count all the votes together, remain in East Timor after the vote. Vote and have YOUR say in East Timor's future.") From the UNAMET website, http://www.un.org/peace/etimor99/POSTERS/p4tt.jpg.

No U.N. personnel carried arms in East Timor. When we left the compound we were shot at, and during the siege it became customary to wear flak jackets when walking out of doors inside the compound. Worse, we were powerless to assist East Timorese who needed protection, a fraction of whom called us in desperation when telephone lines were still functioning. We could only guess how many were killed in the aftermath of the vote because of our powerlessness.

This situation inevitably gave rise to another question: Why did the United Nations not deploy peacekeeping forces to protect its personnel and the people of East Timor? Although UNAMET was never formally asked for advice on this issue, as early as July some of us began informally to convey to DPA and DPKO officials, and to any visitors who would hear us (including various U.S. government and congressional delegations), our belief that an armed force must be deployed *before* the vote.

The answer we heard was that it would be impossible to deploy peacekeepers without Indonesian approval, or without invoking chapter 7 of the U.N. Charter. And, because it was assumed that neither of these things would happen, it was unrealistic to push for or to expect peacekeepers. We were also told, as early as July, that it would take too long—three months at least—to deploy such a force, so there was no point in discussing a preballot deployment in any case. The more practical and cost-effective approach, a series of memoranda from New York explained, was to insist that the Indonesian authorities live up to their obligations for maintaining peace and security.

As far as we could make out from Dili, these arguments were put most forcefully by DPKO, with the strong backing of two key states in the Core Group, the United States and the United Kingdom. Whoever the architects of the policy were, that line prevailed at least until September 9 or 10, when there was a dramatic shift in attitude within the Core Group, supported by DPA, by the Security Council delegation then visiting Jakarta, and by the secretary general himself.

On September 12—facing unprecedented diplomatic and financial pressure—the government of Indonesia did agree to accept a Multinational Force (MNF), and shortly thereafter the U.N. Security Council passed a resolution lending its support to a swift deployment. That resolution, moreover, invoked chapter 7 of the U.N. Charter and gave the MNF authority to use "all necessary means" to restore security, facilitate humanitarian assistance, and permit UNAMET to carry out its mandate. Finally, notwithstanding the earlier claim that a force would take months to assemble and deploy, the MNF was on the ground within a week of the Security Council resolution.

And that was not all. Even as the siege continued, U.N. agencies and private nongovernmental organizations began to coordinate a major humanitarian relief effort that was set in motion within days of the MNF deployment. Simultaneously, U.N. staff in Darwin met East Timorese leaders, including Xanana Gusmão, and plans were being drafted there and in New York for an accelerated transfer from Indonesian to U.N. authority. Meanwhile, a rare special session of the

The Shrine of Remembrance

In the language of images
the images of words
and unuttered thoughts
I can feel the distance getting closer.

The Shrine of Remembrance.
On the eleventh hour of the eleventh
    day of the eleventh month
the sun shines on the altar.
A minute of silence for the fallen
    soldiers.
Fallen white soldiers
Let's walk up the shrine.
A pyramid at the top and an angel too.
Muddy shoes clapping on cemented
    steps.
Let's warm our hands on the flame of
    remembrance.
Naa, let's just walk up.
Shall I tell my friend about the
    promise?
Naa, we helped them because we
    wanted to.
Now it's up to them whether they
    keep the promise or not.
I'm not looking for a saviour in the
    white Monument.
Although, when I'm standing at its top
my gaze can reach the land in the
    shape of a crocodile
where grandfather mountain meets the
    sky
and where makikit* glides
over the morning fog
above the village
tramped by steel boots.
My gaze becomes makikit's.
In the sky I follow

the woman with dust-coated feet.
She sways in and out of the mist.
Her head carries a clay pot.
She treads the dirt path to the
    mountain spring,
passing the sleepy soldier drooped
    against his gun.
She dodges through the rain-sprayed
    gums,
hiding her fear of rape from shafts of
    sunlight.
Her feet moistened with mud,
reach the forest green mountain
where the spring sparkles
in between stones and logs.
I can feel the distance getting closer.
My feet become hers
plunging in the crystal, clear water,
splashing up the stream.

Streaks of muddy water drift down the
    mountain.
Muddy, brown, cloudy, water.
I walk into her dream.
Misty, hazy, foggy, water.
I feel earth throb up the soles of my
    feet.
Motherland is alive.
I see my reflection in her brown water.
She sees her reflection in my brown
    eyes.
White leaflets land on the stream.
"Your friends will not forget you."
I can feel the distance getting closer,
    closer,
here on the summit of the shrine
of remembrance of the fallen white
    soldier.

—Elizabete Lim Gomes

This poem was written in August 1998. In 1999 an Australian-led peacekeeping force was in East Timor. The terrible betrayal that distanced the East Timorese from Australians has been redeemed. Thank You, Australia. (ELG)

Editor's note: "The Shrine of Remembrance" is a huge memorial to Australian soldiers who died in World War I (and later wars). It is located in Melbourne.

*makikit = eagle

U.N. Human Rights Commission was convened, and a resolution passed on September 27 that called for the formation of an international commission of inquiry to investigate possible crimes against humanity and breaches of international humanitarian law in East Timor. This meant that there was now a chance—though in view of strong resistance from China and other states, admittedly a rather distant one—that East Timor would have an international criminal tribunal, like those that had been established for Rwanda and Yugoslavia.

ANOTHER UNITED NATIONS FIASCO?

What then will be the legacy of this mission for the people of East Timor and for the United Nations? Were those of us who worked with UNAMET party to another United Nations fiasco? Some preliminary conclusions are possible.

The cost of the U.N. effort in East Timor was high. In the immediate aftermath of the Popular Consultation, more than half of the population of East Timor was displaced and hundreds, possibly thousands, were killed. In addition, much of the physical infrastructure of the territory was destroyed, and the local economy was left in tatters. The consultation also raised difficult political questions: What would prevent hostile pro-Indonesian forces from attacking or otherwise destabilizing an independent East Timor? How would this new microstate survive economically? And what place if any would East Timorese have within a transitional U.N. administration?

On the other hand, UNAMET achieved something that for more than two decades was said to be impossible, and that even two or three months ago few observers considered possible: a legitimate act of self-determination for the people of East Timor. Although the human costs of that achievement have been high, many East Timorese appear to consider them acceptable, particularly when they are measured against the terrible cost of twenty-four years of Indonesian occupation. And, although it was not part of the original plan, the U.N. mission has spearheaded an unusually strong international humanitarian and economic reconstruction effort that should go some way toward making East Timor a viable new state.

For the United Nations itself, the legacy of the mission is similarly mixed. It is clear that, by accepting a flawed security agreement of May 5, 1999, the United Nations helped to expose the East Timorese people, and its own staff, to unacceptable levels of violence. It also failed to push for the deployment of an armed force in advance of the anticipated postballot violence as many urged it to do. The result of these failures was that many people were killed and displaced.

At the same time, UNAMET avoided the pitfalls of many other U.N. missions and simultaneously established some important precedents. Perhaps most importantly, local U.N. staff and refugees who had sought refuge with the United Nations were not abandoned to their fate, as they had so often been in other places, but were evacuated to safety before international staff was withdrawn. Also encouraging, an effective multinational force was mobilized and deployed with U.N. sanction within a few weeks of the onset of the worst violence. And in its resolution sanctioning the force, the Security Council took the unusual step of citing chapter 7 of the U.N. Charter and of empowering the force to use "all necessary means" to fulfill its mandate. These were important achievements that one can reasonably hope will allow the United Nations to work more effectively in the years ahead.

In short, the United Nations' mission in East Timor was not a fiasco. But, unquestionably, there is a long road ahead, both for East Timor and for the United Nations.

November 16, 1999

POSTSCRIPT

I returned to East Timor in November 1999 to assist UNAMET in preparing for a month of human rights investigations. It seemed a worthy cause, a chance to see that those responsible for the violence of September would be held accountable, but the fact was that I would have accepted any excuse to go back. I wanted to know what had become of friends and colleagues with whom I had lost touch during the chaos. I wanted a chance to say hello and then farewell in my own time, not under duress. I wanted to see and hear first hand whether my thoughts about the referendum had been misguided. I wanted to know whether, in the eyes of East Timorese, the U.N. intervention had been a terrible mistake.

IMPRESSIONS

It was no surprise to see the flattened, blackened buildings, the burnt out vehicles, as we drove from the airport into Dili. I had already seen those sights during a UNAMET reconnaissance patrol on September 14; and later that night I had watched the city smoke and burn from the back of an open truck as we evacuated with some 1,500 East Timorese refugees. More surprising than the devastation was the presence of so many people on the streets, evidence of an almost miraculous rebirth of the city so soon after its destruction.

When we drove through Dili on September 14, clad in flak jackets, conscious of danger, there were virtually no people in sight—only scavenging black pigs, a handful of soldiers and militia men wearing red and white bandanas, loading up trucks with loot, heading for the border. Now just over a month later Dili, though still a burnt out shell, was alive with people, humming with the unmistakable signs of human vitality. On the road from the airport, near Comoro, a bustling market had sprung up, where women sold vegetables, fruit, Indonesian cigarettes, bottled water, and the occasional can of Coke. Along the road people headed home to rebuild, carrying pieces of wood and metal scavenged from around the city and blue tarps distributed by humanitarian agencies.

Over the next few weeks, small shops began to sprout up in the corners of buildings that had not quite burned to the ground. Not far from the governor's office in downtown Dili, the brand new "Speed Café" began to serve good East Timorese coffee, cold drinks, and an occasional grilled fish to a delighted clientele of expatriates and locals. At about the same time, a good Portuguese restaurant opened replacing the popular "Totonito's" that had been burned to the ground by the militias in September. Like thousands of others, the proprietor had been forced to flee Dili, but she had used her time in exile to purchase basic supplies to restart the restaurant upon her return.

These were not isolated cases. Throughout the country there was remarkable optimism and energy in the face of terrible loss. Walking in the middle of Dili one morning in mid-November I became conscious of an unusual, swelling sound. Following a crowd that rushed through the old governor's compound, I turned a corner and saw what must have been twenty-thousand people surging down the street, many of them holding brooms high in the air. In front was resistance leader Xanana Gusmão, who had recently returned to East Timor after years in custody in Jakarta. He too carried a broom on high, a symbol of his call that day for people to begin the task of cleaning and rebuilding their new country.

The same pattern was evident outside of Dili. The small town of Manatuto, about two hours east of Dili along the beautiful north coast, had been so systematically burned by militias and Indonesian army troops in September that when I visited in November fewer than 20 percent of buildings remained intact. Yet the walls still standing were filled with defiant graffiti, including one message that read "Shattered but free!" (*Biar dihancurkan asal merdeka!*), and another that said simply "Freedom is sweet" (*Merdeka enak*).

Of course, not everything was rosy. Surveying the scene in November, it was abundantly clear that the violence and the forced evacuation, the near total destruction of the physical infrastructure, and the sudden collapse of the entire administrative apparatus had left deep scars and had created vast new problems. It had become common to refer to East Timor's condition as "ground zero."

At the UNAMET compound, recently cleaned and refurbished by Gurkha soldiers, there was excitement and optimism but it was tinged with sadness. Many of the local staff—office assistants, drivers, translators and others—had returned, either from the mountains or from exile in West Timor and Australia, to resume their posts. They seemed happy enough to be back at work, but conversations often turned to the horrible events of September, to the loss of loved ones and friends.

Outside the U.N. compound in Dili, among the most visible signs that all was not well were the seamy hotels and bars that had been thrown up within days of the arrival of international forces. One such hotel, a collection of portable containers lined up in rows on land reportedly leased from a departing Indonesian army officer, quickly gained a reputation for selling more than rooms. On the other side of town, the Dili Hotel had become the main watering hole for a rapidly expanding expatriate community that included not just thousands of humanitarian aid workers, U.N. staff, and InterFET soldiers, but a variety of schemers and "entrepreneurs" hoping to capitalize on the absence of taxes, a legal system, or a police force in this state in formation.

RIGHTS

Beyond Dili the most pressing sign of the mounting problems in November were the estimated 150,000 refugees who then remained in camps in West Timor. The problem was not strictly a humanitarian one; indeed it never had been. The majority of the refugees would and could have been returned safely to East Timor except for the fact that the camps were patrolled, with TNI acquiescence, by pro-Indonesian militia. Intent on thwarting the result of the August ballot, these militiamen spread rumors of fighting and chaos in East Timor and threatened refugees who expressed interest in returning. Despite a number of visits from international figures, including the U.S. representative to the United Nations, Richard Holbrooke, the problem remained unresolved months after the violence.

The refugees, moreover, were only the most visible manifestation of a much larger problem—the legacy of twenty-four years of systematic human rights violations by Indonesian forces and their local allies. The events of September had stimulated strong international pressures to investigate, at the very least, the violations of 1999 and to bring those responsible to justice. Accordingly, in early November a team of U.N. human rights experts came to East Timor to conduct a joint investigation. About a week later a delegation from a special unit of Indonesia's Human Rights Commission visited to conduct its own investigation. Later in the month a U.N. Commission of Inquiry visited the country to conduct the inquiry called for by the Human Rights Commission in its resolution of September 27.

Notwithstanding serious resistance from the Indonesian government and its allies, and enormous logistical obstacles on the ground, the U.N. experts and the U.N. Commission of Inquiry conducted serious and credible investigations. The quality of their reports owed a great deal to the valuable cooperation they received from local nongovernmental organizations, from eyewitnesses, and from UNAMET staff. The reports they subsequently released highlighted the responsibility of Indonesian military officers for the violence both before and after the ballot and proposed that further investigations should be conducted with a view to bringing those responsible promptly to justice. These visits helped to generate hope that some sort of international tribunal might finally be established to bring those responsible to account.

The same could not be said for the visit by members of the Indonesian Commission on Human Rights that took place in mid-November. Indeed, when they heard about the planned visit, many East Timorese activists and political leaders were very angry. Some took the view that the delegation should not be welcomed, and all agreed that sensitive information and eyewitnesses should not be made available to the delegates.

There was understandable suspicion about the motives of the Indonesian delegation. After all the same body had failed utterly to curtail or even speak out against the rampant violations that had occurred in the preceding months and years. (Indeed, some commission members had been part of the Indonesian government apparatus that had openly supported pro-Indonesian campaigning and militia violence.) It was widely suspected that the inquiry had been set up primarily to undermine demands for an international tribunal.

In a number of respects, however, the Indonesian investigation surprised the critics. First of all, in a break from past practice, the commission included a number of respected human rights activists and lawyers. These activists and lawyers had been outspoken in their criticism of the military and the government and insisted on questioning high ranking military and civilian officials once they had returned to Jakarta. Second, the commission report, released in January 2000, accused military and government authorities of responsibility for "crimes against humanity" and called for the indictment of thirty-two named individuals, including the former armed forces commander, General Wiranto, and several other military officers.[1]

Citing the commission's report, Indonesian president Wahid called for Wiranto to resign from his post as Coordinating Minister for Political and Security Affairs. After a tense standoff, during which Wiranto refused to step down and Jakarta rumbled with rumors of a coup, Wahid prevailed and Wiranto was dismissed. These developments suggested just how much had changed in Indonesian politics. Two years, even two months earlier, it would have been unimaginable that an Indonesian human rights body would accuse high ranking military officers of crimes against humanity, or that a civilian president would face off against Indonesia's most powerful general and win.

At the same time the actual impact of the commission's investigation remained far from clear. The main problem was that the commission itself did not have the power to indict; it could only urge the attorney general to conduct investigations after which he would decide whether indictments were warranted. And while the new attorney general, Marzuki Darusman, was known to have a genuine concern for human rights and the rule of law, it was by no means certain that he would be able to unearth evidence sufficient to indict those named. Nor was it clear that he would have the political support to push hard for such indictments or convictions. Even among those who believed that the commission members had acted in good faith there was concern that their dramatic report might simply be used as a foil by the military to deflect demands for an international inquiry and tribunal.

By early 2000 it seemed clear that this was exactly what was happening. Eager to restore good relations with Indonesia, and in particular with Indonesia's armed forces, the United States and other major powers began to soften demands for an international inquiry, suggesting that an Indonesian judicial process might suffice. At the same time, the U.S. Department of Defense began quietly to restore international military education and training (IMET) programs that had been cut in mid-September in protest against the military's involvement in the postballot violence. That softened position was endorsed by a resolution of the U.N. Security Council in February shortly after the secretary general returned from a visit to Dili and Jakarta. Under the circumstances, chances for an international tribunal began to look increasingly remote.

TENSIONS

In addition to these problems, there was also, in November, an unmistakable undercurrent of tension between East Timorese and the various United Nations' and other international bodies that had started to appear on the scene in late September. The tension was heightened by a perception that some of these international bodies were displaying an unseemly haste in mending fences with Indonesian authorities.

By all accounts, the international armed force (InterFET) that entered East Timor in late September had done an excellent job of restoring order, putting a swift end to militia violence, and managing the delicate task of getting the TNI out of the country by the end of October. But between late September and early November, for example, Australian forces raided the Dili home of a prominent leader of the National Council of Timorese Resistance (CNRT), Leandro Isaac, on three separate occasions. The explanation provided was that they had acted on intelligence tips that the house was a militia hideout. It is hard to believe that Australian intelligence was so poorly informed or coordinated that it could have made such a mistake three times over. Whatever the truth was, the incidents left a bitter taste in CNRT mouths.

Likewise, the international humanitarian organizations that arrived on the heels of InterFET achieved a good deal in extremely difficult circumstances, distributing tons of food and other humanitarian necessities, and assisting both internally displaced people and refugees to return to their homes. Yet by November the CNRT leadership was complaining openly about the arrogance of the international agencies and of their refusal to cooperate with CNRT in the planning and implementation of humanitarian operations.

Part of the problem was that neither InterFET nor the humanitarian agencies had an especially firm grasp of the recent history of East Timor, nor were they inclined or equipped to establish meaningful relations with East Timor's political, religious, and social leaders. That task was left to UNAMET, which had been asked to fill in until the U.N. Transitional Administration in East Timor (UNTAET) could be properly established. UNAMET was also called upon to fill the gaping hole that had been left by the sudden collapse of the entire political, legal, and administrative infrastructure.

UNAMET's work in this pretransitional period was hampered by a number of factors. First and foremost, in the crucial weeks and months after the crisis, UNAMET remained seriously understaffed and underresourced. The work of establishing a new political, administrative, and economic infrastructure was carried out by a handful of UNAMET staffers, most of whom had stayed on after the ballot. Physically and emotionally exhausted, working and living in difficult circumstances, and feeling that they were not adequately supported by U.N. headquarters in New York, this small group fairly quickly grew demoralized, and a number resigned. Reinforcements finally began to flow in mid-November, with the arrival of the head of UNTAET, Sergio Vieira de Mello, and his immediate staff. But the intervening months of violence and of political and administrative vacuum had already taken a serious toll.

The toll was evident in the growing strain in relations between CNRT and various international organizations. In addition to the earlier noted points of friction with InterFET and the humanitarian agencies, CNRT made a number of decisions that appeared to challenge or to impinge upon U.N. authority. One day in November, for example, Xanana Gusmão swept into the UNAMET compound accompanied by several of his own fully armed soldiers. Although it was later explained that InterFET had agreed to this arrangement, it was nevertheless a startling break with established protocol under which no arms were to be carried within the compound. In another apparent flexing of political authority, CNRT established its new headquarters in the town of Aileu, precisely on the site where the United Nations had begun to establish one of its district offices. After a few days of rather delicate discussions, the United Nations decided to move its offices elsewhere.

To those of us who had been with UNAMET's Political Affairs office through the summer, these signs of CNRT irritation toward the United Nations were worrying. It seemed to us that in the months before the ballot, UNAMET and CNRT had developed a good working relationship, characterized by mutual respect and frequent face-to-face communication. The apparent collapse of that relationship did not bode well for the period of transition. Yet the tension between UNTAET and CNRT was also understandable. The goal of ridding East Timor of Indonesian forces had finally been achieved after twenty-four years, and CNRT could rightly claim responsibility for that victory. It could also fairly speak on behalf of the hundreds of thousands of people who had died in gaining it. It was hardly surprising that CNRT wished to play a greater role in governing and rebuilding the country as soon as possible.

In short, as troubling as the tension between the United Nations and CNRT at first appeared to UNAMET old-timers, some came to view it as an understandable and perhaps even positive development—an indication that the people of East Timor were eager to take responsibility for their political future, and that East Timor's tradition of robust political opposition had survived the devastation of September.

Of course, the tensions that simmered in the postballot period were not only between CNRT and the various international agencies. The uncertainty and the vacuum of political power also gave rise to, or provided opportunities for the expression of, differences of opinion within CNRT, and among East Timorese more generally. In November differences were already emerging, for example, over issues of language, differences in perspective among generations, and between those associated with Falintil and those who worked in support movements underground.

REFLECTIONS

The differences in CNRT ranks that were already simmering in November 1999 seem likely to become more pressing as East Timor moves toward independence. Among the key questions are these: Who beyond the CNRT leadership should be permitted to speak on behalf of the people of East Timor? How much room should there be for the expression of opposition to the CNRT leadership? And what mechanisms or institutions should be established to channel such alternative viewpoints? The ways in which these questions are addressed now will provide some clue to the sort of political system that East Timor will have in coming years.

Similarly, the manner in which past violations of human rights are handled now will profoundly affect the prospects for success in bringing about political reconciliation among East Timorese, in ensuring future respect for the rule of law in East Timor, and in establishing a workable relationship with Indonesia. It will also influence the shape and direction of Indonesia's own continuing political transition, as well as the credibility and strength of international human rights norms and institutions. For all of these reasons, it must be hoped that key international players—in particular the United States, Australia, and the United Nations—will not renege on their earlier promises to ensure that past violations are properly investigated and those responsible brought to justice.

In addition to these questions about the future, a crucial question remains about the past. Was the United Nations right to proceed with the August 30 ballot under the poor security conditions that then prevailed? Seeing the physical destruction of East Timor, and hearing the stories of those who survived the violence, one cannot feel anything but the most profound regret, perhaps even shame, that security was entrusted to the Indonesian armed forces, and that international peacekeepers were not mobilized in advance of the ballot. At the same time, no one who has had a glimpse of Timor Loro Sae, so full of hope in spite of everything, can seriously doubt that it was right to proceed with the vote.

March 12, 2000

NOTE

1. *Komisi Penyelidik Pelanggaran Hak Asasi Manusia di Timor Timur, "Laporan Penyelidikan Pelanggaran Hak Asasi Manusia di Timor Timur,"* Jakarta, 31 January 2000.

6

The Militia, the Military, and the People of Bobonaro

Peter Bartu

Minister of Defense/Commander of the armed forces, General Wiranto has declared that the Indonesian Armed Forces is not a wild band of men who can be put on trial by anyone. The army always complies with official orders and always acts in conformity with the laws in force and with human rights.

"We have done the best we could in keeping within the law, acting with discipline and basic human rights," he said.—Suara Pembaruan (*The Voice of Renewal,* Jakarta), October 3, 1999

BACKGROUND

As a political officer with the United Nations Assistance Mission in East Timor (UNAMET) I reported on political developments in the volatile western districts of East Timor from May 22 to September 2, initially from Dili and then from Maliana, the capital of Bobonaro along the border with West Timor or Nusa Tenggara Timur province.

The situation in Bobonaro district was fluid and uncertain for the entire period of the Popular Consultation during which the East Timorese could choose to accept or reject the autonomy package offered by the Indonesian government. The local authorities repeatedly made it clear that they had not signed the May 5 Agreements and they offered only begrudging cooperation to UNAMET. Elite members of the District Administration (who stood to lose all if the autonomy option lost) and the Indonesian National Armed Forces (TNI), who would have to withdraw from East Timor, pulled out all stops to improve the chances of pro-autonomy vote. A parallel track of coercion and violence was pursued through militia proxies. The militia groups gradually fell apart over the different phases of the UNAMET–run consultation. The East Timorese people and rank-and-file militia members passively rejected their instructions and ultimately many left the organization. By the time of the consultation on August 30, 1999, the TNI and the Indonesian police (*Polri*), including East Timorese in both units, became increasingly responsible for all violence and intimidation. The precision and confidence with which they executed their strategies indicates coordination from the highest levels.

CONSULTATION STRUCTURES

UNAMET divided East Timor into eight regional centers based on population density and logistical considerations. A political officer was assigned to each center and worked alongside a Regional Electoral Coordinator (in charge of technical aspects of the consultation), a regional U.N. Civilian Police chief (responsible for advising *Polri* on their security obligations under the Agreements), and a small team of military liaison officers who maintained contact with the TNI. Through July and August UNAMET had up to sixty international staff working in at least twenty-two separate locations throughout Bobonaro district.

To assist with implementing the agreements, the *Polri*, the TNI, and the Indonesian Foreign Ministry (*Deplu*) each assigned English-speaking liaison officers to work alongside UNAMET and the predominantly East Timorese district administration. Typically, *Polri* liaison officers had served on U.N. missions before, in countries such as Namibia, Cambodia, and Bosnia. They worked alongside their local counterparts, many of whom were intimately involved in the prointegration cause. Other elements of *Polri* included the *Kontigen Lorosae*, specially formed units that augmented the regular *Polri* and also police Mobile Brigade (*Brimob*) units including *Brimob* special forces. *Deplu* representatives dealt with the district administration, monitored UNAMET's adherence, or otherwise, to the Agreements and reported to the Indonesian Task Force led by Ambassador Agus Tamizi in Dili. The TNI liaison officers were a bridge between UNAMET and the TNI and in the main reflected a consistently singular and insular view of the process at odds with the broader perspective of their *Polri* and *Deplu* counterparts who had external experience.

Over time the dynamics among the liaison officers provided unique insights into their respective institutions. Under the Agreements the official elevation of the *Polri* to the central position for all security issues was irksome for the TNI. The military resented being sidelined but ultimately used their "diminished role" to avoid taking responsibility for the actions of the militia, whom they clearly controlled. While the *Polri* were formally separated from the TNI on April 1, 1999, they still came under the command of Defense Minister General Wiranto, who was also the chief of staff of the armed forces. However, they were never given the power to meet their security obligations. In the circumstances, many

Polri were frightened of their new role, some were frustrated and others were resigned to the charade in which they had to participate. As one senior officer confessed: "If we arrest a militiaman, Dili and Jakarta will tell us to let them go. If we shoot one of them, then we know they will attack our [district] headquarters." On only one occasion in mid-May did *Polri* attempt to apprehend militia in Maliana—for the theft of cars and motorcycles looted from proindependence houses. A three-hour gunfight ensued when the militia and the TNI fired on the *Polri*.

BOBONARO DISTRICT

East Timor is divided into thirteen districts, loosely but not exclusively based on the Portuguese administrative structure that cohered the traditional *liurai* feudal system, linguistic groupings, and often formidable geography into a system of regencies. Bobonaro, the fourth largest district (*kabupaten*) with some one hundred thousand people, incorporates six subdistricts (*kecamatan*) stretching from the northern littoral to the southern mountains and dense jungle that define the border with Cova Lima District. The Loes river and a chain of mountains along the east separate Bobonaro from Liquiça district, the central and coffee-rich district of Ermera and Ainaro district to the southeast. The border with West Timor is similarly demarcated by a series of hills, towering limestone ridges, and waterways. The road network, expanded and improved under Indonesian rule, and constantly under repair due to the impact of the October–February wet season, traverses the northern coastline, ridges, and mountains that link the capital Maliana to the outlying subdistricts. Maliana, a subdistrict in its own right, is centrally located on a large rice-growing plain. Traditional paths hug the coast, lowland areas, and valleys and rise through mountain passes providing alternate routes, means of escape, and refuge for Falintil guerrillas and their supporters.

Bobonaro had better road links with Atambua in West Timor than it did with Dili. Each Sunday men would flock from West Timor (where gambling was prohibited) to while away hours at cock fights and gambling games at the border towns of Batugade and Balibo. In general terms, with such good infrastructure, Bobonaro was more developed than other parts of East Timor. However, commercial activity was concentrated in the hands of a few (notably the Tavares and Monez families) and all imports and exports flowed through West Timor. While bright pupils could one day hope to attend the University of East Timor in Dili, the overall literacy rate in the district was appalling. Fewer than 30 percent of the district electorate were able to sign their names on their registration cards.

SECURITY STRUCTURES

As elsewhere in Indonesia the TNI exercised complete suzerainty over broadly defined security issues. Structurally the TNI mirrored the civil administration and

the *Polri*. The local military commander (*dandim*) Lieutenant Colonel Burhanuddin Siagian explained that he had responsibilities for issues of "geography, de-
mography, population, ideology, cultural defense, social issues, and external
threats." From his Maliana headquarters (*kodim*) Siagian oversaw six subdistrict
commands (*koramil*), below which were the *babinsas*, TNI noncommissioned officers based in each of Bobonaro district's fifty-one villages. Siagian reported to
the Military Sub-Area Command (*Korem* 164) based in Dili. Above the *korem*
level was the Military Area Command (*Kodam*, Udayana IX) based in Denapasar,
Bali. The commander (*pangdam*), Major General Adam Damiri in turn reported
to TNI headquarters in Cilangkap, Jakarta.[1]

Two military figures long associated with East Timor, former military intelligence (BIA) chief Major General Zacky Anwar Makarim and General Gleny
Kauripan, were attached to the Indonesian Task Force in Dili. General Anwar had
been replaced as BIA chief in January 1999 and served as a special advisor on
East Timor to Wiranto before assignment to Dili on June 3.

Siagian, the local military head, claimed that under his command in Bobonaro
district there were four hundred East Timorese troops and that they all supported
the prointegration groups. In mid-July Siagian stated on several occasions that
there were some ten thousand East Timorese serving within the TNI and the *Polri*
throughout East Timor and that their "strength had to be noted." Siagian was
clearly disdainful of the East Timorese and the East Timorese National Liberation Army (Falintil); "they have no strategy," he would say. A product of the
TNI system, it is difficult to imagine that he had any capacity for independent
action. Posted to Bobonaro district on October 1, 1997, he oversaw the creation
of the militia system in his district. It is possibly his success in this endeavor that
saw his district military command named "top *kodim*" in the whole of Udayana
IX command in August 1999.

THE IMPORTANCE OF BOBONARO DISTRICT

In early July, Falintil members from Sector IV rated Bobonaro district third in
terms of violence and intimidation behind Liquiça and Cova Lima districts.[2] By
August, Bobonaro district had climbed to the number one spot, edging out Cova
Lima and way ahead of Liquiça, where militia activity went underground in the
wake of the political fallout following a militia ambush on a UNAMET–led humanitarian convoy on July 4, in clear view of the district police station. In terms
of the organization of the militia, Bobonaro district appears to have been a model,
as indicated by the emergence of documents in other districts pertaining to their
financing and coordination.

Also, the self-proclaimed head of all militia groups in East Timor, *panglima*
(supreme commander) João Tavares, had his nominal base in Maliana. A complex
man, at sixty-nine years old his fighting days were long behind him. Among local

Blind Eyes, Blue Eyes

Turn a blind eye
Yes you—blue eyed leader
Look the other way
Yes you—blue eyed statesman
Who pretends not to see
Our pain, our suffering
Our blood runs deep in your conscience
Why is it that you do not look
Are we not brothers
What have I done to you
That you cannot look into my brown eyes
Blue eyes, blind eyes
Your eyes are not my brown eyes
Learn from past mistakes
And you shall be admired
Choose to take a stand
And walk out of your shadow of shame
Blind eyes, your eyes
Blue eyes, blind eyes
Shame on you
Shame on your person
Your lies bring pain to your nation
Once a wise man said
Those words that sound so true

Oh what a tangled web we weave
Once we first learn
To deceive.

—Emanuel Braz

residents his name inspired hate, fear, and, for some, grudging respect. Several noted that when Tavares had been *bupati* (district head) of Bobonaro "no one died." He "protected East Timorese" and prevented the worst TNI excesses in the period 1976 to 1986. Tavares owned houses in Maliana, Atabai, Atambua, Kupang, and Dili and was reported to have an apartment in Jakarta. Of his nine children, eight had successfully completed university courses. One was an Indonesian diplomat and one, aptly nicknamed "the King," was the village chief of Balibo. Tavares liked to boast that when he was *bupati*, the roads were good and the people were happy. His personal influence also extended to other districts. For example the *bupati* of Ermera district, Constantino Soares, was a Tavares protégé.

Tavares claimed to have a working relationship with Xanana Gusmão. Reportedly when the two men were close to striking an accord between the militias and Falintil on April 11, 1999, their talks failed, most likely due to the overnight surge in militia operations on the same date.[3] To a certain extent Tavares was but one prop in the TNI's elaborate orchestration of East Timor's political affairs. As the process unfolded, Tavares, ill with malaria and often bedridden, was frequently unable to explain the structure of his organization, and he did not have a grasp of militia activities in wider East Timor. On certain days he appeared as what he was—a sick old man at the beck and call of the TNI—and accorded minimum respect. TNI controllers followed him everywhere and he never met UNAMET alone.

Bobonaro district was important for several reasons. Close to the West Timor border, along with Cova Lima district and the Ambeno enclave, it was always prominently linked in "secession plans" espoused in public by militia chiefs. That is, in the event that East Timor became independent, the TNI and their proxies hoped to retain this and other western districts as part of Indonesia. The *bupati* Guilherme Dos Santos made no secret of his antipathy toward the United Nations or of his indignation that the consultation process had been forced upon him. The militia structure in Bobonaro district was the most developed in terms of organization and funding. It consistently rated among the districts with the highest incidences of political violence; it was also the first district evacuated by UNAMET after the August 30 consultation and before the announcement of the results that catalyzed general mayhem across East Timor. The TNI–militia relationship was anchored in strategies devised as far back as 1994 where homegrown East Timorese forces would bear the brunt of field and urban operations against Falintil and proindependence supporters. Attempts to develop the militia into an institution in its own right, separate from the TNI, ultimately failed during UNAMET's tenure.

MILITIA ACTIVITY FROM MAY 1998 TO JUNE 1999

When UNAMET's advance team of some ten people arrived in Dili in mid-May the town was still in a state of shock after the April 4–6 massacre of independence supporters in Liquiça church and the subsequent April 17 *Aitarak* (Thorn) rampage in Dili where as many as thirty people were cut down in Manuel Carrascalão's house, including his seventeen-year-old son, Manuelito. The chiefs of the National Council of Timorese Resistance (CNRT) were in hiding (David Diaz Ximenese) or under police protection (Leondro Izaacs). The *Aitarak* militia that operated without restraint under Eurico Guterres patrolled Dili. Information was scanty. The East Timorese human rights nongovernmental organization Yayasan Hak and the Catholic Church had unique and valuable insights into all districts, and many East Timorese volunteered information, unsolicited by UNAMET, in circumstances of considerable personal risk. But it was not until the end of May that UNAMET began moving into the field and was in a position to verify many of the allegations concerning the militia. Discussions and interviews with local institutions and the population during several visits to the western districts—the Ambeno enclave, Cova Lima, Bobonaro, Ermera, and Ainaro districts—revealed that in a broad sense the formation and expansion of the militia and their activities was a direct response to proindependence initiatives.

For example, several militia members from the Maliana-based *Dadurus Merah Putih* (Red and White Typhoon) explained that their recruitment and plans commenced in May 1998 as a direct response to the formation of CNRT—the umbrella organization for all proindependence groups in East Timor—in April. They claimed that *Halilintar* was the "senior" militia group in East Timor. Reportedly in existence since 1973, it had lain dormant from 1976 ("when it was the same as the TNI") before being reactivated, most likely in 1994 in parallel with *Kopassus* and Prabowo Subianto's *Gada Paksi* (*Gadu Penegak Integrasi* or Guards to Uphold Integration) initiative.[4] *Halilintar* was "led" by João Tavares but under the command of *Korem* 164—TNI headquarters—in Dili. It operated in Maliana

Figure 6.1   An old man who has been beaten by the Indonesian military is tended by the nervous inhabitants of a small hamlet in the mountains. Courtesy: Steve Cox.

and Atabai subdistricts of the Bobonaro district, but may also have had wider responsibilities for establishing and raising other militia groups. Certainly it had a close relationship with *Satgas Intel* (*Satuan Tugas Intellijen*, SGI), the *Kopassus* intelligence unit that oversaw its reestablishment, tended to its logistic needs, and provided bodyguards to Tavares and training for its senior cadre.[5]

Internal TNI documents smuggled out of Dili in late 1998 noted that *Halilintar* had a strength of 121 in August 1998. In July 1999 UNAMET was informed by the *Halilintar* chief in Atabai that it had a strength of 121 hard-core or cadre members, many of whom had been with João Tavares since 1975. The consistency in strength numbers over the period suggests a continuity in the group and, by association, a specific function separate from the other militia groups, which were firmly anchored in precise geographical areas and whose numbers fluctuated as men joined or deserted. Certainly, financial statements for militia funding in Bobonaro district had separate budget lines for *Halilintar*, whereas the other subdistrict militia groups were lumped together. The same statements also identified expenditures for the *Kopassus* chief in Bobonaro district (Dan Satgas Tribuana).

By October 1998 at least eleven militia groups were operational throughout East Timor. Like *Halilintar*, two other notorious groups were established early and at strategic locations in the western districts: *Mahidi* (Dead or Alive for Integration) was centered around Cassa in southern Ainaro district, at the crossroads between Manufahi, Ainaro, and Cova Lima districts. *Besi Merah Putih* (Red and White Iron) was based out of Maubara, on the border between Liquiça, Ermera, and Bobonaro districts. These three "senior" groups were ideally placed to control the movement of the population in and out of the western districts and also to partition East Timor by forcing those districts to secede if the need arose.

These groups continued to recruit and consolidate through 1998 as did the proindependence groups, creating tension in several districts. According to a church source, in November 1998 proindependence supporters attacked and burnt twelve houses and demonstrated in front of the *bupati's* house in Ainaro district in response to SGI–orchestrated intimidation via *Mahidi* proxies.

Throughout 1999 politically motivated violence carried out by the TNI and the militia correlated with the negotiation timetable leading to the signing of the May 5 Agreements, the June 7 Indonesian national elections, and subsequently with UNAMET's consultation timetable. In broad terms there were three main periods prior to UNAMET's deployment throughout East Timor: January 27 to Easter; Easter to June 1; and June 1 to June 27.

January 27–Easter

Immediately after President B.J. Habibie's January 27 announcement that he would be prepared to let East Timor separate from Indonesia if the East Timorese rejected autonomy, CNRT became more active. Emboldened by what was a conferral of legitimacy, independence supporters in some areas drove around town centers waving the outlawed Fretilin flag. Other CNRT members began preparations for a province-wide campaign. Certainly there was a reinvigoration of nationalist and anti-Indonesian sentiments across the province. One young Javanese doctor in the Ambeno enclave, who had excellent relations with the community in which he lived, described how he was ostracized for several days by a community whose children he had helped deliver.

As many as thirty thousand such Indonesian administrators and public functionaries, perhaps encouraged by Jakarta, terminated their contracts early or simply left for other provinces. In addition, the TNI and their militia protegés stepped up their efforts to exact retribution against the independence supporters, many of whom had shown their hand for the first time. *Mahidi* reportedly commenced operations immediately after January 27 in Ainaro. At the same time TNI–militia operations in Suai reportedly displaced several thousand. On March 22 the "terror situation" began in Zumalai in eastern Cova Lima District. The former militia leader Tomas Gonçalves stated in September that at a special meeting in Dili on February 16 an SGI officer, Lieutenant Colonel Sudrajud, addressed militia chiefs from twelve of the districts and directed them to attack proindependence supporters beginning on May 1. Gonçalves explained that in fact attacks commenced the next day. He also claimed that at a second meeting on March 26, allegedly attended by the governor of East Timor, Abilio Soares, the order was given to attack priests and nuns who sheltered independence supporters.[6] Events in the field suggest that the plan went much further than that. One strand was designed to destroy CNRT and drive its members underground. Another was to continue with the recruitment and establishment of a province-wide militia consisting of all males over the age of seventeen, who were to be organized into a "company" of militia for each of East Timor's sixty-two subdistricts with a "battalion" or senior group based in district centers. A third angle was the province-wide establishment of offices of the political fronts for the integration/autonomy cause, the Forum for Unity, Democracy, and Justice (*Forum Persatuan, Demokrasi dan Keadilan*, FPDK) and the East Timor People's Front (*Barisan Rakyat Timor Timur*, BRTT).

In two months a comprehensive strategy was implemented to ensure the systematic control of the whole population, irreversibly altering the political space in favor of the proautonomy cause.

Easter–June 1

In this period the TNI and the militia teamed up to drive all independence groups and their supporters underground, beginning with the shocking events in Liquiça on April 4–6 when militia, the TNI, and the *Polri* participated in the massacre of independence supporters sheltered in the Liquiça church. Seemingly overnight, a systematic and widespread campaign against those backing independence was begun by the militia groups, led by the TNI, who maintained within their *kodim* headquarters across East Timor, lists of independence supporters. Government officials, village chiefs, and the male population over the age of seventeen were particularly targeted and forced to declare their support for integration. It was a time of extraordinary pressure on the community at large.

In the west, simultaneous operations were carried out in the Ambeno enclave (April 10), Bobonaro (April 12), and Ermera (April 10–11) at precisely the time that João Tavares was meeting Xanana Gusmão in Jakarta to discuss reconciliation. In the enclave the militia group *Sakunar Merah Putih* (Red and White Scorpion) took over the streets with automatic weapons and chased the only overt CNRT member (one of two doctors) out of town. In Bobonaro district the terror began on April 12 when the district finance chief, Manuel Soares Gama, was killed in an ambush on the road to Kailaco. The military commander, Siagian, and his intelligence chief, Lieutenant Sutrisno, had six people suspected of being Falintil supporters killed on the spot on the grounds that Falintil had been behind the ambush. The weight of evidence suggests that Gama was killed by a combined *Halilintar*/SGI/TNI team, as a pretext for a district-wide crackdown against proindependence supporters.[7]

Those who did not flee were forced to "accept the red and white" and fly the Indonesian flag outside their houses. To not do so was an open invitation to attack. In Bobonaro district, CNRT chiefs Manuel Marghalene (believed killed on September 8 in Maliana) and José Andrade Da Cruz had their houses burnt and looted and were forced to take refuge in the police station, where they remained until late July. Another leading CNRT figure, Pedro Gomez, fled to the hills with his seven-year-old son where he hid for nearly two months, during which his house was destroyed and his car was stolen. On May 24 he was captured by militia from Bobonaro subdistrict *(Hametin Merah Putih* or Red and White Vice) and taken to Maliana. On June 1 he was forced to sign a petition with José Andrade, Manuel Marghalene, and Francisco Margo at a BRTT rally in Maliana. The four men "dissolved the CNRT" in Bobonaro district in a bizarre ceremony in front of a large crowd. Original copies of the signed petition were lodged with the district chief of police and would later be produced as evidence that CNRT had ceded its right to campaign in the district. The provincial chief of the BRTT, Ambassador Lopez da Cruz, used the opportunity to tell all proindependence supporters to leave the district and all residents of the district to "accept autonomy or face fatal consequences."

In Suai, twenty members of CNRT were run out of town in early May and the student office was closed down. By June 1 there were an estimated three thousand people taking shelter in the surrounding hills. Many were unable to escape to Dili on account of militia checkpoints at Zumalai to the east and at Atambua and Batugade along the route to Dili through West Timor.

Other victims in the period were village chiefs who refused to support the "program." Many fled to Dili, losing property and possessions. They were replaced by trusted prointegrationists, some of whom were TNI "pensioners." A small number had dual functions of village chief and militia chief although this was rare in Bobonaro district. One source stated that João Tavares disagreed with Siagian over the plan to recruit all men over the age of seventeen into the new militias. Tavares reasoned that the program would drive all the young men away to the forest and to Dili; it eventually did after Siagian's instructions prevailed. The scale of the social dislocation caused by this one aspect alone was not fully realized until midway through the registration process in late July when the youths returned to register. In all, over one thousand young men returned: 112 to Atabai, 46 to Balibo, 290 to Maliana, 29 to Kailaco, 494 to Bobonaro, and 59 to Lolotoe subdistrict. From the figures, Bobonaro would appear to have been the subdistrict of greatest repression. One resident described the situation there as the worst it had been since 1975.

The notorious *bupati* of Bobonaro district, Guilherme Dos Santos, who described himself as the "Muhammed Ali of all Bupatis," was reported, at least initially, to have favored political dialogue with proindependence student groups. This sentiment was allegedly overturned by Siagian and Dos Santos became an ardent supporter of the prointegration side.

In parallel, the TNI launched a military campaign in those subdistricts bordering the central mountain spine. The operation was designed to separate Falintil from its support base and to remove any ambiguities in the tacit support offered to the group. As admitted by several Falintil supporters this may have been in part a reaction to the ongoing collection of the "revolutionary tax" from villagers.

The combination of militia actions in the urban areas and TNI operations in the interior saw some forty thousand people displaced throughout East Timor in the months prior to the consultation. In the hard-hit Kailaco subdistrict in Bobonaro, for example, some 4,300 people from four villages were brought down from the hills to makeshift camps in the subdistrict capital, where they were placed under militia "protection" and were told that they could not return home until after the consultation. This was done on the pretext that Falintil would attack them. In fact the TNI and the militia burnt many houses and forcibly relocated the villagers. Most of the men had run to Dili or taken refuge in the mountains. Those who remained were co-opted into the subdistrict militia *Gumtur Merah Putih* (Red and White Thunder) under the direction of the intelligence chief Sutrisno.

By mid-May most TNI objectives in Bobonaro district had been met. CNRT had gone underground, its leaders in hiding or under police protection. Officials in the district administration had sworn allegiance to autonomy. Those who had not had been forced to flee. Village chiefs in several areas had been replaced or sidelined, and the youths and men remaining were rapidly being forced into the ranks of the new militia, funding for which had been distributed at the beginning of the month.

In the remote and proindependence subdistricts of Bobonaro and Lolotoe recruitment methods included holding youths hostage in militia chiefs' houses,
beatings, and generally unfulfilled promises of rice and salaries. In the house of
Alberto Leite, the militia chief of *Hametin Merah Putih* in Bobonaro subdistrict
town, some thirty-seven men had been held under effective house arrest until the
beginning of June when they were released "to go and vote for *Golkar*" in the
impending Indonesian national elections.

In early May in Lolotoe, the young men were called into "peace meetings"
where they were forced to swear allegiance to the "red and white." After two
teachers were killed for refusing to join, a Falintil company under "Deker" killed
three TNI soldiers on May 16 in an ambush during which they spared the life of
the militia commander, Juni Frewea. It was the only action by Falintil in Bobonaro district—their relative inaction a measure of their own weakness probably
more than of adherence to orders from Xanana Gusmão, which forbade any repri-
sal by the guerrilla force. Church sources alleged that in response the TNI
rounded up six hundred people and killed an unknown number in the villages
closest to the ambush site.

With all opposition out of the way and before UNAMET's arrival, the militia
and the district administration commenced the "socialization" process. This involved an extensive series of village, subdistrict, and district-level meetings and
"festivities" across East Timor's 422 villages, 62 subdistricts, and 13 districts,
paid for from the province's social development fund. This heavy-handed program extolled the virtues of autonomy (the economic benefits of integration, development, and so on). Having effectively silenced CNRT, militia activities refo-
cused on further recruitment, military-style training for their rank and file
conducted by the TNI, and the Indonesian national elections.

June 1–June 27 (UNAMET's Arrival in Bobonaro District)

Around the end of May the militias began a campaign to ensure that all East
Timorese participated in the national elections on June 7. Militia groups visited
villages and inspected people's registration cards. Those without them were
beaten. All were told that voting was compulsory. The militia and their sponsors
wanted to hold credible national elections with maximum turnout, with a view
to undermining the UNAMET consultation since, by participating in the June 7
elections, the East Timorese would have proved their desire to be part of Indonesia. Accordingly, militia violence abated in this period and a "peace" of sorts
commenced. At the same time there was a belief in Bobonaro district that the
consultation would not necessarily proceed. Guilherme Dos Santos stated on June
3 that the population was not sure if it wanted the consultation: "There are two
ways of casting a ballot. One is to vote and the other is not to vote. It is the
people's choice."

Perhaps the most significant political change involved the harmonization of all prointegration and proautonomy groups and the security institutions. Specifically, Ambassador Lopez da Cruz, the chief of the BRTT, who had previously advocated a separate, peaceful approach to autonomy, began campaigning with the FPDK and also warned of violence if autonomy were rejected. Generous funding for the socialization process allowed for the disbursement of significant payoffs to the district authorities, the military commander, the police chief, the district mayor, the district judge, and so on. The socialization funds also bankrolled the militia cadres, providing them with status and an institutional role in what was a "whole of government approach" by Jakarta in assisting the autonomy cause.

THE MILITIA IN BOBONARO DISTRICT

After the Indonesian national elections, the BRTT and FPDK chiefs and the militia continued the socialization process. Pressure was maintained on proindependence groups, but perhaps because of their absence (they had already fled or gone underground) an uneasy peace reigned in Bobonaro district. UNAMET's gradual deployment into the countryside at this time had an impact as well. By the end of June the militia had been established in all six subdistricts, their status formalized in a ceremony in Dili in June where the militia were given the appellation of *PAM Swakarsa* (Volunteer Community Security). It was an attempt to place the establishment and organization of the militia on a quasilegal foundation. A member of the *Deplu* task force benignly described them as a type of "neighborhood watch." A form of paid civilian militia, *PAM Swakarsa* units had first appeared in Jakarta in June 1998 and had been formally established in a special session of the People's Consultative Assembly (MPR) in November 1998 amid much controversy. In East Timor they had first been established in Dili (only) on April 19, 1999, and were financed from the provincial budget.

Militia groups in Bobonaro district were organized on a geographical basis with a "company" at each subdistrict forming an overall "battalion" for the district. As discussed, João Tavares's personal force, *Halilintar* (Lightning/Thunderbolt), was the senior group. Although based in Atabai it had wider responsibilities for coordinating the western region or Sector IV of the militia structure that included Cova Lima district and the Ambeno enclave. Below *Halilintar* were six subdistrict groups as shown in Table 6.1. For the rank and file and the population the names were essentially meaningless. More important were the strong men who ran the separate groups.

TRENDS AND DISCONTINUITIES

Broadly speaking, the militias had three levels of command and status. At the bottom of the chain was the rank-and-file militia who represented males press-

Table 6.1   Militia Groups in Bobonaro District

Subdistrict	Militia Group	Date Name Adopted	Group Commander
Maliana	*Dadurus Merah Putih* (Red and White Typhoon)	May 1998	Sergeant Domingos Dos Santos (serving TNI soldier)
Balibo/Batugade	*Pemuda Benteng Batugade* (Batugade Fortress Youths), also known as *FIRMI Merah Putih* (unknown acronym)	July 1999	Ruben Tavares (nephew of Panglima Tavares and son of Jorge Tavares)
Atabai	*ARMUI Merah Putih* (Atabai is Ready to Die for Integration)	July 1999	José Amaral Leite (a long time protégé of Panglima Tavares and also chief of *Halilintar* in the subdistrict)
Kailaco	*Gumtur Merah Putih* (Red and White Thunder)	April 1999	Adau Abu
Bobonaro	*Hametin Merah Putih* (Red and White Vice)	June 1999	Alberto Leite (TNI Pensioner)
Lolotoe	*Kaer Metin Merah Putih* (unknown name)	June 1999	Juni Frewea (son of subdistrict chief, José Vicente)

ganged into the organization from April 1999. Their major duty was to report each evening at 6 p.m. and serve until 6 a.m. at sentry posts near their villages where they monitored movement in and out of the villages. In fact the system functioned as a control mechanism whereby on any evening higher level cadres could determine the exact location of all able-bodied males over the age of seventeen. Those who fell asleep, deserted their post, or failed to turn up were beaten or punished. One punishment involved being tipped upside down in an oil drum full of water from which the victim had to extricate himself. Militia duty was hated as it meant that people were exhausted during the day and often unable to tend their farms and gardens.

Training obligations included weapons drill with mock rifles and physical exercise, along with instructions about how to deal with UNAMET and lectures on the benefits of autonomy. Each Saturday muster parades were conducted at subdistrict *koramils* where the new "line" and the latest news was disseminated. Each night in Maliana the sentry posts would ring cowbells on the hour. By the end of July, and before the end of the registration process, the cowbells were silent on account of wholesale desertions by the rank and file. Faced with such large-scale "civil disobedience" the TNI and the militia could do little. The focus changed when the rank and file were summoned to attend specific proautonomy campaign activities or events like the Indonesian National Day celebrations on August 17. Again truants were beaten.

The second-level militia were the "cadres" selected from more trusted East Timorese. These cadres were allocated resources such as radios and motorbikes and were given command positions. They were responsible for mobilizing manpower in their areas and also for collecting and disseminating information. One platoon commander from *Dadurus Merah Putih* stated that his other responsibilities included monitoring all the villages in his area for Falintil and proindependence supporters, checking on fund-raising activities for Falintil and CNRT, and checking on "corruption"—thrice monthly.

The highest tier within the militia consisted of the subdistrict chiefs and their lieutenants. Their backgrounds varied considerably. Some were East Timorese serving within the TNI, others were TNI pensioners. Several were next of kin to high-ranking district officials. One was a lecturer from the University of East Timor who doubled as deputy head of the FPDK. A few had been with João Tavares since 1975. Top-tier commanders were privileged with extra resources and funding and attended key meetings in Dili until just after the registration period when coordination of militia activities shifted to Atambua. District activities until then were coordinated from the *bupati's* office, through which funding passed, or the *kodim*.

As the TNI's need for plausible denial grew, the FPDK and the BRTT picked up the responsibility for the tactical coordination of district operations in concert with the *bupati*. However, these operations always had TNI and SGI oversight, often with career officers from other provinces.

By mid-August TNI–militia designs for the postconsultation period became evident; they planned to eject UNAMET, seal the district, cut the power, evacuate communities to West Timor, carry out retributive attacks on proindependence supporters, and destroy all facilities. In Bobonaro district these actions commenced before the announcement of results on September 4. All the evidence suggests that in early August the assessment that the proautonomy camp would lose had already been made. Militia leaders from throughout East Timor were briefed at meetings in Dili in this period and told what to do.

Several second-level militia commanders sought accommodation with CNRT because they did not want to participate in such plans and also because they did not want to live in Atambua after the consultation. Throughout the consultation CNRT had been denied any political space whatsoever and never opened an office in the district. On the one day that they had campaigned, all of their supporters were subject to house visits by militia, the TNI, and in some cases SGI. From mid-August through the campaign period (August 14–17) the TNI and the militia stepped up their activities, which included several murders, house burnings, widespread intimidation, and the indiscriminate terrorizing of whole communities. The *Polri* never once intervened and in several cases were accessories through either their prior knowledge or inaction. In the week preceding the consultation up to forty militia members from *Dadurus Merah Putih* decided to take their chances in the hills and left the group, following the majority of the population.

On August 27, the last day of the campaign, the militia rampaged through Memo, a village in Maliana subdistrict. Three villagers were killed and twenty houses were razed in an incident that TNI liaison officers initially described as a "Falintil attack." Many of the proautonomy participants were believed to be from West Timor—to make up the numbers given the increasing absence of militia from Bobonaro district.

At dawn on August 30 the sun rose over thousands of voters who had emerged from hiding to cast their ballots. By 2 p.m. Maliana town had emptied with proindependence supporters returning to the hills and proautonomy supporters to Atambua. On September 2, two UNAMET local staff members were shot dead by a TNI sergeant who doubled as the militia chief of a Maliana suburb. The killings capped weeks of intimidation against UNAMET local staff. On at least two occasions the *dandim*, Lieutenant Colonel Siagian, had personally told local staff that they would be killed after the consultation. That night the militia began to burn Maliana. As they left the district on September 3, UNAMET observed members of the TNI directing the remaining militia members to burn and destroy specific houses and buildings in the town associated with UNAMET and proindependence groups. The *Polri* remained in their police station singing songs.

CONCLUSION

The TNI was heavily involved in all aspects of militia activity in Bobonaro district aimed at ensuring a proautonomy vote in the Popular Consultation. At the higher levels the subdistrict militia leaders were coordinated and directed by the *dandim* and his intelligence chief from the *kodim* and from the *bupati's* office. At the subdistrict level the militia was either directly commanded by TNI personnel or directly supported by *koramil* staff. At the village level the militia worked hand in hand with military posts and *babinsas*.

In early August, after the successful registration of some 450,000 East Timorese (well above the 380,000 registered for the June 7 Indonesian national elections), it was clear that the autonomy package would be rejected. The proautonomy camp and its TNI backbone shifted their headquarters to Atambua and began preparations for the postconsultation period. Alarmed at the impending carnage, the lower and midlevel order of the militia began to fragment. In the days following the consultation the TNI emerged as primary architects of the plan to destroy Bobonaro district—a plan they implemented with confidence and precision.

POSTSCRIPT

On September 22 the Indonesian National Human Rights Commission established the Commission for Human Rights Violations in East Timor (KPP-HAM) to "gather facts, data and information concerning violations of human rights that occurred in East Timor from January 1999 until the Parliament Ruling of October 1999 that ratified the results of the Popular Consultation." In its January 31, 2000, report the commission listed, among others, four Bobonaro district officials suspected of involvement in crimes against humanity: the mayor, Guilherme Dos Santos; the district military commander Lieutenant Colonel Burhanuddin Siagian; the head of military intelligence, Lieutenant Sutrisno, and the *Halilintar* commander, João Tavares.[8]

The Indonesian government has stated that those responsible for grave violations of international humanitarian and human rights law in East Timor will be brought to justice through Indonesia's national judicial system.[9]

NOTES

1. Key Officers in Jakarta included: General Wiranto the Armed Forces Commander (*pangab*) and also Defense Minister; General Subagyo Hadisiswoyo, the Army Chief of Staff (KSAD); his assistant for operations and former East Timor Commander from September 1994–May 1995; Major General Kiki Syahnakri (who replaced Muis Noer after martial law was declared in East Timor on September 7); Major General Muchdi Purwopranjono, *Kopassus* Commander; Major General Tiasno Sudarno, BIA Commander; and General Ruhsmanhadi, the National Police Chief.

2. Falintil had divided East Timor into four sectors: I–IV. The Sector IV commander was Ular Rate. In Bobonaro district Falintil was divided into two companies: North Company commanded by "Rocke," and the more active South Company commanded by "Deker." UNAMET met with Falintil on a number of occasions, but Falintil's lack of military strength and their eventual self cantonment in early August meant that throughout the consultation, they had little influence as a group on the course of events.

3. The two men also met on May 5, June 18, the end of July, and August 4. At the June Dare II reconciliation talks in Jakarta it seemed that they were again in sight of a genuine breakthrough, but nothing came of them.

4. The *Gada Paksi* was established in 1994 by Prabowo as a means of co-opting young East Timorese into the integration cause, in part due to the increasing gains by proindependence student groups. Members were assisted into small businesses and given military and intelligence training in Jakarta. Many militia cadres in Bobonaro declared their occupation as "businessman" before they joined the militia.

5. In early June 1999 the author witnessed the inauguration of a "new" militia unit of

some four hundred youths in Maucola (halfway between Suai and Zumalai) in Cova Lima district. The organizing "team," which included at least one SGI officer, was composed of TNI officers and the chief of the *Mahidi* chapter from Zumalai, one Vasco da Cruz. Several people at the site referred to the team collectively as *"Halilintar* 612" or "Battalion 612."

6. Tomas Gonçalves had been initially recruited by the Indonesian State Intelligence Coordinating Agency (Bakin) in 1975 and trained at Atambua for covert operations under the command of then *Kostrad* Major Yunus Yosfiah, the officer in charge of the attack on Balibo. Following the consultation, Gonçalves returned to East Timor after a period of hiding in Macau.

7. Most sources stated that Gama was killed by TNI/SGI/*Halilintar*. Only one source said he was killed by Falintil because he was carrying wages for the militia to Kailaco. A report of the Indonesian Commission for Human Rights Violations in East Timor (KPP-HAM) dated 31 January 2000 noted that Falintil was "presumably" responsible for the ambush on Manuel Gama's convoy. A second investigation by the East Timorese Human Rights nongovernmental organization Yayasan Hak entitled *Intelektual pun Bisa Membunuh Belajar Dari Maliana, Timor Timur (Intellectuals Can Kill. A Study from Maliana, East Timor)* dated November 1999 alleged that, according to parish records and other government officials, the district military commander was personally involved in Gama's death.

8. See *Executive Summary: Report on the Investigation of Human Rights Violations in East Timor*, 31 January 2000.

9. Letter dated 18 February 2000, from the president of the Security Council to the secretary general of the United Nations.

7

Taking the Risk, Paying the Price: East Timorese Vote in Ermera

Helene van Klinken

In mid-June 1999, I arrived in East Timor to work as a political affairs officer with the newly established United Nations Assistance Mission in East Timor (UNAMET). Political officers were stationed in eight regions where UNAMET had headquarters. I was delighted to be sent to the beautiful district of Ermera, situated in the hills one hour's drive south of Dili.[1] As you approach Gleno, the district center, Mt. Ramelau, the highest mountain in East Timor, dominates the skyline. It is a picturesque, fertile, coffee-growing area. People are friendly and open, and the welcome to UNAMET was unbelievable. Children would pop out of fragrant coffee gardens as we drove past, waving and calling in chorus, "UNA-MET, UNAMET!"

My job as a political affairs officer was to meet everyone—villagers, Indonesian government personnel, police and military officials, church leaders, proautonomy and proindependence supporters, students, pro-Indonesian militia and the proindependence guerrilla army—and report to UNAMET's Dili headquarters what they were saying and hoping for, and whether or not it was possible for the Popular Consultation to proceed.[2]

More than five hundred United Nations volunteers from many nations formed the electoral staff who registered 450,000 eligible voters over a period of twenty-two days from July 16 to August 6, 1999. After that they conducted voter education, informing people of the voting process, especially the fact that it was secret and that votes would not be counted in villages or districts. Finally they organized the ballot on August 30, 1999. Prior to the ballot the two sides, those who accepted autonomy and those who rejected autonomy, could campaign for approximately ten days, up to August 28.

"TWO SIDES"

Indonesian authorities have always presented the problem in East Timor as between two opposing sides of East Timorese, and since 1975 they have exploited rivalries. They encouraged the brief civil war in 1975 and in the lead up to the 1999 ballot they again fanned these rivalries.

The proindependence side operated under the umbrella organization CNRT, National Council of Timorese Resistance, with its armed wing, Falintil. The backbone of the pro-Indonesian side was civil servants who were hurriedly organized into two civilian political groups just prior to the vote.

WHO WERE THE MILITIA?

Militias have been part of Indonesia's military strategy in East Timor since 1975. However, beginning in late 1998, in response to a wave of proindependence expression following the resignation of President Suharto, the militias were greatly expanded through a combination of payments and forcing East Timorese youth to join their ranks. Each district had its own militia. In early April 1999 groups already operating in Ermera district joined together and expanded their ranks to become the Ermera-based *Darah Integrasi* (Blood of Integration). *Darah Integrasi* called itself a battalion. In each subdistrict there was a company of the *Darah Integrasi*. They claimed 1,500 members, but according to informants the number of committed members was in the low hundreds.

Miguel Soares Babo was the *Darah Integrasi* commander while his brother Antonio dos Santos was second-in-command. Antonio, a low-ranking TNI officer, said he was on "civilian duty." He was the real force and spokesperson. Miguel was not taken seriously because he was often drunk and prone to abusive language.

The difficulty for UNAMET was to understand the exact nature of the militia. Indonesian government officials described the militia in terms of existing civil defense categories in the Defense Act, but the description changed all the time.[3] In August we were told we now had to refer to the militia as Forces Struggling for Integration (*Pasukan Perjuangan Integrasi*). At this time they mysteriously evolved into a guerrilla army that, we were led to understand, had formed "spontaneously" to fight for integration with Indonesia. Interestingly, they organized themselves to copy the Falintil command structure.

ERMERA PRIOR TO APRIL 1999

The Indonesian president, B. J. Habibie, first mentioned offering wide-ranging autonomy to East Timor in June 1998. In Ermera district, and elsewhere in East

Timor, by contrast, support was building for a referendum on independence. Falintil was able to take advantage of the political confusion in Jakarta by, for the first time, openly patrolling the roads leading in and out of Ermera. Also for the first time, CNRT opened an Ermera office, with a fully functional organizational structure at the district level, as well as the subdistrict and village levels. They even talked about having established a "parallel government."[4] University students who originated in Ermera traveled around the district holding demonstrations and calling for a referendum on independence. A foreign visitor described the atmosphere to me as a "Prague Spring."

Conversely, many Indonesians living in Ermera felt frightened. Some local youths caused distress by calling openly for them to return home. The wife of one high government official told me that youths came into the yard of the local primary school and used a megaphone to tell Indonesians to leave. After February 1999, her young children refused to attend school in Gleno. In other places, especially Dili, some proindependence supporters did burn shops, markets, businesses, and sometimes the homes of collaborators and non-Timorese. Members of the armed forces and their families were particular targets of such attacks.

In Ermera, long-standing East Timorese supporters of Indonesia made peace with their Timorese brothers and sisters, joining the proindependence side. Even Timorese soldiers who had fought for Indonesia sought reconciliation with Falintil. Many people told me that Timorese in Ermera were united.

In an attempt to resolve the tensions between East Timorese and the district council, the ex–district head of Ermera, Tomas Gonçalves, sponsored reconciliation meetings between the various parties.[5] On March 24, 1999, CNRT and others signed an agreement to respect each other and work together, but three weeks later the CNRT office was burnt down.

Towards the end of February 1999, eleven people were killed in Ermera under mysterious circumstances. Suspects were arrested by the police and the victims were reported to be militia.[6] The police commander said he suspected proindependence Ermera youth. At the end of April, the decaying corpses were placed in the local health clinic in Gleno, where flies blackened the windows, to the horror of the whole town. The Indonesian authorities used these deaths to discredit CNRT.[7]

APRIL–MAY 1999

Attacks on CNRT

With the growing likelihood of a Popular Consultation, a savage crackdown began in Ermera on April 10, 1999, when a CNRT supporter and member of local parliament, Antonio Lima, was killed and the CNRT office was burnt down. The crackdown began five days after the widely reported massacre of CNRT supporters in a church in nearby Liquiça. The Ermera district CNRT leader, Eduardo de Deus Barreto, was arrested and charged with "extorting money and coercing people to join CNRT." All remaining CNRT leaders fled to the hills. CNRT members told me they were disappointed by the Indonesians' betrayal of the March 24 reconciliation agreement. The Indonesians responded that the deaths of the eleven justified their actions, though the murders occurred before March 24.

During the days that followed, many more proindependence people were killed. People said that the killings were done by Indonesian police and military in uniform who patrolled the streets searching for and shooting CNRT leaders and well-known proindependence supporters. CNRT estimated twenty-nine killed. But with some 2,500 people forced into hiding in the hills, it was difficult to know who might still be alive. Killing continued in different subdistricts of Ermera throughout April and May.

In some areas of East Timor, Falintil had maintained long-term control of a few villages, reaching some sort of modus vivendi with local military posts. One such "liberated area" was Fatubolo village, close to Gleno. On April 10 most senior Ermera CNRT officeholders fled into this Falintil-controlled territory, while some went to Dili, which was also considered safe. When I later visited the Falintil base I met a subdistrict head, many village heads, successful business people, and other community leaders. One CNRT officeholder, Germenino Amaral dos Reis, who had some protection as a member of the local parliament, had returned to Gleno to serve as the spokesperson for CNRT in Ermera district.[8]

Civil servants who were prepared to sign statements promising to support autonomy could come out of hiding on April 24, 1999. Those who refused were threatened with losing their jobs or even death. Many stayed in hiding in the hills. CNRT itself was forced to formally "disband" on April 26 by engaging in a (chicken) blood-drinking oath-taking ceremony and declaring that they were disbanding voluntarily. Later they told me that the killing of their members would continue as long as they refused to capitulate.

Militia and TNI Posts

While there have long been military outposts in remote areas of East Timor, the numbers of these posts in Ermera was now greatly increased, many of them established after the crackdown in April and May 1999. A military post was usually a simple structure of bamboo and local materials, with the telltale tall communications antenna. Four Indonesian officers and about ten East Timorese TNI members were typically stationed at a post.

A group of about twenty militia, mostly locally recruited, was also stationed at each post, testimony to the close link between militia and military. When UNAMET visited villages, the militia would often hide in the coffee gardens or in a house and refuse to talk to us. The local people would always secretly indicate their presence.

THE ARRIVAL OF UNAMET

The UNAMET political office had to determine if the situation was secure enough to proceed with voter registration. As the time for registration approached it was clear this was not the case, and the start of registration was delayed for several days. However, the United Nations decided to proceed and to reassess the situation half way through registration, after ten days. In Dili the UNAMET political office drew up a list of six security conditions, all of which needed to be addressed for the ballot to be fair. One of these was that the TNI had to move out of village posts and back to their barracks.

The new military posts established in April and May 1999 were in villages where support for Falintil had been strongest. In these villages the people were aggressively proindependence, and on the arrival of UNAMET they registered complaints with us most often. The story of contact with a village best paints a picture of the relationship between UNAMET and the military in the period mid-June to mid-July.

On my first day in Ermera, a group of people from Talimoro village, situated on the mountain slopes directly behind our district UNAMET headquarters, came with a complaint. Their location made it somewhat easier for them to sneak into our headquarters, out of sight of the police mobile brigade that was guarding us, stationed directly across the road.[9]

They informed us about a meeting in their village that had been organized by the village military official and village head and guarded by soldiers from the village military post. They said the village head told the meeting that UNAMET would be present for only two months and so wouldn't be able to protect them, and if they didn't choose autonomy they would all be killed, including women and children. The villagers were worried because they had been ordered to attend another such meeting in a few days, when the names of those who supported the position of the village head would be collected.

UNAMET police contacted the Indonesian police complaining that such a meeting broke the tripartite agreement by Indonesia, Portugal, and the United Nations specifying terms for the consultation, in that there were threats and compulsion to attend a meeting in relation to the ballot and "campaigning" was taking place prior to the specified time. On the day appointed for the follow-up meeting in the village I accompanied the UNAMET police to this village. We discovered that the meeting was canceled and the military post vacated. We all were very pleased, and naively thought that this would be the pattern as we fanned out into more remote villages—that the TNI would move out of villages back to barracks, at least at the subdistrict level.

Ten days later, the villagers from Talimoro returned in alarm to tell us that the soldiers were back at their post. When the UNAMET military liaison officers asked the subdistrict military commander about this, the latter explained he was told that the village military official from Talimoro village had requested the return of the soldiers to help guard the village against Falintil.[10] From that day on, we received numerous complaints from the Talimoro villagers about the activities of these soldiers. In the middle of the night the soldiers threw stones on the roofs of houses of people known to have housed Falintil soldiers in the past. They shot randomly into the air to intimidate people. They broke into homes saying they had received information that Falintil soldiers were attacking the occupants. Most often they were drunk, and frequently they terrorized female members of the household, sometimes spending all day lying around inebriated in a house, making it impossible for the owners to care for their children or to cook.

Contact with Government Officials

The many government officials, subdistrict and village heads, and village secretaries who remained in hiding and refused to sign statements supporting autonomy were replaced by the authorities with people who were persuaded or bribed to support integration with Indonesia. As village heads are supposed to be elected, these officeholders were all, strictly speaking, illegal. I met one local subdistrict head, who I had heard from UNAMET electoral staff had been quite uncooperative in helping them find a suitable center. But this same official, when I met him in the home of friends and family, was a different man. He was vociferously anti-Indonesian, but impressed on me how I had to keep his secret. Amazingly he assured me that most of the other "proautonomy" officials in the district, right to the highest level, were just like him.

By contrast, Amaral and other CNRT leaders were inspiring people who did not sell their souls, even though they lived with constant threats and in fear. They believed leaders had a responsibility to stand up for and protect the little people, who were the ones who always suffered. Amaral would always say that Timorese have to be honest but tell a few lies, and that even while they are afraid they must also be brave. When facing a tiger, you have to be careful or you'll get caught by one of his teeth, he would say.

Some village heads told us how they accepted the large sums of money they were given by the district head, to be used to persuade the people in their village to vote for autonomy, but then urged support for independence. They told me they accepted the money because it was needed to develop their village.

Contact with Ordinary People

When UNAMET arrived in Ermera we found the people traumatized and fearful. Streets were deserted, the market scarcely operational. But the mood changed

Rai Inan, Motherland

Rai Inan is not above. Rai Inan is not below.
Rai Inan is my mother. The land is her body.
Earth is her flesh. Water is her blood.
Wind is her breath. Fire is her weapon.

Hold me, Mother

I want to bang my head on the wall.

Hold me, Mother

I want to smash faces.

Hold me, Mother

Burn away the rage that drips with my blood, Mother

Heal me with your warmth, Mother.

Rai Inan is not above. Rai Inan is not below.
Rai Inan is my mother. The land is her body.
Earth is her flesh. Water is her blood.
Wind is her breath. Fire is her warmth.

—Elizabete Lim Gomes

markedly when people saw with their own eyes that the world did care. UNA-MET local staff told of the overwhelming welcome they received in mid-June when they first ate at a stall. People gave them money and a free meal. They told them how glad they were that the United Nations had finally come. Soon afterwards the market became once more the busy hub of town, and people were seen out along the roads, doing more than just the essential.

Indonesians seemed to have no idea of the breadth of support CNRT enjoyed. One Balinese government official told me that he believed that 70 percent of people in Ermera wanted East Timor to remain part of Indonesia.

Contact with Militia

In contrast to pro-independence supporters, militia in Ermera made no attempt to contact UNAMET on our arrival in June. Mostly because we were bombarded with information and complaints from the proindependence side, it was some time before we ourselves were able to initiate contact with the militia.

Over a period of time, we were able to develop personal relationships with the militia. I often visited their headquarters and had cordial conversations with their members. The commander hooted with delight on one occasion when I turned up in a red T-shirt and white jeans, and he suggested he would not mind if I wore red and white, the Indonesian colors, rather than United Nations blue, all the time! Some militia members told me they believed that Timorese could be united because they were all brothers, which is not exactly inaccurate. Give any Timorese a few minutes together and they will find a family relationship, even if remote—such as that their grandmothers are second cousins. Indeed, it was my impression that if the TNI had not interfered, Ermera would have had no militias.

CNRT'S EFFORTS TO FIND A PLACE IN THE SUN

On the first day of registration people turned out in the hundreds, queuing like sardines in a tin. It was as if they were finally doing something they really wanted to do. Parties were held at registration centers. They were joyful places. After the ten-day registration period, it was as if the Timorese people had taken the decision into their own hands. No matter what the security situation was like they were going to vote in what they believed was the only chance they had.

UNAMET had to make a judgement as to whether there were equal opportunities for both sides. For CNRT in Ermera it was a constant struggle, though they philosophically said, "We've been campaigning for twenty-four years. Our people know what they want." Nevertheless they were not passive and implemented strategies to raise their profile. However, compared with other districts, they were given little space, perhaps because Ermera had been one of the most active proindependence strongholds in East Timor prior to April 1999. After the arrival of UNAMET, CNRT was able to open offices in most districts, but in Ermera they were too afraid to reopen their office.[11] There were never any Xanana or CNRT posters displayed in town as appeared in some other districts, and they did not dare to openly distribute their election material.

CNRT in Ermera decided in July, in the middle of the registration period, that the leadership and members who had been displaced since April 10, 1999, would return home to participate in the Popular Consultation and to open their office. They sought support of the Ermera district council in doing this, citing the May 5 Agreements between Indonesia, Portugal, and the United Nations: that as the representatives of the proindependence side they should have equal rights with the proautonomy side and be able to operate openly. They invited the police commander to attend a ceremony to be conducted in the hills near Gleno. The Falintil commander, who intended to wear his full Portuguese general's uniform, would "hand over" the CNRT members to the district police commander, in a ceremony signifying that while they had been protected by Falintil since April, now their safekeeping would be in the hands of the Indonesian police.

They were very excited about this event, hoping to encourage the many other displaced people in East Timor to follow their example. They were adamant that they would not leave the hills only to live in a compound, with police protection, as was the case for the internally displaced people who had undertaken a similar "reconciliation" in Suai. They talked of returning triumphantly in a convoy of six to eight hundred people, in the light of international media, putting Ermera on the map. They wanted to meet with the district council in the town hall, then return to live at home with their families. Senior UNAMET officials from Dili agreed to attend as observers, and a date was set.

However, at the very last minute the plan had to be canceled, as the district military commander said he could not guarantee their security. Possibly he did not want attention to focus on the numbers of displaced persons in Ermera district. CNRT was very disappointed, but they also now had to face the reality that the Indonesians, because of the military's hard-line position, would not fulfill their obligations under the May 5 Agreements to create a safe situation within which independence supporters could operate freely.

Registration and Campaigning

CNRT put all its effort into registering the people. CNRT members who had to stay in hiding registered wherever they could, mostly in areas where Falintil held control. They often requested the protection of UNAMET, but we were unable to offer them even this basic security.

Registration was a resounding success, numbers far exceeding estimates. I did not meet any Timorese in Ermera who had wanted to register but were unable to do so. As a result of this success, in some ways UNAMET slipped into a false sense of what we could achieve.

The next step was the campaign, a period of about ten days prior to voting day. As CNRT had no office and their leadership was in hiding, the proautonomy forces felt they had the upper hand. Militia provided the "crowds" at the autonomy campaigns. Public servants, who were obliged to support autonomy, led the rallies. The militia traveled around all day in trucks, campaigning whenever and wherever they could find a crowd. Some of these militia complained to UNAMET local staff about having to "yell party slogans all day," without even being given food.

In the end CNRT canceled all but two of its six planned rallies, because of threats to ordinary people who might have attended the events, especially those held far from the main UNAMET headquarters. One rally was held in Railaku in the north on August 18. The participants, mostly students from Gleno, were escorted the half-hour drive there by UNAMET and Indonesian police, after their convoy was threatened by militia. No locals dared attend.

People felt somewhat safer attending a second rally in Gleno, where on August 26 approximately two thousand locals gathered. As CNRT was about to begin its rally, one of its leaders was called by the district police commander, who told him that he could not guarantee the security of public servants who took part in the rally, and he suggested they withdraw. This was a problem as all the speakers were public servants! After some negotiation, the rally proceeded. In spite of the threats, the speakers were strident, demanding an end to colonialism, corruption, collusion, and nepotism in East Timor.

Reconciliation

There were strong indications that Timorese from both sides wanted to resolve their differences peacefully. In this they requested the mediation of UNAMET. The militia commanders were particularly keen to meet with Falintil. The district police commander was supportive of such a meeting. In mid-June he himself visited Falintil in the area it controlled (Region IV) and saluted its commander, whose code name was Ular (Snake) before shaking hands. The Timorese were jubilant about this meeting, claiming it was the first time in twenty-four years an Indonesian official had openly recognized Falintil. However, after some time it became clear that the district military commander was against any such rapprochement. He would always say he could not guarantee security.

After Falintil moved into cantonment, the militia talked of also doing so but never did. They claimed they had gone further by actually surrendering weapons, but the *Darah Integrasi* commander, Miguel Babo, and his brother, the deputy commander, continued to show weapons at campaign rallies to remind voters that this is what they faced if they rejected autonomy.

UNAMET sponsored several reconciliation meetings. Under some UNAMET pressure both sides eventually agreed on a statement they could sign on August 12, 1999. They agreed to stop threats, not to carry weapons, to respect the legal authority, and not to take unilateral action.

Cantonment, Celebration, and Flag Raising

So how did CNRT convey their message to the people, given that the right to campaign and open an office was basically denied them?

At every subdistrict and village level there were CNRT secretaries, who carried the message, albeit clandestinely. Priests and nuns also provided moral leadership, many at great personal risk. On the occasion that Bishop Carlos Filipe Ximenes Belo came to Ermera Lama, the old cathedral town ten kilometers from Gleno, he told the people that this ballot was a once-only opportunity given to them by the international community. They should not be afraid, but vote according to their conscience, remembering they were choosing the future for their children and grandchildren.

A group of university students was also instrumental in spreading the message.[12] Some two hundred of them originating in Ermera returned to their homes and villages to explain to people the registration and voting process and to gather information about human rights abuses. They were in constant conflict with the authorities, who claimed they "angered" the "people."

After an agreement between Falintil commanders and senior Dili UNAMET officials, Falintil guerrillas moved into cantonment. One of these areas was located in Ermera district, in Poetete village.[13] On August 10, this movement into cantonment in Ermera was celebrated in style with a large party to which UNAMET officials were invited from Dili and Gleno.

August 20 was Falintil Day, their twentieth anniversary and the first time they had been able to celebrate it openly. Many East Timorese saw and met with the guerrillas for the first time at a campaign rally of eighteen thousand people. The shops and streets of towns in Ermera district were deserted. The militia, with their police and TNI escorts, were angry to find no one at the village where they had planned a rally. On their way home the next day, they vented their anger by attacking villagers and destroying homes of people who had just returned from the Falintil anniversary celebration.

Two days before the ballot, CNRT held a flag-raising ceremony in the cantonment. As the flag slowly rose under the intense tropical glare, men hugged each other, their tears flowing unashamedly. The cantonment was by far the most interesting place in Ermera district, alive with hope and indeed forgiveness.

Police Inaction against Crimes Committed by Militia and the TNI

Reports that UNAMET received about incidents involving the militia were passed to the Indonesian police, as they were responsible for investigation. But little action was ever taken, despite promises, and no militia member was ever arrested. After the ballot, the police commander told the UNAMET police commander that he had been ordered "from above" not to interfere with the actions of the militia. This led to a ludicrous situation on the day of voting, after the center in Gleno was attacked by militia. The district police chief secretly confided that he could solve the militia situation in twenty-four hours if given a free hand. Instead of being able to do this, it seemed the only thing he could do was to take personal responsibility. He sat in the sun for hours in the Gleno polling station grounds in order to ensure that the militia allowed voting to continue. I observed militia standing nearby, no doubt plotting their next move.

Many Timorese reported incidents to UNAMET in which the TNI acted together with the militia in threatening and bashing, in addition to the TNI's crimes of April and May. After some time, UNAMET police were told by the Indonesian police that they could not handle any incidents involving the TNI and that reports of these incidents should be passed to the military. Indonesian law stipulates that crimes by the military must be handled in a military court. UNAMET military liaison officers duly reported complaints about TNI members and incidents involving them to the Indonesian military commander, but there was never any feedback or notification of action.

Polling Day and Its Aftermath

Voting day, Monday, August 30, unlike registration, was not a jubilant occasion. Bishop Belo, in a pastoral letter read in all churches the previous day, exhorted people to go home afterwards to pray, and keep on praying. Don't do anything to provoke, he told them, presumably meaning "don't celebrate." By 7:30 on the morning of the ballot, we heard on our UNAMET radios that most people were already waiting in line to vote, and this was the case everywhere in East Timor. Many people had traveled the previous evening to their polling centers as voting had to take place where you registered. A small number of people were intimidated after registration and left the areas where they had registered, so were unable to vote. Despite all the fears that voting might be disrupted, 98.5 percent of those registered cast their ballots.

The militia attack on our Gleno polling station at midday came as a surprise, as Ermera was by this time considered safe, although it was always a knife-edge situation. The U.S. ambassador to Indonesia, Robert Gelbard, had come to view voting there and was in the yard when shooting broke out and rocks were thrown at the walls of the polling station. The Timorese could hardly believe their luck, to have the ambassador of the superpower actually witness this attack. After several hours and an attempt to address the militia's complaints, the polling station was reopened. About three hundred of the approximately 2,500 registered voters at this polling station were too frightened to return after the attack.

Meanwhile, in a distant subdistrict of Ermera, Atsabe, over three hours' drive away, an even more disturbing attack was taking place. As the Baboi Leten polling station was closing, a TNI officer and militia, all armed with automatic weapons, approached the station. They demanded that UNAMET's local Timorese staff be handed over to them, accusing them of forcing the people to vote to reject autonomy. The lone UNAMET police officer was unable to defend the local staff and witnessed two being bashed with poles and kicked. Two Indonesian police mobile brigade members stood by doing nothing, but the UNAMET police officer was quite convinced that if they had interfered they would also have been attacked by the militia. One of the victims was taken away by UNAMET staff when their police escort arrived to take them back to Atsabe town, but he later died. The UNAMET police officer believes that the other was killed, and almost certainly also a third, who was taken off in the car of the TNI member. The next day it took many hours of negotiation for the remaining local Timorese staff, together with the ballot boxes, to be evacuated by helicopter from Atsabe to Dili.

Even the boxes in Gleno were not removed without incident. New militia arrived in town the day after polling. We were never able to talk to them and find out their identity. We asked the district military commander if they were *Aitarak*; he seemed to agree. The rumor was that the new militia was inserted because *Darah Integrasi* had never been "effective." They tried to prevent the helicopter from picking up the ballot boxes, but not with sufficient determination to succeed. During this attempt, UNAMET staff saw Indonesian police mobile brigade members handing traditional weapons to the militia.

The evening after the ballot, the burning of houses of CNRT leaders began. A twelve-year-old girl came to the UNAMET headquarters to report that her house was burnt, together with her family's store of rice and corn. She described the grenade planted by a militia member in her mother's flower plot, which was supposed to prove her father was a Falintil member, thus providing the pretext for burning the house.

UNAMET staff was never able to visit the families whose homes were destroyed after the ballot. During the day we were basically hostages in our compound. All staff had to move together into one of two areas, well-guarded by the police mobile brigade. We could only travel between our houses and the headquarters, along one main route. Militia roamed around Gleno with jerry cans of petrol looking for the next house to target. A UNAMET police patrol was threatened by machete-wielding militia, so that was the end of their patrols.

Somewhat to my surprise, we were able to make one last visit to the cantonment, on Thursday, September 2, after the ballot but before the announcement of the result. While there were militia roadblocks to the north so that we needed police escorts to travel to Dili, there were none to the south. The only people we saw on our trip were militia. The markets were closed in the towns through which we passed. All houses had their shutters locked and were deserted, many already burnt. No one was working, and no children greeted us from the coffee gardens. It was as if winter had come to beautiful Ermera.

It was comforting to see that so many people were safe in the cantonment, but they feared for many of their friends. There were many requests to check the whereabouts of family members. They implored us to tell UNAMET that peacekeepers were needed before the announcement of the result. Could UNAMET help with food and medicines, as people were already flocking there? It was difficult to walk away knowing there was probably nothing we could do to help.

On September 3 I went to Dili, never imagining our headquarters would be burnt in just over a week and that I would not be able to return. As the situation deteriorated, counting of votes was accelerated and the announcement of the result brought forward to Saturday, September 4, in the hope that a clear result might help stabilize the situation.

On the day of the announcement and just after, an uneasy calm settled over Dili, like the calm before a storm. No one went into the streets to celebrate the clear 78.5 percent victory for the proindependence side, an astounding victory against all odds. Even as the announcement was being made, a group of angry militia from Atsabe, where the three Timorese UNAMET staff had been killed on polling day, arrived in Dili demanding that their complaints about the ballot be heard and considered in the final count. It was small comfort to them to be told by UNAMET that they were the first to hear the official result. They left in a rage and razed Atsabe to the ground. In Dili all day I answered the phone in the political office. One caller, monitoring military radio, reported he'd heard that attacks on CNRT and independence supporters would begin at 1 p.m. Several people phoned saying they had been ordered to get ready to leave immediately for West Timor and asked what UNAMET advised them to do. The tragic thing was that we could do nothing.

In Ermera, the district police commander finally told the remaining UNAMET staff he could not guarantee UNAMET security, and the UNAMET headquarters in Ermera was evacuated on September 6. Between September 12 and 14 there was some armed contact between Falintil and militia backed by the TNI, including an unsuccessful attack on the cantonment.

The Indonesian police left Gleno on September 8. The TNI and the militia began their campaign where they forced an estimated thirty thousand people from Ermera district to West Timor. They then gradually withdrew, looting and burning as they went. Most of Gleno and Atsabe towns were burnt. All the relatively new and valuable government, military, and police offices and essential facilities in Gleno were destroyed. Other towns not along this route were less damaged.

People in the cantonment survived, eating cassava and sweet potato. Their greatest fears were for family and friends taken to West Timor. At least forty people are known to have been killed including a prominent female CNRT leader, Ana Lemos, murdered on September 13, 1999.

CONCLUSION

The destruction of East Timor following the ballot did not surprise East Timorese, although they fervently hoped the international community would protect them. After the close of voting on August 30, all active members of CNRT in Ermera fled their homes to hide in the cantonment. Many left behind their families, who were later taken to West Timor. In Ermera they seemed to have no forewarning of this strategy on the part of the militia and the TNI.

The UNAMET military liaison officers stationed in Ermera believe this plan was probably conceived by TNI liaison officers. In Ermera there were seven TNI liaison officers sent from Jakarta to liaise between the UNAMET military officers and the TNI. Their task was to accompany the UNAMET officers wherever they went. After the first few weeks they rarely turned up as arranged. One senior officer was conspicuously angry at the enthusiastic reception local people gave to UNAMET. I witnessed this particular officer's reaction to villagers who openly criticized the action of soldiers at a TNI post in a village. He later told UNAMET

Birth in the Great Mountain Tatamailau

Maria lies down
layered stones cool her pain
thick shrubs hide her cries
ancient trees mother her thoughts
while standing crosses witness
the sun blazing on her giving birth
unrest caught her in the great Mountain Tatamailau
for her dwelling lingers in the sand lined town
swarmed by smothering growls
awaiting rest to douse
its burning shore once again
Maria lies down
blind fate chose her bed
in the abeyant altar of the mountain folk
oblivion obscures the rising chants
of the great Mountain Tatamailau
latent wisdom reminds her
that bloodshed invoking strength
grants tomorrow lasting rest
her fleeing baby born today
grasping sense might and place
untamed vision flaring faith
shall ripe real her longing
for rest.

—Elizabete Lim Gomes

The story of creation told by the Mambae ethnic group, "The Walk of Ina Lua—The Walk of Our Mother," tells of how the land of Timor was formed. Maromak, the Shining One, in other words God, united with a spirit, Ina Lua. From their union, Ina Lua gave birth first to Mount Ramelau then to other smaller mountains and trees, rocks, people, and animals. The great mountain Ramelau is the highest mountain in East Timor. It is the oldest of the Timorese ancestors, a grandparent who is wise and powerful. Ramelau marks the beginning of all material life in the island. Ramelau is also called Tatamailau, which in Timorese means "grandfather."

that while the vote would be secure, he thought there would be a problem after-wards—there could be an "emotional outburst." One is tempted to conjecture that they were responsible for planning the postballot mayhem, a view supported by a large cache of documents found in Dili military headquarters after the TNI withdrawal.[14]

The fact that the East Timorese were determined to vote in full awareness of the danger led most UNAMET staff to view them with genuine admiration. The Timorese believed there was no other option than to take this risk. They seemed to be well aware that Indonesia could withdraw the offer of the ballot if peace-keepers had been made a precondition. Bishop Belo worked tirelessly to encour-age them to take this unique opportunity. Ten years previously he had written a letter to the United Nations secretary general pleading that such an opportunity be given to his people.

The Timorese often expressed their disappointment at the security arrange-ments even before the ballot. The fact that the tripartite agreements placed secur-ity in the hands of the Indonesian police was ludicrous to them. "When you've been in East Timor for a while you will understand why that is impossible," they would say to us. I had visited East Timor on several occasions previously and had lived for many years in Java throughout Suharto's repressive New Order era, so understood their fear.

The fact that there was relative calm on the day of the vote, and even the day of the announcement, gave those of us in the political office some hope that perhaps Indonesia had decided to let East Timor go honorably, as foreign minister Ali Alatas had repeatedly said it would do. We thought there was a chance that for Indonesia the political cost on the world stage would be too great to do anything disastrous after the people's will was known. We certainly thought there would be trouble, but never anticipated so violent a response.

However the East Timorese, while disappointed that the response of the inter-national community did not come earlier, did not criticize UNAMET. I visited Ermera briefly again in November 1999. People smiled and told me that it was worth it, that they'd been suffering for a long time and now finally they were free. We sat on the steps of the military barracks and they joked about no longer needing to worry about who was watching them. They walked the streets at night without fear. Graffiti etched on many burnt out buildings said it all, "Although it's razed to the ground, the important thing is that now we're free" (*Biar hangus, yang penting merdeka*).

NOTES

The views in this article are the author's own and are not necessarily the official UNA-MET position. This essay is dedicated to Ana Lemos, a wonderful East Timorese activist who became a friend in Ermera. She was tortured and murdered on September 13, 1999.

1. Ermera is one of East Timor's thirteen districts (*kabupaten*). Each district consists of several subdistricts (*kecamatan*). Each subdistrict is made up of several villages (*desa*), which in turn consist of several hamlets (*kampung* or RK). In Ermera district there are five subdistricts, with about fifty villages altogether. Each level of organization has its own administrator: district head (*bupati*, in Ermera, Constantino Soares), subdistrict head (*camat*), village head (*kepala desa*). At the district level there is a district police headquarters (*polres*) and district military headquarters (*kodim*). The heads of these are, respectively, the district police commander (*kapolres*, in Ermera, Lt. Col. Pol. Drs. Erry T. B. Gultom), and the district military commander (*dandim*, in Ermera, Col. Muhammad Nur). There are military and police equivalents at the subdistrict level. In each village there is also a military official, a noncommissioned officer (*babinsa*).

2. The term *referendum* was deliberately avoided as Indonesia had long refused to permit a referendum on independence.

3. The 1982 Defense Act sets out the role of trained civilians (*rakyat terlatih* or *ratih*). The total population has the responsibility to enforce the law. People receive rudimentary military training and can be called on to assist government, military, or police for particular tasks.

4. Indonesian police claimed that the problem was that CNRT extorted money. I know little about CNRT's tax-collecting practices at that time.

5. Tomas Gonçalves, a long-standing supporter of Indonesia. However, after militia attacks in April 1999 he fled Ermera and went into hiding in Macau, where he confessed to his involvement in forming militias.

6. *Kompas* (1 May 1999) suggests they may have been *Aitarak* members.

7. I concluded that those murdered were militia, and that Falintil, CNRT or their followers were somehow involved in the murder, but whether it was ordered by the leadership, I do not know. CNRT protested that the police insisted on investigating these murders but refused to even take evidence concerning the many proindependence people killed by militia, police, and military.

8. In 1997 he was elected as a member of Suharto's *Golkar* party in the local assembly (DPRD II). In April 1999 he was expelled from the party and excluded from the assembly.

9. The Indonesian Police Mobile Brigades (*Brimob*) are something like riot police. Indonesia was responsible for security of the ballot, and a large *Brimob* force, called *Kontingen Lorosae*, was sent to East Timor for this purpose. All registration centers, UNAMET headquarters, and UNAMET staff accommodation were guarded by its officers.

10. In Ermera there were three UNAMET military liaison officers who were the contacts with the Indonesian military.

11. Many of the offices operated for only a short time before they were attacked or burnt.

12. The university students mostly belonged to *Dewan Solidaritas Mahasiswa Timur Timor* (East Timorese Students' Solidarity Council). The Ermera branch was called *Dewan Mini Mahasiswa Ermera* (Ermera Students' Mini Council). Some belonged to East Timorese organizations from outside East Timor, mostly Java, Bali, and Sulawesi. In Ermera they were very well organized.

13. Ermera is in Region IV of the Falintil command structure. Region IV is the largest region, located in the west. There was a north and a south cantonment in Region IV, the northern one being close to Gleno town.

14. Richard Lloyd Parry, "Letters Reveal How Indonesian Generals Planned Repression," *The Independent*, 5 February 2000, 1, 15.

8

Grassroots in the Field—Observing the East Timor Consultation

Charles Scheiner

BACKGROUND

Since the Indonesian invasion in 1975, "the question of East Timor" has been on the agenda of the United Nations. The Security Council passed two resolutions urging Indonesian withdrawal, and the General Assembly passed eight. Yet the governments of the world declined to resolve the situation or obtain justice for the East Timorese people. In fact, most of the major powers, following the example of the United States, provided Indonesia with military, economic, and diplomatic support. They calculated that the advantages of a close relationship with the Suharto regime outweighed the horrors his military inflicted on strategically insignificant East Timor.

For the first fifteen years of the occupation, Indonesia closed the territory to outside observers in an effort to smother global concern about their illegal invasion. They had considerable success; Western media and governments ignored the ongoing slaughter of two hundred thousand East Timorese. Through the 1980s in most of the world, East Timor was the quintessential obscure lost cause, followed only by a tiny fringe of hard-core activists. Solidarity and human rights campaigns mounted in the aftermath of the invasion had waned, and only a handful of people were aware that the atrocities continued. Media coverage, which had always been rare, became nonexistent.

Throughout this period, the West increased its economic, military, and political ties with Jakarta. The United States in particular shipped massive quantities of weapons to the Indonesian army, including many of those used with most deadly effect in East Timor. Every year, U.S. taxpayers hosted Indonesian soldiers for training to "improve their professionalism." And the U.S., British, Australian, and European governments continued to run interference for Indonesia in the United Nations and other international fora.

But for the persistence of the East Timorese resistance, the story might have ended there. When Indonesia opened the territory to foreigners beginning in 1989, the East Timorese organized an underground civilian movement to complement the guerrilla struggle. On November 12, 1991, they staged a large, peaceful demonstration at Santa Cruz cemetery in Dili and were attacked by Indonesian soldiers firing U.S.–supplied M-16 automatic rifles. When the shooting stopped, at least 271 East Timorese lay dead; perhaps two hundred more were murdered in Indonesian military hospitals over the next few days.[1]

Unlike most previous massacres, this one was witnessed by international journalists, whose reporting briefly broke through the global media blackout. (See Allan Nairn's congressional testimony in this volume.) A few governments suspended aid to Indonesia and many uttered harsh warnings. More lastingly, the Santa Cruz massacre catalyzed the reemergence of a worldwide solidarity movement. The East Timor *Action* Network (ETAN) was formed in the United States, and similar organizations in Europe, Canada, Japan, and Australia expanded or began their support for East Timor. In Portugal, widespread grassroots activity forced the government to advocate East Timorese rights in European and international circles.

SOLIDARITY GROWS

In the United States, ETAN built on existing networks and the internet to achieve a nationwide presence, developing a dozen local chapters and several thousand members by 1996. Although protests were held at Indonesian consulates and educational events were organized all over the country, the main focus was on Washington. ETAN saw the U.S.–Indonesia military relationship as the most effective lever with which to pressure Jakarta to withdraw from East Timor. ETAN challenged military aid, weapons sales, and military training in an effort to increase the cost to Indonesia of remaining in East Timor to a point where continued occupation ceased to be worthwhile.

From 1992 through 1996, ETAN's all-volunteer grassroots campaigns blocked several weapons sales, pressured Congress into barring U.S. military-training aid, and raised the profile of East Timor in both the mainstream and alternative media.[2] Similar campaigns were growing throughout Europe and other parts of the world. From 1994 onward, the Asia-Pacific Coalition on East Timor (APCET), centered in the Philippines and including groups from East and Southeast Asia, Australia, and Oceania, brought public pressure to Indonesia's own neighborhood.

The International Federation for East Timor (IFET) had been formed in 1991 by groups from Europe, Japan, and North America and began to coordinate the campaigns of international non-governmental organizations (NGOs) to petition the United Nations and otherwise influence transnational governmental processes. Other conduits, including the internet, Christian church networks, and regional conferences, strengthened international cooperation among grassroots activists on East Timor, coordinating closely with East Timorese leaders both inside the occupied territory and in exile.

When the Nobel Peace Prize was awarded to East Timorese leaders José Ramos-Horta and Bishop Carlos Filipe Ximenes Belo at the end of 1996, ETAN was able to capitalize on the attention on East Timor, using newly available resources and media access to hire field organizing staff and open an office in Washington. Over the next two years, ETAN and others continued to expose and erode the remaining U.S. support for the Indonesian military, and to get the U.S. government to acknowledge East Timorese human and political rights. In 1997 Congress barred the use of U.S.–supplied weapons in East Timor. After the 1997 Asian economic crisis, the U.S. lost confidence that Suharto could continue to reliably protect its interests. As dissent increased in Indonesia, Washington was less willing to back the dictatorship. Congress had banned U.S. military training aid for Indonesia in response to grassroots pressure since 1992, but Pentagon training persisted quietly in Indonesia until it was exposed in early 1998. Before Suharto fell, Congress had built upon administration unease and Indonesian dissent to suspend all remaining U.S.–Indonesian military training. Then as B. J. Habibie came into office, the U.S. Senate unanimously supported an internationally supervised referendum on East Timor's political status.

U.S. grassroots and congressional pressure on the U.S.–Indonesia military relationship may be one reason that Suharto's ouster in 1998 was not a reprise of the mass slaughter that consolidated his military coup in 1965—Washington policymakers let their friends in the Indonesian armed forces know that the U.S. would not support a military takeover this time.[3]

SETTING THE STAGE

In 1992, Indonesian foreign minister Ali Alatas called the international outcry over East Timor "a pebble in the shoe, not a major issue but causing a nuisance. It would be a great pity if, because of this question, Indonesia is not able to play a greater role in the world."[4]

Six years later, Alatas and newly anointed President Habibie were dealing with an intractable economic crisis. With his hold on power tenuous, President Habibie sought increased Western and Japanese support. Together with Alatas (who remained foreign minister until President Wahid took office in late 1999), he suggested allowing the East Timorese people to vote on an autonomy plan to remain Indonesia's twenty-seventh province. They believed that the electorate, with sufficient incentive and threats, would support the plan, and make the pebble disappear. For the first time in twenty-four years, Jakarta entered substantive negotiations with the United Nations and Portugal in an effort to resolve the East Timor issue.

The Indonesian military (TNI) did not share Habibie's and Alatas's confidence that Jakarta would win the vote and stepped up its creation and arming of East Timorese paramilitary groups (so-called militias) to terrorize the East Timorese and prevent them from voting for independence. By using militias instead of its own units, the TNI hoped to be able to plausibly deny involvement in the terrorism. From late 1998 onward, the TNI's militias escalated their violence against proindependence East Timorese, and against the civilian population in general. By early 1999, massacres were a weekly occurrence, and tens of thousands of East Timorese had been driven from their villages.

As international activists, ETAN and the other IFET member groups tried to bring these developments to the attention of the negotiators. On March 30, for example, IFET gave a videotape of an Australian TV program[5] to Secretary General Kofi Annan and wrote:

> We have been concerned by recent statements by your office and by the Indonesian government that disarmament of the paramilitaries and withdrawal of Indonesian soldiers from East Timor are not seen as prerequisites to the "ballot consultation" in which the East Timorese people are to accept or reject Indonesia's offer of autonomy. As this program makes clear, a U.N.–conducted East Timorese vote in the current atmosphere of terror would be a mockery of everything the United Nations stands for.[6]

The negotiations continued, and Indonesia and Portugal were approaching agreement with the secretary general on leaving Indonesia responsible for security before and during the vote. On April 5 and 6, militias massacred more than fifty refugees in Liquica; ten days later they rampaged through Dili, murdering a dozen refugees in the home of prominent independence advocate, Manuel Carrascalão as well as his teenage son. ETAN brought a survivor of the Liquiça massacre to the United States and Europe in late April, where he testified before Congress and met with officials from the United Nations and several governments, as well as with media and religious leaders, before seeking safety in Portugal.[7]

On April 21, Indonesian defense minister General Wiranto flew to East Timor and proclaimed a cease-fire between militias and the East Timorese resistance. The militias never intended to honor the agreement; they inflicted new atrocities hours after signing. The proindependence forces, who had unilaterally refrained from military confrontation for several months, felt compelled to sign to maintain credibility with the pro-Jakarta international community and to refute Jakarta's propaganda that East Timor would erupt into civil war if the TNI withdrew. Wiranto, whose legal responsibility should have been to order the arrest of perpetrators of violence against civilians, did nothing to restrain the militia forces. IFET again expressed its concern to the secretary general and the Indonesian and Portuguese

Foreign Ministers, who were in New York negotiating the final details of a consultation agreement scheduled to be signed on May 5:

> [T]he paramilitary violence persists, and Indonesia has made no significant efforts to control it. Murders continue daily, militia leaders exhort their coerced followers to assassinate proindependence leaders and human rights workers with impunity, and tens of thousands of internal refugees live in fear for their lives. . . .
> As soon as the 5 May accord is signed, the United Nations must assume responsibility for creating and preserving law and order in East Timor, and for protecting public safety. The Indonesian military has been there illegally for twenty-three years, and their occupation has taken more than two hundred thousand East Timorese lives. . . . It will be impossible for the United Nations to conduct a meaningful assessment of East Timorese public opinion if those forces—one party to the conflict—are controlling the situation on the ground.[8]

Although the secretary general and other U.N. officials were fully aware of the danger of the Jakarta-backed militias, they were unable to persuade any national government to make this issue public. The agreement signed on May 5 set the stage not only for the August 30 vote, but also for the terrorism and destruction that preceded and followed it.[9]

The secretary general and others have since excused allowing the Indonesian military to retain control in East Timor during the referendum process by saying that Jakarta would not have signed the agreement under any other terms, and there would have been no vote.[10] They believed that China, at Indonesia's request, would have vetoed any Security Council resolution that did not leave the TNI in charge, and that the East Timorese leadership and public wanted the vote to take place while the window of opportunity was open. However, neither the United States nor any other government put even the slightest pressure on Indonesia to improve the agreement by accepting international responsibility for security. If the international community had threatened in April to curtail or cut off economic and/or military cooperation with Indonesia, as they finally did in mid-September, the May 5 Agreements would have been different and the postballot devastation could have been avoided.

THE ACTIVISTS' DILEMMA

People around the world who had worked for years to advance East Timor's human and political rights pondered how to make the best of a bad situation. We supported the desire of the East Timorese people (as expressed by the leader of the National Council of Timorese Resistance (CNRT), Xanana Gusmão) that the consultation proceed, and sought ways to help make the vote free, fair, and peaceful. Many activists joined the United Nations Assistance Mission in East Timor

(UNAMET), the United Nations' mission that was to carry out the referendum,[11] and played key inside roles in making that process go smoothly.

IFET, having little confidence in governments that had acquiesced or conspired to deny East Timorese rights for the past quarter century, chose to support and monitor UNAMET and the parties to the vote from inside East Timor. UNAMET's parameters were defined by the May 5 Agreements and resulting Security Council resolutions; their personnel were constrained by U.N. protocol to refrain from expressing criticism of member states or public dissent from established U.N. positions.

The IFET Observer Project (IFET-OP) became the largest of the dozen international observer delegations in East Timor. There were also about a dozen Indonesian observer groups, with both pro- and antiautonomy biases. Because IFET-OP was a U.N.–accredited project, its observers were nonpartisan, taking no position on whether people should vote for autonomy or independence. IFET-OP did, however, strongly support their right to vote in a free and fair election, without intimidation, and frequently reported actual or potential infringements on that right. Most IFET members expected that East Timorese voters would choose independence if given the chance, but the decision was theirs, and the observers went to make certain that it was freely made.

IFET volunteer observers, recruited from every continent and trained in advance, began arriving in East Timor in June. Most field teams lived with East Timorese families or in rented houses for several weeks before the vote, monitoring the registration and campaign phases, building relationships with the local people, and attempting to communicate with all sides (although the militia were rarely willing to talk). By August 30, 125 U.N.–accredited IFET observers from twenty countries were deployed in eighteen teams, covering every district in the territory. They observed balloting at 135 of the two hundred polling centers.

The UNAMET mission, hired and directed by the U.N., was charged with conducting the referendum, only the third U.N.–run election in history.[12] UNAMET had about 450 nonpolice international staff and about four thousand local staff, barely enough to implement the mechanics of the vote on a very tight timetable. The U.N. mission was also limited by diplomatic compromises, institutional goals, insufficient international political will, and its hierarchical structure. IFET-OP, the Carter Center, and other groups were independent observers, with fewer constraints. Although IFET members had campaigned against the long, brutal, and illegal Indonesian occupation, they were committed to genuine self-determination for the East Timorese and to expose problems and recommend solutions whenever logistics, intimidation, or political factors threatened to undermine the process.

IFET-OP relayed what they and the local population observed to the United Nations, the media, and world governments. The IFET teams lived with families, walking through villages and staying visible in the hope that the presence of international observers would augment the limited U.N. presence outside Dili and help deter militia violence. In addition, IFET-OP would be global eyes, voices, and hands—a direct link between the East Timorese people and grassroots people around the world, unmediated by governments or journalists. Through the international network of East Timor support groups that had developed since 1991, IFET-OP would inform and lobby governments to make the consultation as free as possible.

OBSERVING THE CAMPAIGN

The observers quickly saw that the problem of leaving security in Indonesia's hands was not just theoretical. IFET-OP's first in-country report described a July 4 militia attack on a humanitarian aid convoy in Liquiça "while the police and military stood idly by." Although the convoy included international aid workers, U.N. staff, foreign journalists, and an IFET observer, police did nothing while the militias assaulted the humanitarian workers with rocks and machetes. IFET-OP pointed out that the humanitarian crisis—thirty to sixty thousand people had been forced from their homes by militias, many for months on end—"directly affects the validity of the vote" and called on the Indonesian government to disarm the militias and bring their leaders to justice, to fulfill its commitment "to ensure an 'environment devoid of violence or other forms of intimidation' as a 'prerequisite for the holding of a free and fair ballot in East Timor.' "[13]

On August 6, in Same (a town in southern East Timor), the IFET-OP team witnessed and reported a militia assault on a recently opened student proindependence campaign headquarters. This was the first of many attacks on the proindependence campaign; CNRT offices in many towns were fire-bombed or worse. IFET-OP concluded that the election would not be free and fair if one side could not campaign publicly.

The IFET Observer Project served as an alert system for the U.N. Civilian Police, often asking these unarmed advisors to intervene in difficult situations (they were very cooperative and efficient, given their strict limitations of their mandate and resources).

In addition to sending reports to observers' home governments and to the U.N. ambassadors of the Security Council countries, IFET-OP teams often briefed foreign delegations and reporters in East Timor. Visiting parliamentarians found them accessible, informed, and forthcoming; journalists found their readers could identify with the grassroots IFET-OP volunteers. Although the international visitors to East Timor appreciated IFET-OP (the Canadian and Finnish ambassadors to Indonesia provided funding; U.S. embassy officials were frequent visitors), there was little response from the United Nations in New York or from capitals around the world. Privately, U.N. staffers in New York appreciated IFET-OP's reports, which confirmed internal information from UNAMET, but could be freely distributed. But publicly, the United Nations and governments rarely responded; they took no effective action to redress the Indonesian military/militia terror.

The largest accredited Observer Project was *Komite Independen Pemantau Pemungutan Suara* (Independent Committee for Direct Ballot Monitoring; KIPER), a joint Indonesian–East Timorese mission that hoped to deploy more than five hundred observers. However, KIPER volunteers were limited by lack of resources and particularly targeted by militia violence. In addition, many of their East Timorese members resigned as observers in order to take a partisan role in the campaign. KIPER was initiated by Solidamor, a group of courageous Indonesians who had taken tremendous risks for several years, opposing the Suharto regime by supporting East Timorese self-determination. They were much appreciated by the East Timorese and in the forefront of grassroots prodemocracy activism in Indonesia.

The two sides agreed to campaign on alternate days, but the "reject" autonomy (i.e. support independence) side was usually prevented from public campaigning by militia threats, as IFET-OP repeatedly reported. When the East Timorese people got to know the observers better, they often confided in the foreigners or asked them for help.[14] IFET-OP also received reports and heard rumors of preparations for widespread retaliation after the vote.[15] On August 17, at the start of the campaign, IFET-OP reported "warnings by government officials and proautonomy spokespersons of large-scale violence if the East Timorese people reject the autonomy option in the August 30 vote, along with widespread reports of arms shipments entering the territory" and recommended "that the international community work diligently through the United Nations to broaden the UNAMET mandate as it relates to security, and to increase significantly the numbers of U. N. security personnel in East Timor *before* the August 30 vote."

Seeing no response, IFET-OP wrote a public letter from Dili to the U.N. secretary general on August 24, describing "pervasive fears within the East Timorese population that the Indonesian military-backed militias will launch a wave of terror around, or shortly after, the time of the ballot."

Many in the IFET-OP project were pacifists with principled views against military force. When IFET-OP's letter to Annan recommended "a much larger international security presence, preferably armed, to maintain security following the vote" several of IFET-OP's country coordinators (who relayed IFET-OP reports to media and officials in their own countries and campaigned for their recommendations) stood aside from the decision. But the IFET observers in East Timor, like every East Timorese person[16] they spoke with, could see no other choice.

As IFET-OP's reports became more outspoken, the observers' presence increasingly irritated the pro-Indonesian side. Militias often threatened them; on three occasions they surrounded IFET-OP vehicles, brandishing weapons at the occupants for extended periods. An East Timorese IFET driver was kidnapped (and later released unharmed) in Liquiça. Another team, listening to radio conversations between *Kopassus* and local militia, heard their own murders being ordered.[17] But they avoided the trap, and no IFET-OP people were injured. It became clear that the general militia orders were to intimidate foreigners, not to harm them.

CNRT's enthusiasm overcame caution on the Thursday before the vote, and a twenty-thousand–person rally was followed by a joyful caravan all over Dili. Although that day was mostly peaceful, the militias retaliated on Friday, killing about a dozen people in various parts of the city. For the first time, sharp international reaction pressured Indonesia to curtail the violence, but a siege mentality pervaded Dili, and most people stayed home until Monday's vote.

On Saturday, August 28, IFET-OP reported that

the upsurge in violence over the last two days places the entire consultation process in jeopardy. . . . Unless the United Nations and the international community take

Figure 8.1   Polling place in Gleno, East Timor, on voting day, attacked an hour and a half earlier. Courtesy: John M. Miller.

quick and decisive action to stem the violence, the results of Monday's balloting will be contaminated by fear.

Decisive action was not forthcoming. The U.S. State Department portrayed the latest violence as a new development. State Department spokesman James Foley said: "The United States is deeply concerned by these changes in the security situation." Foley claimed that Washington had relayed its concern directly and repeatedly to the "highest levels" of the Indonesian government but noted: "Despite the assurances we have received, violence and intimidation continue to pose a great risk to the success of the U.N.–administered vote. Urgent remedial attention and action is required."[18]

Foley's statement exemplifies hypocritical U.S. diplomacy, where a public façade obscures a more significant signal behind the scenes.[19] Habibie and Alatas— the officials at the "highest levels" who had given assurances to Washington— were not in control of the situation. A different message went to those in charge: between August 11 and 25, the U.S. Navy conducted CARAT-99 joint exercises with the Indonesian Navy off Surabaya.[20] The Pentagon was simultaneously training Indonesian soldiers (ostensibly in non-military subjects) at the National Defense University (Ft. McNair, Washington, D.C.) and in California,[21] and other U.S.–Indonesian military and economic business continued as it had since before Habibie took office. IFET-OP and UNAMET's reports of violence in East Timor and the less-than-heartfelt pleas from the State Department were destined to be ignored.

THE VOTE—AND ITS AFTERMATH

August 30 was a glorious day. Most voters went to the polls before dawn, hoping that darkness would reduce the likelihood of militia attack. They waited patiently for hours to cast their ballots, a brief interregnum after twenty-three years of horrific sacrifice. Although there were a few violent incidents, the day was generally peaceful and nearly everyone voted before noon. By the time the polls closed, 98.6 percent of the registered voters had transcended intimidation.

Counting took five days, and during that time, the threats and violence mounted rapidly. By September 1, four East Timorese U.N. workers had already been murdered, militia roadblocks were proliferating, and many of the East Timorese who lived and worked with IFET observers now felt that proximity brought risk, not safety. IFET-OP withdrew four observer teams from the field and decided to pull the rest back to Dili and Baucau within the next few days. As many East Timorese men had already fled to the hills, families sought our help in increasing numbers, imploring us to shelter women and children in our houses. It was agonizing to tell them that we could not guarantee their safety. We saw ourselves as under threat and believed our foreign status no longer shielded against violence.

Like some awful Greek tragedy, the situation in East Timor moved inexorably toward catastrophe. Although the August 30 vote stands as a monument to the dedication of local and international UNAMET personnel and the incredible courage of the East Timorese people, the ensuing disaster was not only predictable, but could have been prevented at any time from April to mid-August.

On September 2, IFET-OP assessed the Consultation Process, finding that the voting itself was administered in a free and fair manner, but that security was still inadequate and the East Timorese lived in a state of "fear for their lives."

The vote was announced on Saturday morning, September 4: 78.5 percent for independence. Most IFET observers, now in Dili, watched it on CNN. The group clapped once, an embarrassed lapse of nonpartisanship.[22] Throughout the day, IFET-OP received reports of increasing violence—the destruction of East Timor had begun in earnest.

On Sunday, conditions only got worse, and many IFET-OP observers left with most other foreigners on hastily chartered flights. About fifty remained in East Timor, although virtually continuous gunfire and widespread militia activity forced them to abandon several houses in Dili. Sunday evening, the office of Yayasan Hak (the leading East Timorese human rights group) was attacked; police intervened only after an hour of shooting, and only in response to U.S. embassy complaints that an American IFET-OP observer was inside.

Later that night, the IFET headquarters was temporarily evacuated by local police—too much gunfire, too close. Monday morning, September 6, half of the remaining observers were evacuated by the Royal Australian Air Force. Two dozen stayed—the only group of foreigners outside the U.N. compounds (UNAMET had retreated from the countryside to compounds in Dili and Baucau) or the Australian consulate. Throughout the day, they took reports of atrocities (people murdered in Bishop Belo's residence; a thousand forced from the Red Cross office, which was then destroyed; attacks on the Australian ambassador's car; thousands of East Timorese loaded at gunpoint onto ships and trucks). As long as phones worked, IFET could relay what was happening to the media and governments, most of whose representatives had already fled.[23]

Like the East Timorese people, the remaining IFET observers kept thinking of 1975, when the international community had abandoned East Timor, allowing the Indonesian military to kill two hundred thousand people with impunity. IFET-OP was one of the last links between the destruction of East Timor and a world that was running away. But as the day proceeded, IFET-OP came to believe that the rules had changed, that foreigners were now targets. With East Timor being destroyed around them, the IFET-OP observers still in Dili took the Monday night evacuation flight to Darwin, along with some hundred UNAMET personnel. The last IFET observers were evacuated the next day from Baucau, along with Bishop Belo.

Things Fall Apart

I was staying with seven other IFET-OP observers at a home in the Kampung Alor neighborhood of Dili, close to an *Aitarak* militia post. Natercia, who rented us the house, had five children, including two teen-aged daughters. They came by on Friday evening, September 3, 12 hours before the results were to be announced. Natercia asked if her daughters could stay with us, since she was taking her sons to the mountains. She was sure the militia would attack the next day; they had already burned some pro-independence houses in the neighborhood. "If my family isn't all in one place," she told us, "some of us will probably survive."

We told Natercia that her daughters were welcome to stay, but that if we were evacuated, our governments would probably not allow her children to come with us. She took her sons to the mountains, leaving her daughters sleeping on the floor. But before the sun rose, Natercia came back and took the girls away.

I went to work, and the overwhelming vote for independence was announced that morning. When I returned home that afternoon (we were not going out after dark), new Indonesian flags flew in front of every house on the street. The *Aitarak* militia had visited each home, threatening to kill people if they were pro-independence. The flags were evidence that, although four out of five East Timorese had voted for independence, none lived on our block.

In this climate of terror, there was no place to obtain food, and we resigned ourselves to a hungry evening. But the doorbell soon rang. Maria, whom we had hardly met, lived across the street. She brought us dinner and breakfast to show her appreciation for our coming to her country. She had not evacuated because she didn't think her 18-month-old son could survive in the hills. I don't know what happened to them—the entire neighborhood has been destroyed.

—extracted from Charles Scheiner, "Things Fall
Apart," *Estafeta*, vol. 5., no. 3, Autumn 1999.

In Darwin, IFET-OP held press conferences and pressured the Australian government. Most observers soon returned to their home countries to lobby for international military intervention.

In the two weeks before InterFET forces arrived, 650,000 East Timorese people (three-fourths of the population) were driven from their homes, and virtually all the towns were destroyed. Thousands, perhaps tens of thousands, of people were murdered. Almost all of the twenty houses IFET-OP rented in East Timor were looted, then demolished, and their local staff dispersed to Australia, Indonesia, and the mountains of East Timor. The whereabouts of some are still unknown.

FOLLOWING UP

The IFET Observer Project presented information at the emergency session of the U.N. Human Rights Commission in Geneva in late September. Although IFET offered to provide the U.N. investigating team with detailed information about Indonesian crimes in East Timor, they were never contacted.

IFET also testified on October 6 at the General Assembly in New York. They pointed out that a fundamental error made by the U.N. was "failing to listen to the East Timorese people, whose knowledge and observations, if heeded, would have averted the recent disaster." In retrospect, that statement may be simplistic. Perhaps it is an intrinsic element of the U.N., composed of national governments, not to heed the cries of people who have no government to represent them.

With the development of the UNTAET administration, many of the same mistakes are being repeated. Not only does the international community defer to Indonesian sovereignty over the East Timorese who were kidnapped and taken to West Timor,[24] but the interim UNTAET government makes autocratic decisions that the people of East Timor will have to live with for years.[25] The international war crimes investigation seems to be deferring to the Indonesian one, and both have limited jurisdiction that excludes all crimes committed before 1999.

In spite of the devastation of September, most East Timorese do not regret that the U.N. followed CNRT's recommendation to proceed with the ballot, although they wish that the international community had acted to prevent the post-ballot holocaust. As one older East Timorese man said shortly before voting day, "They've been killing us for twenty-four years. They'll kill us whether we vote or not. This is the only chance we will have to show the world that East Timor wants independence, and we must use it." Although the world has forgotten, most East Timorese know in their bones that Indonesia's invasion and occupation of East Timor in the 1970s and 1980s was far more brutal than the vengeful destruction that followed their 1999 vote for independence.

In May 2000, IFET launched *La'o Hamutuk* (Tetum for "Walking Together") as a joint East Timorese/international project to transmit East Timorese concerns to international agencies, governments, and the U.N. The *La'o Hamutuk* staff, based in Dili,[26] publishes regular bulletins, reports, and e-mail updates analyzing the reconstruction and development process. Perhaps this time, the international NGO community will be more effective in influencing the powers of the world to listen to the needs and respect the judgments and rights of the East Timorese people.

NOTES

1. For a vivid description of the underground and how it was organized, as well as the Santa Cruz massacre, see Constâncio Pinto and Matthew Jardine, *East Timor's Unfinished Struggle: Inside the Timorese Resistance* (Boston: South End Press, 1997); and the interview with Pinto in this book.

2. For detailed recounting of the grassroots campaign in the United States, contact ETAN (P.O. Box 1182, White Plains, N.Y. 10602, U.S.A.). Their website, <http://www. etan.org>, contains past annual reports and newsletters that document this history.

3. The grassroots success at building congressional and political awareness of Indonesia's crimes was extremely frustrating to Suharto's backers. One of their responses was to resort to time-tested Indonesian methods of buying influence in Washington, which resulted in the 1996 Clinton-Riady-Lippo-Suharto campaign contribution scandal.

4. Interview published in *Tempo,* 28 March 1992.

5. *A License to Kill,* produced by Mark Davis and broadcast by the Australian Broadcasting Company on 19 March 1999. Copies available from ETAN. The program vividly portrays militia-military cooperation and shows Indonesian military and political officials, including Ali Alatas, denying that reality.

6. Letter from IFET's U.N. representative (the author of this chapter) to Secretary General Kofi Annan, 30 March 1999 <http://www.etan.org/ifet>. The text of this and other IFET and IFET Observer Project communications are available on this Web site.

7. The East Timor *Action* Network published these testimonies as a pamphlet "Paramilitary Violence in East Timor," ETAN, May 1999.

8. Letter from IFET's U.N. representative, 3 May 1999.

9. For a warning to the international community from an East Timorese human rights leader, see Aniceto Guterres Lopes, "East Timor's Bloodiest Tradition," *New York Times,* 5 May 1999, 25(A).

10. For a description of the secretary general's thoughts and efforts during this period, see Afsané Bassir Pour, "La lutte solitaire de Kofi Annan" in *Le Monde,* 31 October/1 November 1999.

11. UNAMET consisted of approximately one thousand international U.N. staff and volunteers who carried out the vote, including unarmed civilian police advisors, military liaison officers, and electoral officers.

12. The others were in Cambodia and Namibia. With little relevant experience to draw on, the U.N. did an outstanding job developing the mechanisms for the East Timor vote in a short, tense period.

13. Between June and September 1999, IFET-OP issued nine reports and numerous press releases and letters to Annan, Habibie and others. All are available at <http://www. etan.org/ifet>.

14. I was an IFET-OP observer. Shortly after arriving in Dili on August 12, I went to visit the family of an East Timorese friend in exile. After five minutes of pleasantries, they were in tears, explaining their terror of militia violence after the ballot results were announced and imploring us to allow them to seek refuge in the IFET-OP headquarters. Such requests were repeated by different people dozens of times all across East Timor in the weeks leading up to the ballot.

15. In mid-August, a CNRT official gave IFET-OP a list of shipments of large quanti-

ties of automatic rifles and other weapons that he alleged had just been delivered to militia groups across East Timor. The numbers were so large (many thousands) that IFET-OP wrote off the information as incredible and reported it only in general terms, as a rumor. Although most East Timorese people understood the scope of the military's postballot plans, IFET observers, like UNAMET and the U.N. officials in New York, deluded themselves into believing that their dispassionate foreign intellects had a better grasp of the situation than the East Timorese people who had lived with Indonesian military rule for a quarter of a century. We were wrong.

16. CNRT and most East Timorese proindependence supporters had called for armed U.N. peacekeepers since before the May 5 Agreements, but IFET and IFET-OP had not, advocating rather that armed Indonesian militia, police, and military should be disarmed and withdrawn. The armed pro-independence forces, Falintil, had refrained from initiating clashes since the beginning of 1999; during the referendum process they were voluntarily confined to cantonment areas. Although the militias had similarly agreed to cantonment, they frequently violated it.

17. A translated transcript of these radio conversations was published as "Apt Pupils," *Harper's Magazine*, December 1999, 34.

18. State Department Regular Washington Briefing, 26 August 1999.

19. See the testimony by Allan Nairn in this volume.

20. Lt. Cmdr. Cate Mueller, "CARAT '99 Enters Final Phase in Indonesia," U.S. Navy News report #NS3802. 24 August 1999. This exercise—Cooperation Afloat Readiness And Training—would seem to be of dubious legality, given the congressional ban on Pentagon training of the TNI.

21. Rajiv Chandrasekaran, "U.S. Resumes Training Plan for Officers of Indonesia," *Washington Post*, 19 February 2000, 21(A).

22. Two Australian activists, arrested for alleged illegal campaigning, watched the announcement on TV at a Dili police station. They report that the police were genuinely surprised by the outcome of the vote, having deluded themselves that Indonesia would win or that it would be close enough to discredit with alleged irregularities.

23. On the afternoon of September 6, 1999, I had a telephone conversation with a well-known reporter for a leading U.S. newspaper who had evacuated to Jakarta a few days earlier. He asked about rumors he had heard of militia members defecting to the TNI. Although he had covered East Timor for many months, he still did not understand that the militias were operating under direct command of Indonesia's military.

24. As of this writing, six months after the vote, more than one hundred thousand East Timorese remain in military- and militia-controlled camps in West Timor (Indonesia), slightly fewer than half of the refugees who fled or were taken there in early September. Two-thirds would probably like to return to East Timor, but a militia propaganda campaign has convinced them that conditions there are unlivable. The U.N. High Commission for Refugees and other international groups have been denied access to many of the camps. An estimated five hundred to one thousand people, mostly children, have died there as a result of inadequate food, health care, and sanitation. Although the U.N., the U.S. government, and others have repeatedly asked Indonesia to disarm the militias, allow international access to the camps, and facilitate the return to East Timor of those refugees who wish to go home, the current climate of terror, isolation, and disinformation keeps them virtual hostages.

25. The author spoke on a panel at U.N. headquarters on February 17, 2000 with several hundred NGO representatives, U.N. staff, and diplomats present. When I raised the issues of inequity and insensitivity between internationals working in East Timor and the local population, most people accepted my description of the problem as an apartheid-like economy. Their explanation was that this always happens in crisis response situations. Once again, the East Timorese are suffering from international "business as usual."

26. *La'o Hamutuk* (The East Timor Institute for Reconstruction Monitoring and Analysis/*Institut Permantauan dan Analisis Reconstruksi Timor Loro Sa'e*), Dili, Timor Loro Sa'e. Mobile phone: (61)(0408)811373, land phone: (670)(390)325013, email: lhproject @one.net.au, <http://www.etan.org/lh>.

Part III

East Timor, the United States, and the World Community

9

East Timor, the United States, and International Responsibility: "Green Light" for War Crimes

Noam Chomsky

It is not easy to write with feigned calm and dispassion about the events that unfolded in East Timor in 1999. Horror and shame are compounded by the fact that the crimes are so familiar and could so easily have been terminated. That has been true ever since Indonesia invaded in December 1975, relying on U.S. diplomatic support and arms—used illegally, but with secret authorization—even new arms shipments sent under the cover of an official embargo. There has been no need to threaten bombing or even sanctions. It would, very likely, have sufficed for the U.S. and its allies to withdraw their participation and to inform their close associates in the Indonesian military command that the atrocities must be terminated and the territory granted the right of self-determination that has been upheld by the United Nations and the International Court of Justice. We cannot undo the past, but should at least be willing to recognize what we have done and to face the moral responsibility of saving the remnants and providing ample reparations, a pathetic gesture of compensation for terrible crimes.

The latest chapter in this painful story of betrayal and complicity opened after the referendum of August 30, 1999, when the population voted overwhelmingly for independence. Atrocities mounted sharply, organized and directed by the Indonesian military (TNI). A Security Council mission gave its appraisal on September 11:

> The evidence for a direct link between the militia and the military is beyond any dispute and has been overwhelmingly documented by UNAMET over the last four months. But the scale and thoroughness of the destruction of East Timor in the past week has demonstrated a new level of open participation of the military in the implementation of what was previously a more veiled operation.

The mission warned that "the worst may be yet to come. . . . It cannot be ruled out that these are the first stages of a genocidal campaign to stamp out the East Timorese problem by force."[1]

Indonesia historian John Roosa, an official observer of the vote, described the situation starkly: "Given that the pogrom was so predictable, it was easily preventable. . . . But in the weeks before the ballot, the Clinton administration refused to discuss with Australia and other countries the formation of [an international force]. Even after the violence erupted, the administration dithered for days,"[2] until compelled by international (primarily Australian) and domestic pressure to make some timid gestures. These limited measures sufficed to induce the Indonesian generals to reverse course and to accept an international presence, illustrating the latent power that has always been at hand, overwhelmingly so since Indonesia's economic collapse in 1997.

These recent events should evoke bitter memories among those who do not prefer what has sometimes been called "intentional ignorance."[3] They were a shameful replay of events of twenty years earlier. After carrying out a huge slaughter in 1977–78 with the support of the Carter administration, the regime of General Suharto felt confident enough to permit a brief visit by members of the Jakarta diplomatic corps, among them U.S. Ambassador Edward Masters. The ambassadors and the journalists who accompanied them recognized that an enormous humanitarian catastrophe had been created, reminiscent of Biafra and Cambodia. The aftermath was described by the distinguished Indonesia scholar Benedict Anderson. "For nine long months" of starvation and terror, Anderson testified at the United Nations, "Ambassador Masters deliberately refrained, even within the walls of the State Department, from proposing humanitarian aid to East Timor," waiting "until the generals in Jakarta gave him the green light" —until they felt "secure enough to permit foreign visitors," as an internal State Department document recorded. Only then did Washington consider taking some steps to deal with the consequences of its actions.[4]

While Clinton followed suit from February through August 1999, the Indonesian military implemented a scarcely veiled campaign of terror and intimidation, and as he "dithered" in the final weeks, most of the population were expelled from their homes with unknown numbers killed and much of the country destroyed. The air force that was able to carry out pinpoint destruction of civilian targets in Novi Sad, Belgrade, and Ponceva a few months before lacked the capacity to drop food to hundreds of thousands of people facing starvation in the mountains to which they had been driven by the TNI forces armed and trained by the United States and its no less cynical allies. The administration also took no meaningful action to rescue the several hundred thousand captives held by paramilitaries in Indonesian West Timor, probably elsewhere too, though no one is investigating.

By year's end, 100,000–150,000 or more people remained in West Timor as "virtual prisoners," Amnesty International reported, "trapped in makeshift camps and living in a state of constant fear under the rule of the militia groups that destroyed East Timor, . . . often intimidated, harassed, extorted and in some cases sexually assaulted and killed." This is "the only place in the world where UNHCR [U.N. High Commissioner for Refugees] workers are heavily escorted by police and army troops where they go into camps," the agency reported, adding that "the moment an East Timorese expresses a desire to leave the camps and go home, their life is in danger." Perhaps five hundred had died "due to inadequate sanitation and medical care," officials said, mostly children, victims of diarrhea and dysentery. "Every day, many of the people are dying from malaria, respiratory infections and acute gastro-intestinal diseases," says Arthur Howshen, a volunteer doctor. "There is also a lack of food, shortages of rice are common, and there are also a lot of children suffering from vitamin A deficiency." With the onset of the rainy season, conditions are even worse than when they were driven from East Timor. Touring camps on both sides of the border, U.S. assistant secretary of state Harold Koh reported that the refugees are "starving and terrorized," and that disappearances "without explanation" are a daily occurrence.[5]

To bring these crimes to an end has easily been within Washington's power, as before.

At last report, the U.S. had provided no funds for the Australian-led U.N. force InterFET (International Force in East Timor); Japan, long a fervent supporter of Indonesia, offered $100 million and Portugal $5 million. That is perhaps not surprising, in the light of Washington's failure "to pay any of the $37.9 million assessed for the startup costs of the United Nations civilian operation in Kosovo, which Washington supported in the Security Council." At the same time, the Clinton administration asked the United Nations "to reduce the size" of its small peacekeeping force in East Timor.[6]

In Kosovo, preparation for war crimes trials began in May 1999, in the midst of the NATO bombing campaign, expedited at the initiative of Washington and London, which also provided unprecedented access to intelligence information. In East Timor, investigations were discussed at leisure, with numerous delays and deference to Jakarta's wishes and sensibilities. "It's an absolute joke, a complete whitewash," Lucia Withers, a spokeswoman for Amnesty International, informed the British press: it will "cause East Timorese even more trauma than they have suffered already"; a leading Indonesian role "would be really insulting at this stage." Few seriously expect that the United States or the United Kingdom will release vital intelligence information, and the Indonesian generals are reported to feel confident that their old friends will not let them down—if only because the chain of responsibility might be hard to snap at just the right point. By mid-January, U.N. officials said that a tribunal was unlikely. U.S. Ambassador Richard Holbrooke and others "are pinning their hopes on an internal tribunal held by Indonesia, whose military controlled East Timor from 1975 until August and is blamed by human-rights groups for the atrocities." It was claimed that China and Russia are blocking a tribunal, an obstacle that the West cannot think of any way to overcome, unlike the case of Serbia.[7]

On January 31, 2000, the U.N. International Commission of Inquiry on East Timor issued a report calling for an international human rights tribunal under United Nations' auspices. Its mandate should be "to try and sentence those accused by the independent investigation body of serious violations of fundamental human rights and international humanitarian law which took place in East Timor since January 1999." "It is fundamental for the future social and political stability of East Timor," the commission concluded, "that the truth be established and those responsible for the crimes committed be brought to justice. Every effort has to be made to provide adequate reparation to the victims, for only then can true reconciliation take place."[8]

On the same day, an Indonesian government Commission of Inquiry issued a "damning report" condemning "the Indonesian military and its militia surrogates" including former army chief General Wiranto.[9] Indonesian president Abdurrahman Wahid, then at the Davos conference in Switzerland, called upon Wiranto to resign his cabinet post and promised to pardon him if he was convicted. U.N. High Commissioner for Human Rights Mary Robinson expressed her "hope that efforts to hold those responsible for the atrocities in East Timor accountable will go on so that there is no impunity." But that is "not very likely," correspondent Dan Murphy observed: "Support within the U.N. for a war-crimes tribunal is low." Crucially, support in the great powers is not merely "low" but negative. The general attitude is expressed by the editors of the *Washington Post*: "But before a Bosnia-style tribunal is created, Indonesia should be given a chance to judge its own"—and to pardon them if convicted, as the president announced at once.[10]

Australian U.N. correspondent Mark Riley reported from New York that the United Nations "is set to ignore the strong advice of its own human rights body for a war-crimes tribunal in East Timor, instead deferring debate on the issue until Indonesia's probe into the killings is completed. The decision is a political victory for the Jakarta [government], which has argued that it should be left alone to investigate allegations of atrocities on what it considers was its sovereign territory."

Sonia Picado, head of the U.N. inquiry commission, was not optimistic, Riley reported further, recognizing "that there is little prospect of the U.N. Security Council supporting an international war crimes tribunal." "The East Timorese deserve compensation—moral and material compensation—because their families and their country have been devastated," Picado said, and "the United Nations has to give that to them": "It cannot be provided through an Indonesian tribunal." Picado "had no faith in the ability of a planned Indonesian tribunal to deliver justice to the East Timorese people." "It is just not feasible for [the Indonesians] to create a tribunal out of the blue and bring their own generals to justice," she said. Furthermore, no meaningful tribunal can be held in Jakarta because "East Timorese people remained scared of the Indonesian authorities and most were reluctant to travel to Jakarta to give evidence to a government tribunal. How can they expect the military courts in Indonesia to bring justice to the people of East Timor?" But "East Timor deserves not to be forgotten," and with an international tribunal unlikely, she recommended a South African–style Truth and Reconciliation Commission with commissioners from East Timor, Indonesia, and U.N.–appointed members, with powers to indict or pardon, meeting outside Indonesia.[11]

Australian Asia correspondent Lindsay Murdoch commented that "grave doubts exist that the guilty will be brought to justice. Indonesia's legal system is riddled with corruption and has a poor record when dealing with human rights abuses." Indonesian attorney general Marzuki Darusman is "a respected human rights advocate," but "the task he faces in bringing some of the country's most powerful people to justice appears daunting, if not impossible," as illustrated by President Wahid's apparently having "buckled to pressure from General Wiranto" by declaring that he would be pardoned if found guilty: "Any such pardon would be outrageous," Murdoch wrote.[12]

"You cannot have one-sided justice in human rights cases," Picado said. It is fairly safe, however, to predict that one-sided justice is the most that can be anticipated, and even that is a dubious prospect. Furthermore, it is hardly likely that the guilty parties, particularly the United States and the United Kingdom, will consider providing the "moral and material compensation" they owe to the victims, and there is no call for such action.

Leaving any trials to Jakarta has various advantages to Indonesia's international collaborators: East Timorese are unlikely to testify, pardons have already been announced, the pressures to evade the facts will be strong, and the great powers are immune from inspection. But even in an international tribunal the possibility that Western leaders would be held accountable for their responsibility is so slight as hardly to merit comment. Only by attaining a remarkable level of "intentional ignorance" can one fail to perceive that the international judicial process, like other aspects of international affairs, is subject to the rule of force, which overrules considerations of justice, human rights, or accountability.

In East Timor, the peacekeeping forces and the U.N. mission "have neither the means nor the authority to track down those responsible" for crimes, and little evidence is being unearthed: "In contrast to Kosovo, where human-rights investigators began work as NATO forces took control on the ground, the United Nations in East Timor has no such capability."[13] "Meanwhile, in East Timor, the evidence of crimes against humanity—and so the chance of successful prosecutions—is literally rotting away because of inadequate resources." U.N. civilian police are finding many bodies and mass graves, but have no resources to investigate them. "The need for forensic experts is very, very urgent," said David Wimhurst, spokesman for UNAMET. "Neither InterFET nor UNAMET is able to do this properly at the moment. It is crucial that investigative teams come into

Dili as soon as possible. . . . When NATO went into Kosovo, teams of police, forensic scientists, and lawyers from the International War Crimes Tribunal in The Hague were at work within days, sealing off and cataloguing mass grave sites. In East Timor, a few harassed policemen have the task of exhuming the bodies and collecting what evidence they can."[14]

The delays ensure that little will be found, even if forensic experts are ultimately sent. Much of the evidence was destroyed by the TNI, bodies have been buried by local people, and more will be washed away or eaten by animals, Australian doctor Andrew McNaughtan informed the press, giving details; he has worked in East Timor for seven years. Isabel Ferreira, who coordinates the East Timor Human Rights Commission in Dili, added that "when the rainy season begins, all the bodies will be washed away into the rivers and there will be no evidence left to investigate." Kosovo was swarming with police and medical forensic teams from the United States and other countries in the hope of discovering large-scale atrocities. In contrast, InterFET had ten investigators, no morgue, and no forensic capabilities. Australian forensic pathologists confirmed that with further delay, tropical heat and the onset of the rainy season would eliminate most evidence. U.N. administrator Sergio Vieira de Mello pleaded again for forensic experts and facilities at the end of November, in vain. A month later it was announced that "international forensic experts will arrive in January to help in investigations of mass graves" and to compile information on crimes, four months after the arrival of InterFET, long after tropical rains and other factors have significantly reduced the likelihood of revealing the truth.[15]

The distinction between the two most prominent atrocities of 1999 is clear. In Kosovo, there was a desperate need for tribunal indictment (for crimes committed after the bombing began, as the indictment reveals); and "proving the scale of the crimes is also important to NATO politically, to show why 78 days of airstrikes against Serbian forces and infrastructure were necessary," by the intriguing logic, conventional in Western doctrine, that crimes provide retrospective justification for the NATO bombing of which they were the anticipated consequence.[16] Putting logic aside, at least the immediate agent of the crimes is an official enemy, while in East Timor, the agents of the crimes were armed, trained, funded, and supported by the United States and its allies from the beginning through the terrible denouement, so it is best to know as little as possible about them.

Though Jakarta had indeed considered East Timor to be "its sovereign territory," nevertheless no actual issue of sovereignty arose in this case, as distinct from Kosovo, which the United States and its allies insist must be under the sovereignty of the Federal Republic of Yugoslavia (specifically Serbia), probably out of fear of a "greater Albania." Even Australia, the one Western country to have granted de jure recognition to the Indonesian annexation (in large measure because of its interest in joint exploitation of Timorese oil), had renounced that stand in January 1999. Indonesia's "sovereign rights" were comparable to those of Nazi Germany in occupied Europe; they rested solely on great power ratification of aggression and massacre in this Portuguese-administered territory, which had been formally placed under the United Nations responsibility. Nonetheless, the non-existent claim to sovereignty was accorded the most scrupulous respect under the principles of the new humanism that had been proclaimed a few months earlier,[17] while those assigned responsibility for security proceeded to kill and terrorize.

In the light of the absence of any legitimate claim to sovereignty, and the refusal to send peacekeeping forces until after the Indonesian generals agreed to withdraw, having at last been informed by Washington that the game was over, the term "intervention" is out of place. A fortiori, the issue of "humanitarian intervention" does not arise, though this is one of the rare cases when it is possible to speak seriously of humanitarian intent, at least on the part of Australia, or more accurately, its population, who were bitterly critical of the government's failure to react.

As TNI forces and their paramilitaries were burning down the capital city of Dili in September 1999, murdering and rampaging with renewed intensity, the Pentagon announced that "a U.S.–Indonesian training exercise focused on humanitarian and disaster relief activities concluded Aug. 25," five days before the referendum.[18] The lessons of this training were quickly applied in a familiar way, as all but the voluntarily blind must recognize after many years of the same tales, the same outcomes.

One gruesome illustration was the coup that brought General Suharto to power in 1965. Army-led massacres slaughtered hundreds of thousands in a few months, mostly landless peasants, destroying the mass-based political party of the left, the Indonesian Communist Party (PKI), in "one of the worst mass murders of the twentieth century," the CIA concluded, ranking with "the Soviet purges of the 1930s, the Nazi mass murders during the Second World War, and the Maoist bloodbath of the early 1950s."[19] This Rwanda-style slaughter elicited unrestrained euphoria in the West and fulsome praise for the Indonesian "moderates," Suharto and his military accomplices, who had cleansed the society. Secretary of Defense Robert McNamara informed Congress that U.S. military aid and training had "paid dividends"—including half a million or more corpses—"enormous dividends," a congressional report concluded. McNamara informed President Johnson that U.S. military assistance "encouraged [the army] to move against the PKI when the opportunity was presented." Contacts with Indonesian military officers, including university programs, were "very significant factors in determining the favorable orientation of the new Indonesian political elite" (the army). The U.S. had "trained 4,000 Indonesian army officers—half the total officer corps, including one third of the general staff," two Australian analysts observe.[20]

The United States is a global power, and policies tend to be consistent worldwide. Not surprisingly, at the same time, the same planners were helping to insti-

Figure 9.1   Dili, 1998. Hermanegildo das Dores Soares, 21, and his cousin were collecting wood from the side of the road when an Indonesian soldier shot him six times in the leg and chest. The seriously injured boys had to catch public transport to the nearest town, but the health center in Manatuto was not equipped to treat such serious wounds, and Herman died of loss of blood on the way to Dili. Ten thousand people attended his funeral at Santa Cruz cemetery on 18 May 1998. The death of her third and youngest son seriously affected Rosa Dores Soares's emotional health and soon after this photo was taken her daughter found her outside the family home in west Dili throwing stones and screaming abuse at Indonesian soldiers on patrol. Her daughter has since arranged for her to be sent to live in Portugal. Courtesy: Ross Bird.

tute murderous military terror states elsewhere, on the principle, explained by McNamara to National Security Advisor McGeorge Bundy, that it is the task of the military to remove civilian leaders from office "whenever, in the judgment of the military, the conduct of these leaders is injurious to the welfare of the nation," a necessity in "the Latin American cultural environment," and likely to be carried out properly now that the judgment of the military is based upon "the understanding of, and orientation toward, U.S. objectives" as a result of the military aid and training provided by the Kennedy administration.[21]

So matters continued for three decades of military aid, training, and friendly interaction with Suharto, the great mass murderer and torturer who was "at heart benign," the London *Economist* explained, unfairly condemned by "propagandists for the guerrillas" in East Timor and West Papua (Irian Jaya) who "talk of the army's savagery and use of torture." The unnamed propagandists were the major human rights groups, the Church, and others who failed to see the merits of "our kind of guy," as the Clinton administration admiringly described Suharto when he was welcomed to Washington in October 1995. His son-in-law General Prabowo, "the leader of Indonesia's paramilitary death squads, who has authorized mass killings and rapes" and was finally sent to Jordan as an embarrassment after the fall of Suharto, was "an 'enlightened' military leader who deserved to have his demands treated promptly and with courtesy by British politicians," according to British defense minister George Robertson, "liberator of oppressed muslims of Kosovo."[22]

Direct U.S. support for Indonesian occupation forces in East Timor was hampered after they massacred several hundred people in Dili in 1991. In reaction, Congress banned small arms sales and cut off funds for military training, compelling the Clinton administration to resort to some intricate maneuvers to evade the legislative restrictions. The State Department commemorated the anniversary of the Indonesian invasion by determining that "Congress's action did not ban Indonesia's purchase of training with its own funds," so the training can proceed despite the ban, with Washington perhaps paying from some other pocket. The announcement received scant notice and no comment in the press, but it did lead Congress to express its "outrage," reiterating that "it was and is the intent of Congress to prohibit U.S. military training for Indonesia" (House Appropriations Committee): "We don't want employees of the U.S. government training Indonesians," a staff member reiterated forcefully, but without effect.[23]

Government-approved weapons sales total over $1 billion since the 1975 invasion, including $150 million during the Clinton years; government-licensed sales of armaments increased from $3.3 million to $16.3 million from fiscal 1997 to 1998.[24] As atrocities peaked in 1977–78, the United Kingdom, France, and others joined the United States in providing arms for the killers as well as diplomatic protection. Britain's Hawk jets proved to be particularly effective for killing and terrorizing civilians. The current Labor government continued to deliver Hawk jets secretly to Indonesia, using public funds, as late as September 23, 1999, two weeks after the European Union had imposed an embargo, several days after InterFET had landed, well after it had been revealed that these aircraft had been deployed over East Timor once again, this time as part of the pre-referendum intimidation operation, two weeks after the Indonesian air force had deployed Hawk jets at the Kupang Airbase in West Timor "to anticipate any intrusion of foreign aircraft into the eastern part of Indonesian territory, especially East Timor," also installing an early warning radar system in Kupang. Foreign Secretary Robin Cook, the author of the new "ethical foreign policy," explained that "the government is committed to the maintenance of a strong defense industry, which is a strategic part of our industrial base," as in the United States and elsewhere. For the same reasons, Prime Minister Tony Blair later gave "the go-ahead for the sale of spare parts to Zimbabwe for British Hawk fighter jets being used in an African civil war that has cost tens of thousands of lives."[25]

These are altogether unsurprising illustrations of the new humanism, a grand new era in world affairs led by the United States, now "at the height of its glory,"[26] and its British partner.

In 1997, the Pentagon was still training Indonesian military forces. The programs continued into 1998 under the code name "Iron Balance," "hidden from legislators and the public" because they were in violation of the clear intent of congressional restrictions. "Principal among the units that continued to be trained was the *Kopassus*—an elite force with a bloody history—which was more rigorously trained by the United States than any other Indonesian unit," according to Pentagon documents. Training focused on "military expertise that could only be used internally against civilians, such as urban guerrilla warfare, surveillance, counter-intelligence, sniper marksmanship, and 'psychological operations.'" Among commanders trained were those implicated in the renewed outburst of violence in 1999, as well as earlier massacres, including Krasas (1983) and Dili (1991). "Loyal" Timorese also received U.S. training. Britain was carrying out similar programs.[27]

In November 1998, *Kopassus* forces arrived in a port town in East Timor, entering in disguise along with the first of five thousand new TNI forces recruited from West Timor and elsewhere in Indonesia. These became the core elements of the paramilitaries ("militias") that initiated massive violence in operation "Clean Sweep" beginning in February 1999, with "the aim, quite simply, . . . to destroy a nation." As senior military adviser, the TNI command sent General Makarim, a U.S.–trained intelligence specialist with experience in East Timor and "a reputation for callous violence"; he was also assigned the role of liaison with the U.N. observer mission. The plans and their implementation were, surely, known to Western intelligence, as has been the case since the planning of the 1975 invasion.[28]

There is substantial evidence from many sources that from the beginning of 1999, the atrocities attributed to militias were organized, directed, and sometimes carried out by elite units of *Kopassus*, the "crack special forces unit" that had "been training regularly with U.S. and Australian forces until their behavior became too much of an embarrassment for their foreign friends," veteran Asia correspondent David Jenkins reports; though not their friends in Washington, it appears. These forces are "legendary for their cruelty," Benedict Anderson observes: in East Timor they "became the pioneer and exemplar for every kind of atrocity," including systematic rapes, tortures, and executions, and organization of hooded gangsters. They adopted the tactics of the U.S. Phoenix program in South Vietnam that killed tens of thousands of peasants and much of the indigenous South Vietnamese leadership, Jenkins writes, as well as "the tactics employed by the Contras" in Nicaragua, following lessons taught by their CIA mentors. The state terrorists were "not simply going after the most radical pro-independence people, but going after the moderates, the people who have influence in their community." "It's Phoenix," a well-placed source in Jakarta reported: the aim is "to terrorize everyone"—the NGOs, the Red Cross, the United Nations, the journalists.[29]

Again, U.S. and British intelligence must have known all of this, doubtless far more, and it is hard to imagine that the civilian authorities in Washington and London were unaware of what they were supporting.

In April 1999, shortly after the massacre of fifty or more refugees who had taken shelter in a church in Liquiça, Admiral Dennis Blair, U.S. Pacific Commander, met with TNI commander General Wiranto, assuring him of U.S. support and assistance and proposing a new U.S. training mission, one of several such contacts.[30]

In the face of this record, only briefly sampled, and duplicated repeatedly elsewhere, Washington lauds "the value of the years of training given to Indonesia's future military leaders in the United States and the millions of dollars in military aid for Indonesia," urging more of the same for Indonesia and throughout the world.[31]

The reasons for the disgraceful record have sometimes been honestly recognized. During the latest phase of atrocities, a senior diplomat in Jakarta succinctly formulated "the dilemma" faced by the great powers: "Indonesia matters and East Timor doesn't."[32] It is therefore understandable that Washington should keep to ineffectual gestures of disapproval while insisting that internal security in East Timor "is the responsibility of the government of Indonesia, and we don't want to take that responsibility away from them"—the official stance throughout, repeated a few days before the August referendum in full knowledge of how that responsibility had been carried out. The same stance was officially reiterated well after the referendum, while the most dire predictions were being fulfilled.[33]

The reasoning of the senior diplomat was spelled out more fully by two Asia specialists of the *New York Times*: The Clinton administration "has made the calculation that the United States must put its relationship with Indonesia, a mineral-rich nation of more than 200 million people, ahead of its concern over the political fate of East Timor, a tiny impoverished territory of 800,000 people that is seeking independence." The *Washington Post* quoted Douglas Paal, president of the Asia Pacific Policy Center: "Timor is a speed bump on the road to dealing with Jakarta, and we've got to get over it safely. Indonesia is such a big place and so central to the stability of the region."[34]

The term "stability" has long served as a code word, referring to a "favorable orientation of the political elite"—favorable not to their populations, but to foreign investors and global managers.

In the rhetoric of official Washington, "We don't have a dog running in the East Timor race." Accordingly, what happens there is not our concern. But after intensive Australian pressure, the calculations shifted: "We have a very big dog running down there called Australia and we have to support it," a senior government official concluded.[35] The survivors of U.S.–backed crimes in a "tiny impoverished territory" are not even a small dog.

Figure 9.2   Secretary of Defense William Cohen (left) meets with Indonesian President Suharto at his residence in Jakarta on January 14, 1998. DoD photo by R. D. Ward.

Serious commentators had recognized these realities long before. Twenty years earlier, Daniel Southerland reported that "in deferring to Indonesia on [the East Timor] issue, the Carter administration, like the Ford administration before it, appears to have placed big-power concerns ahead of human rights." Southerland referred particularly to the role of current U.N. Ambassador Richard Holbrooke, who had direct responsibility for implementing Carter's policy and was so little concerned by the consequences—by then, some two hundred thousand killed—that he could find no time to testify before Congress about East Timor, Southerland reports, though "he did have the time, however, to play host at a black-tie dinner later the same day."[36]

The guiding principles were well understood by those responsible for guaranteeing the success of Indonesia's 1975 invasion. They were articulated lucidly by U.N. Ambassador Daniel Patrick Moynihan in words that should be committed to memory by anyone with a serious interest in international affairs, human rights, and the rule of law. The Security Council condemned the invasion and ordered Indonesia to withdraw, but to no avail. In his 1978 memoirs, Moynihan explains why:

> The United States wished things to turn out as they did, and worked to bring this about. The Department of State desired that the United Nations prove utterly ineffec-

tive in whatever measures it undertook. This task was given to me, and I carried it forward with no inconsiderable success.

Success was indeed considerable. Moynihan cites reports that within two months some sixty thousand people had been killed, "10 percent of the population, almost the proportion of casualties experienced by the Soviet Union during the Second World War."[37] A sign of the success, he adds, is that within a year "the subject disappeared from the press." So it did, as the invaders intensified their assault. Atrocities peaked as Moynihan was writing in 1977–78. Relying on a new flow of U.S. military equipment, the Indonesian military carried out a devastating attack against the hundreds of thousands who had fled to the mountains, driving the survivors to Indonesian control. It was then that Church sources in East Timor sought to make public the estimates of two hundred thousand deaths that came to be accepted years later, after constant denial and ridicule of the "propagandists for the guerrillas." Washington's reaction to the carnage has already been described.

Media coverage of East Timor had been fairly high prior to the Indonesian invasion, in the context of concerns over the collapse of Portuguese fascism and its imperial system. As Moynihan observed, coverage declined as the U.S.– supported aggression and slaughter took its toll; in the national press it reached zero as the atrocities peaked in 1978. Journals were similar. Such coverage as there was during the worst atrocities kept largely to State Department fabrications and assurances from Indonesian generals that the population was fleeing to their protection. By 1980, however, the story was beginning to break through, though only rarely the U.S. role, which remains well hidden to the present. By then, it was also becoming clear that the atrocities were comparable to Cambodia in the same years, though in this case they were major war crimes in addition, in the course of outright aggression supported by the great powers.

The first reports caused considerable annoyance. Commenting in a journalism review, Asia specialist and foreign correspondent Stanley Karnow said he could not bring himself to read a story on East Timor that had just appeared: "It didn't have anything to do with me," he said. His colleague Richard Valeriani agreed, because "I don't care about Timor." Reviewing a book that gave the first extensive account of what had happened, and the unwillingness to report it, former *New York Times* Indochina correspondent A.J. Langguth dismissed the topic on the grounds that "If the world press were to converge suddenly on Timor, it would not improve the lot of a single Cambodian."[38]

Langguth's observation is surely accurate. More important, it captures lucidly the guiding criteria for approved humanitarian concerns: atrocities for which we bear responsibility, and which we could easily mitigate or terminate, do not "have anything to do with" us and should be of no particular concern; worse still, they are a diversion from the morally significant task of lamenting atrocities committed by official enemies that we can do little if anything about—though when the Vietnamese did end them in this case, Washington was presumed to have the obligation to punish them for the crime, by severe sanctions, backing of a Chinese invasion, and support for the ousted Khmer Rouge ("Democratic Kampuchea," DK).

Some nevertheless felt uneasy that while bitterly denouncing atrocities in Cambodia, we were "looking away" from comparable ones in Timor—the standard rendition of the unacceptable truth that Washington was "looking right there" and acting decisively to escalate the atrocities. That quandary was put to rest in 1982 by the State Department, which explained that the Khmer Rouge–based DK is "unquestionably" more representative of the people of Cambodia than the resistance is of the East Timorese, so therefore it is proper to support both Pol Pot and Suharto. The contradiction vanishes, as did the grounds for its resolution, which remain unreported.[39]

For the next twenty years the grim story continued: atrocities, complicity, and refusal to submit. By 1998, some rays of hope began to break through. By then Suharto had committed some real misdeeds and was therefore no longer "our kind of guy": he had lost control of the country after the financial crisis and was dragging his feet on implementing harsh IMF programs. Debt relief had been granted to "our kind of guy" after he took power, but not to the two hundred million Indonesians who are now compelled to pay the huge debts accumulated by Suharto and his cronies, amounting now to over 140 percent of GDP, thanks to the corruption of the regime and the eagerness of the World Bank, the IMF, and Western governments and financial institutions to provide lavish funds for the ruler and his clique.[40]

On May 20, 1998, Secretary of State Madeleine Albright called upon Suharto to resign and provide for "a democratic transition." A few hours later, Suharto transferred formal authority to his hand-picked vice president, B. J. Habibie. The events were not, of course, simple cause and effect, but they symbolize the relations that have evolved. With Suharto gone, the way was paved for the first democratic election in forty years—that is, the first election since the parliamentary system had been undermined in the course of the U.S. clandestine operations of 1958 that aimed to dismantle Indonesia by separating the resource-rich outer islands, undertaken because of Washington's concern that the government of Indonesia was too independent and too democratic, even going so far as to permit a popular party of the left to function. The praise for Indonesia's first democratic election in forty years managed to overlook the background.[41]

Habibie moved at once to distance himself from Suharto, surprising many observers. In June 1998, he called for a "special status" for East Timor. In August Foreign Minister Ali Alatas suggested a "wide-ranging autonomy." And on January 27, 1999, Habibie made the unexpected announcement that if the East Timorese were not willing to accept Indonesia's offer of autonomy, then the government would recommend to the People's Consultative Assembly that Indonesia relinquish control of the territory it had invaded and annexed. On May 5, Indonesia and Portugal, under U.N. auspices, agreed that the choice should be made in a referendum scheduled at first for August 8, delayed until August 30.

The military, however, was following a different track, already described, moving even before Habibie's January announcement to prevent a free choice by violence and intimidation. From February through July, three to five thousand East Timorese were killed, according to highly credible Church sources—twice the number of deaths prior to the NATO bombing in Kosovo, more than four times the number relative to population.[42] The terror was widespread and sadistic, presumably intended as a warning of the fate awaiting those foolhardy enough to disregard army orders elsewhere.

The events were reported widely in Australia, to some extent in England. In Australia there was extensive protest along with calls for action to end the atrocities. Though information was much more sparse,[43] there was growing protest in the United States as well. On June 22, the Senate unanimously supported an amendment to a State Department authorization bill asking the Clinton administration to "intensify their efforts to prevail upon the Indonesian government and military" to crack down on the militias, reiterated on June 30 by a vote of ninety-eight to zero. In a July 8 press briefing, in response to a query about the Senate vote, State Department spokesperson James Foley repeated the official stand that "the Indonesian military has a responsibility to bring those militias under control"—namely, the militias it was organizing, arming, and directing.[44] Database searches found no reports of the Senate votes or Foley's comment in the United States.

Braving violence and threats, almost the entire population voted on August 30, many emerging from hiding to do so. Close to 80 percent chose independence. Then followed the latest phase of TNI atrocities in an effort to reverse the outcome by slaughter and expulsion, while reducing much of the country to ashes. Within two weeks, more than ten thousand might have been killed, according to Bishop Carlos Filipe Ximenes Belo, the Nobel Peace laureate who was driven from his country under a hail of bullets, his house burned down and the refugees sheltering there dispatched to an uncertain fate.[45]

TNI forces responsible for the terror and destruction from February have been described as "rogue elements" in the West, a questionable judgment. There is good reason to accept Bishop Belo's assignment of direct responsibility to commanding General Wiranto in Jakarta,[46] not only in the post-referendum period to which inquiry is to be restricted. Well before the referendum, the commander of the Indonesian military in Dili, Colonel Tono Suratman, had warned of what was to come: "I would like to convey the following," he said: "If the pro-independents do win . . . all will be destroyed. . . . It will be worse than twenty-three years ago." On July 24, Suratman met with a police commander and militia leaders at the Dili military headquarters, where they took "the major decisions . . . in the recognition that the pro-integration side was unlikely to win the vote," according to an August 6 report by Australian intelligence officer Wayne Sievers.

Sievers is facing charges for having informed the Parliament's Committee on Foreign Affairs, Defense, and Trade of the secret reports he had sent to the United Nations from his arrival in June, predicting the post-referendum violence and identifying militia leaders as Indonesian intelligence officers, available to the government through the Australian U.N. embassy. A TNI document of early May, when the U.N.–Indonesia–Portugal agreement on the referendum was reached, ordered that "massacres should be carried out from village to village after the announcement of the ballot if the proindependence supporters win." The independence movement "should be eliminated from its leadership down to its roots."[47]

Documents discovered in Dili in October 1999, "and analyzed in Jakarta by Indonesian investigators and Western diplomatic sources, provide evidence . . . that, for months before the referendum on East Timor's independence in August, it was being systematically undermined by Indonesia's top generals," including plans for "the forcible deportation of hundreds of thousands of East Timorese." A Western diplomat who reviewed the documents describes them as "the missing link," showing "a clear chain of command from close to the very top," also expressing his surprise at the "sheer quantity" of the weapons provided to local militia and pro-Jakarta figures. As the May 5 referendum agreements were signed, a letter from General Subagyo to Colonel Suratman, copied to senior military figures, ordered preparations for "a security plan to prevent civil war that includes preventive action (create conditions), policing measures, repressive/coercive measures, and a plan to move to the rear/evacuate if the second option [independence] is chosen." A July document drafted by an officer of a Dili-based regional command, Colonel Soedjarwo, outlines a battle plan directed against what it calls the "Enemy Forces": "not only the guerrillas of the resistance movement, Falintil, but civilians, including unarmed student groups and political organizations." In August, the Dili police department produced "a meticulous plan to evacuate hundreds of thousands of Timorese after the referendum," with extensive detail. The plans were soon implemented, and it would be most surprising if they were not known at least in a general way to Western intelligence.[48]

Citing diplomatic, Church, and militia sources, the Australian press had reported in July 1999 "that hundreds of modern assault rifles, grenades, and mortars are being stockpiled, ready for use if the autonomy option is rejected at the ballot box." It warned that the army-run militias might be planning a violent takeover of much of the territory if, despite the terror, the popular will would be expressed. Leaked official cables reveal the "Australian Government's harsh assessment of the Pentagon's 'overly generous' interpretation of Indonesian army (TNI) involvement with the militias."[49] The Indonesian generals had every reason to interpret the evasive and ambiguous reactions of their traditional friends and backers as a "green light" to carry out their work.

The sordid history should be viewed against the background of U.S.–Indonesia relations in the postwar era.[50] The rich resources of the archipelago, and its critical strategic location, guaranteed it a central role in U.S. global planning. These factors lay behind U.S. efforts forty years ago to dismantle Indonesia, then provide support for the military in preparation for the anticipated military coup, and unbounded enthusiasm for the regime of killers and torturers who brought about a "favorable orientation" in 1965 and for their leader, who remained "our kind of guy" until his first missteps in 1997, when he was abandoned in the usual pattern of criminals who have lost their usefulness or become disobedient: Trujillo, Somoza, Marcos, Noriega, Saddam Hussein, Mobutu, Ceausescu, and many others. The successful cleansing of Indonesia in 1965 was, furthermore, understood to be a vindication of Washington's wars in Indochina, which were motivated in large part by concern that the "virus" of independent nationalism might "infect" Indonesia, to borrow standard rhetoric, just as concern over Indonesian independence and excessive democracy had been motivated by fear that a "communist" (meaning independent nationalist) Indonesia would be an "infection" that "would sweep westward" through all of South Asia, as George Kennan warned in 1948.

In this context, support for the invasion of East Timor and subsequent atrocities was presumably reflexive, though a broader analysis should attend to the fact that the collapse of the Portuguese empire had similar consequences in Africa, where South Africa was the agent of Western-backed terror. Throughout, Cold War pretexts were routinely invoked. These should be analyzed with caution; all too easily, they can serve as a convenient disguise for ugly motives and actions that had little to do with shifting relations among the United States, Russia, and China, not only in Southeast Asia but in Latin America, the Middle East, and elsewhere.

The story does not begin in 1975. East Timor had not been overlooked by the planners of the postwar world. The territory should be granted independence, Roosevelt's senior adviser Sumner Welles mused, but "it would certainly take a thousand years."[51] With an awe-inspiring display of courage and fortitude, the people of East Timor have struggled to confound that prediction, enduring monstrous disasters. Some fifty thousand lost their lives protecting a small contingent of Australian commandoes fighting the Japanese; their heroism may have saved Australia from Japanese invasion. Perhaps a quarter of the population were victims of the first years of the 1975 Indonesian invasion, many more since.

Surely we should by now be willing to cast aside mythology and face the causes and consequences of our actions realistically, not only in East Timor. In that tortured corner of the world there is now an opportunity to remedy in some measure at least one of the most appalling crimes and tragedies of the terrible century that has finally come to a horrifying, wrenching close.

NOTES

Expanded from " 'Feu vert' occidental pour les massacres," *Le Monde Diplomatique*, October 1999.

1. Report of the Security Council Mission to Jakarta and Dili, 8 to 12 September 1999, S/1999/976, 14 September 1999, paragraphs 9, 8.

2. John Roosa, "Fatal Trust in Timor," *New York Times*, op-ed, 15 September 1999, 29(A).

3. Donald Fox and Michael Glennon, "Report to the International Human Rights Law Group and the Washington Office on Latin America," Washington D.C., April 1985, referring to State Department evasion of U.S.–backed state terror in El Salvador.

4. Benedict Anderson, Statement before the Fourth Committee of the U.N. General Assembly, 20 October 1980. For fuller quotes and context, see Noam Chomsky, *Towards a New Cold War* (New York: Pantheon, 1982). On the earlier background, see Noam Chomsky and Edward Herman, *The Political Economy of Human Rights*, vol. 1, (Boston: South End, 1979).

5. Amnesty International (AI) estimated over one hundred thousand refugees in West Timor, by late December. West Timorese officials reported 150,000. At the end of January, the Australian press reported from West Timor that over 150,000 still remained. AI report of 22 December; "Refugees in West Timor Living in Fear: Amnesty," *Australian Associated Press*, Canberra, 22 December 1999. "More than 150,000 East Timorese Begin 5th Month in West," *Agence France-Presse* (AFP), *The Age* (Australia), 31 January 2000. "Up to 500 East Timorese Died in West Timor Camps," *AP*, 13 January 2000; Richard Lloyd Parry, "Forgotten: The Child Refugees of West Timor," *Independent* (London), 24 January 2000, 11. Slobodan Lekic, AP, "U.S. Adds Choppers, Specialists in E. Timor," *Boston Globe*, 10 October 1999. UNHCR, see Human Rights Watch, *Forced Expulsions to West Timor and the Refugee Crisis*, December 1999. According to U.N. figures, 750,000 of East Timor's population of 880,000 were driven from their homes. Seth Mydans, "East Timor, Stuck at 'Ground Zero,' Lacks Law, Order and Much More," *New York Times*, 16 February 2000, 8(A).

6. Barbara Crossette, "U.N. to Begin Taking Refugees Home to East Timor This Week," *New York Times*, 5 October 1999, 12(A); Crossette, "Annan Says U.N. Must Take Over East Timor Rule," *New York Times*, 6 October 1999, 1(A); Joe Lauria, "U.S. Asks U.N. for Trims in Force for East Timor," *Boston Globe*, 8 October 1999, 1(A).

7. Mark Riley, New York, "Atrocities Inquiry Awaits Green Light," *Sydney Morning Herald*, 16 October 1999; Richard Lloyd Parry, Dili, "Jakarta is Given Role in the U.N.'s War Crimes Inquiry," *Independent*, 27 September 1999, 10; Joe Lauria, "Envoys Seek Inquiry by Indonesia," *Boston Globe*, 15 January 2000.

8. United Nations Office of the High Commissioner for Human Rights, "Report of the International Commission of Inquiry on East Timor to the Secretary General," January 2000, transmitted with A/54/726, S/2000/59, 31 January 2000.

9. Keith B. Richburg, "Indonesian Commission Blasts Army; Top Generals Cited In E. Timor Terror," *Washington Post*, *Boston Globe*, 1 February 2000. Also Seth Mydans, "Jakarta's Military Chiefs Accused of Crimes," *New York Times*, 1 February 2000, 11(A); Seth Mydans, "Indonesian General Denies Guilt in Timor Abuses," *New York Times*, 2 February 2000, 8(A).

10. Dan Murphy, "E. Timor Inquiry Taints Top Brass," *Christian Science Monitor*, 2 February 2000, 6; Editorial, "Justice for East Timor," *Washington Post-International Herald Tribune*, 2 February 2000.

11. Mark Riley, "U.N. to Delay Decision on Crimes Tribunal," *The Age*, 31 January 2000; "U.N. Official Doubts Jakarta Probe," *The Age*, 2 February 2000.

12. Lindsay Murdoch, "Wahid Talks Pardon for Defiant Wiranto," *The Age*, 2 February 2000.

13. Cameron W. Barr, "Who Will Investigate Atrocities?" *Christian Science Monitor*, 30 September 1999, 1.

14. Parry, 27 September 1999, see note 7.

15. "Human Rights Activists Decry Slow U.N. Probe in E. Timor," *Kyodo News International* (Dili), 8 November 1999; Sonny Inbaraj, "Rights—East Timor: Investigation into Abuses a Tricky Task," *Inter Press Service*, 10 November 1999; "U.N. Chief in E. Timor Appeals for Urgent Forensic Help," *Japan Economic Newswire*, 28 November 1999; "East Timor to Judge on Crimes, Says Head of U.N. Transition Authority," *AP Worldstream*, AP Online, 24 December 1999.

16. Scott Peterson, "This Time, War-Crimes Trial Is on a Fast Track," *Christian Science Monitor*, 27 August 1999, 1. On the indictment and other documentary sources made public in an effort to justify the bombing, and related matters, see my *The New Military Humanism: Lessons of Kosovo* (Monroe, Me.: Common Courage, 1999), and "In Retrospect," "Afterword" to French translation, excerpted in *Le Monde Diplomatique*, March 2000; *Z* magazine, April 2000, 19–24.

17. For a sample of the rhetorical flourishes and awed self-congratulation, see Chomsky, *New Military Humanism*.

18. David Briscoe, "Cohen: No U.S. Troops for East Timor," *AP Online*, 8 September 1999.

19. Cited by Robert Cribb, ed., *The Indonesian Killings of 1965–1966* (Clayton, Victoria: Monash Papers on Southeast Asia, no. 21, 1991).

20. Brian Toohey and William Pinwill, *Oyster* (Port Melbourne: Heinemann, 1989), 93, censored by the Australian government. For review and sources, see Noam Chomsky, *Year 501* (Boston: South End, 1993), chap. 5.

21. Chomsky, *Year 501*, chap. 7. For more extensive quotes and discussion, see my *On Power and Ideology* (Boston: South End, 1988).

22. John Andrews, "The Extended Family," *Economist*, 15 August 1987, (Indonesia Survey) 4, 16; David Sanger, "Real Politics: Why Suharto Is In and Castro Is Out," *New York Times*, 31 October 1995, 3(A); Nick Cohen, "Labor: Quartermaster to Tyranny in East Timor," *Observer*, 5 September 1999, 31. For more see Chomsky, *Year 501*; Chomsky, *Powers and Prospects* (Boston: South End, 1996); and sources cited.

23. Reuters, "Indonesia Military Allowed to Obtain Training in U.S.," *New York Times*, 8 December 1993, 14(A), a few lines on an inside page; Irene Wu, "House vs. White House," *Far Eastern Economic Review*, 30 June 1994, 18. See Chomsky, *Powers, and Prospects,* for further detail.

24. William Hartung, weapons specialist of the World Policy Institute, "Half an Island, Half a World Away," *KRT News Service*, 16 September 1999; John Donnelly, "Pentagon Reluctant to Isolate Indonesia," *Boston Globe*, 11 September 1999, 1(A).

25. John Gittings, et al., "Cook Faces New Crisis as Hawk Jets Fly In," *Observer*, 26 September 1999, 3; Robert Peston and Andrew Parker, "Public Cash Funded Indonesia Hawk Sales," *Financial Times*, 15 September 1999, 9; "Indonesian Air Force Deploys Hawk Fighter Jets, Radar in Kupang," BBC Summary of World Broadcasts, 13 September 1999 (source: Suara Pembaruan, Jakarta, in Indonesia, 10 September 1999); Richard Norton-Taylor, "In the Swamp," *Guardian*, 2 September 1999, 17. Ewen MacAskill, "Brit-

ain's Ethical Foreign Policy: Keeping the Hawk Jets in Action," *Guardian*, 19 January 2000. On Britain's record, see John Pilger, *Distant Voices* (London: Vintage 1992), *Hidden Agendas* (London: Vintage; New York: New Press, 1998). Also Chomsky, *New Military Humanism*, and sources cited. For recent review, see John Taylor, *East Timor: The Price of Freedom* (London: Zed, 1999); Arnold Kohen, *From the Place of the Dead* (New York: St. Martin's, 1999).

26. David Fromkin, *Kosovo Crossing* (New York: Free Press, 1999). On the favorite illustration and its validity, see Chomsky, *New Military Humanism* and Chomsky, "In Retrospect."

27. Hartung, "Half an Island"; Ed Vulliamy and Antony Barnett, "U.S. Aided Butchers of Timor," *Observer* (London), 19 September 2000, 1; also *Guardian Weekly*, 23 September 1999. A database search on 29 September found no mention in the U.S. media.

28. John Aglionby, et al., "Revealed: Army's Plot," *Observer*, 12 September 1999 (and foreign service); "For Nearly a Year, Generals Hatched Murderous Plan to Block Independence for East Timor and Western Intelligence Services Knew about It," *Globe and Mail* (Toronto), Observer Service, 13 September 1999. For review and background, see Taylor, *East Timor: The Price of Freedom*, and Richard Tanter, "East Timor and the Crisis of the Indonesian Intelligence State," this volume.

29. David Jenkins, Asia Editor, "Army's Dirty Tricks Brigade Unleashed in Fight for Timor," *Sydney Morning Herald*, 8 July 1999; Benedict Anderson, "Indonesian Nationalism Today and the Future," *New Left Review* 235 (May/June 1999): 3–17.

30. Allan Nairn, "U.S. Complicity in Timor," *The Nation*, 27 September 1999, 5–6; Nairn's congressional testimony, this volume.

31. Elizabeth Becker, "U.S.-to-Jakarta Messenger: Chairman of the Joint Chiefs," *New York Times*, 14 September 1999, 16(A).

32. Sander Thoenes, "Martial Law—Habibie's Last Card," *Financial Times*, 8 September 1999, 4; Sander Thoenes, "What Made Indonesia Accept Peacekeepers," *Christian Science Monitor*, 14 September 1999, 6. Shortly after, Thoenes was murdered in East Timor, apparently by the TNI.

33. Gay Alcorn, " 'Too Late' to Send Armed U.N. Force," *Sydney Morning Herald*, 25 August 1999, citing State Department spokesman James Foley; Defense Secretary William Cohen, press briefing, 8 September 1999.

34. Elizabeth Becker and Philip Shenon, "With Other Goals in Indonesia, U.S. Moves Gently on East Timor," *New York Times*, 9 September 1999, 1(A). Steven Mufson, "West's Credibility at Stake, Laureate Says," *Washington Post*, 9 September 1999, 17(A).

35. Peter Hartcher, "The ABCs of Winning U.S. Support," *Australian Financial Review*, 13 September 1999.

36. Daniel Southerland, "U.S. Role in Plight of Timor: An Issue that Won't Go Away," *Christian Science Monitor*, 6 March 1980, 7 (Midwestern ed.).

37. Daniel Patrick Moynihan, with Suzanne Weaver, *A Dangerous Place* (Boston: Little, Brown, 1978), 245–47. Moynihan writes that sixty thousand were reported killed "since the outbreak of civil war." There had been a brief civil war, with two to three thousand killed, months before the full-scale Indonesian invasion in December.

38. Karnow, Valeriani, "The New Foreign Correspondence," *Washington Journalism Review*, March 1980: 39–46. For these and many other examples, see *Towards a New Cold War*, and on the earlier record, Chomsky and Herman, *Political Economy of Human Rights*, the book Langguth was reviewing in *The Nation*, 16 February 1980, 81–84.

39. John Holdridge (State Dept.), Hearing before the Subcommittee on Asian and Pacific Affairs of the Committee on Foreign Affairs, House of Representatives, 97th Congress, 2nd sess., 14 September 1982, 71. On how the quandary was faced, see Chomsky, *Towards a New Cold War*; on the context, Edward Herman and Noam Chomsky, *Manufacturing Consent* (New York: Pantheon, 1988).

40. Binny Buchori and Sugeng Bahagijo, "The Case for Debt Relief," *Inside Indonesia*, January–March 2000. On the role of the IMF, see Robin Hahnel, *Panic Rules* (Cambridge, Mass.: South End Press, 1999).

41. Audrey and George Kahin, *Subversion as Foreign Policy* (New York: New Press, 1995); Chomsky, *Powers and Prospects*. For details on the operations, see Kenneth Conboy and James Morrison, *Feet to the Fire: CIA Covert Operations in Indonesia, 1957–1958* (Annapolis: Naval Institute Press, 1999).

42. Taylor, *East Timor: The Price of Freedom*, citing Church report of 6 August. Arnold S. Kohen, "Beyond the Vote: The World Must Remain Vigilant Over East Timor," *Washington Post*, 5 September 1999, 1(B). For review of the first part of the year, mainly from the Australian press, see Chomsky, *New Military Humanism*.

43. See Edward Herman and David Peterson, "How the *New York Times* Protects Indonesian Terror in East Timor," *Z* magazine, July/Aug. 1999, 82–88; Herman and Peterson, "East Timor: From 'Humanitarian' Bombing to Inhumane Appeasement," *CovertAction Quarterly*, no. 68, Fall–Winter 1999: 4–10.

44. Farhan Haq, "Rights—East Timor: U.N. Announces Delay in Vote," Inter Press Service, 22 June 1999; "Indonesia—East Timor—U.S. Senate Urges Clinton to Support Direct Ballots," *Antara* (Indonesian National News Agency), 2 July 1999. See also David Shanks, " 'Jakarta Oligarchy' Seen as Hidden Hand in Strife," *Irish Times*, 10 July 1999, 14; M2 PRESSWIRE, 8 July 1999, U.S. Dept. of State daily press briefing.

45. Philip Shenon, "Timorese Bishop Is Calling For a War Crimes Tribunal," *New York Times*, 13 September 1999, 6(A).

46. Shenon, "Timorese Bishop," 6(A).

47. Suratman cited by Brian Toohey, "Dangers of Timorese Whispers Capital Idea," *Australian Financial Review*, 14 August 1999, referring to a radio interview "earlier this year." Sievers, Andrew West, "Timor Action Puts Officer in Firing Line," *Sunday Age*, 9 January 2000. Document, Aglionby, et al., "Revealed: Army's Plot." A similar document, dated 5 May 1999, is published in Human Rights Watch, *Forced Expulsions to West Timor*. The Indonesian Investigative Commission for Human Rights Abuses in East Timor "confirmed the existence and validity of the Garnadi Document which ordered the burning of the troubled region" (*Indonesian Observer*, 4 January 2000), referring to a document, denied by the military, authorized from the highest levels of the military command.

48. Richard Lloyd Parry, "Letters Reveal How Indonesian Generals Planned Repression," *Independent*, 5 February 2000, 1, 15.

49. Mark Dodd, "Fears of Bloodbath Grow as Militias Stockpile Arms," *Sydney Morning Herald*, 26 July 1999; Dennis Shanahan, "U.S. Was Warned of Militia Link," *Australian*, 24 September 1999.

50. See sources cited earlier, and for brief review, my "L'Indonésie," *Le Monde Diplomatique*, June 1998.

51. William Roger Louis, *Imperialism at Bay: The United States and the Decolonization of the British Empire, 1941–1945* (New York: Oxford University Press, 1978), 237.

10

The East Timor Ordeal: International Law and Its Limits

Richard Falk

A LETHAL ENCOUNTER: INTERNATIONAL LAW VERSUS GEOPOLITICS

The dynamics of self-determination for peoples under colonial rule have taken various forms. Many of the most tragic outcomes for the peoples concerned arose in settings where the colonial power forcibly resisted claims for decolonization and national independence. In such circumstances, bloody wars tended to ensue, as against France in Indochina and then Algeria, and as against Portugal in its African colonies. The circumstances of the East Timor ordeal were different, but no less costly to the people who lived in that country. Portugal stubbornly maintained colonial rule until it experienced its own revolution in 1974, which was prompted in part by the unpopularity of its insistence on fighting colonial wars. Thereafter, Portugal acknowledged that peoples living in its colonies were entitled to exercise a right of self-determination.

It is at this point that the distinctive character of East Timor's tragedy begins to unfold. As Portugal moved to implement the manifest will of the inhabitants of East Timor in early 1975 to move toward independence, Indonesia evidently perceived an opportunity to extend its borders, and sovereign reach. Indonesia supported a splinter movement in East Timor that advocated integration with Indonesia. As Portugal withdrew from exerting daily control over the affairs of the territory, a brief civil war was fought in August and September 1975 between proindependence and prointegrationist factions; the proindependence faction Fretilin (Frente Revolutionária de Timor–Leste Independente), which had earlier prevailed in local elections, also won the war. Despite this outcome, Jakarta extended its support to the side that lost (politically and militarily) and used the losers' existence to obtain "an invitation" to invade and annex East Timor.

On December 7, 1975, only days after statehood was declared by the proindependence side, Indonesia invaded East Timor, occupied the territory, and imposed a harsh rule upon the people resulting in the death of between one and two hundred thousand East Timorese out of a population total at the time of seven hundred thousand. In other words, the Indonesian invasion amounted to one of the greatest losses of life, as measured proportionately, of any modern war and subsequent belligerent occupation.

To provide these developments with cosmetic legitimacy, the occupying forces established a puppet East Timor Peoples Assembly that obediently expressed its desire for East Timor to become an integral part of Indonesia. Not surprisingly, Indonesia obliged, making East Timor the twenty-seventh province of the country and the first beyond the borders acquired from the Dutch colonial administration. The conquest and annexation of East Timor was condemned in strong language by Security Council and General Assembly resolutions. The incorporation of East Timor into Indonesia was never formally acknowledged by the United Nations, nor was Portugal's role as administrator of the territory ever formally terminated. At the same time, in years subsequent to 1982, the United States supported Indonesia's efforts to remove the East Timor question from the active agenda of the General Assembly, and no further resolutions of censure were thereafter forthcoming. Australia, virtually alone among sovereign states, went further and in 1978 officially recognized on a de facto basis Indonesia's incorporation of East Timor.[1] The general situation, until the events of recent years, was one in which the legal status of East Timor was left in abeyance, while Indonesia's de facto control of the territory was generally accepted as the basis for practical relations with the outside world.

Here is the puzzle that confronts interpreters of this East Timor experience. Gradually, as the process of decolonization became generally accepted as an imperative of international morality, politics, and law, the right of self-determination was implicitly affirmed for all colonized peoples.[2] To fulfill international expectations, the colonial power was supposed to transfer sovereignty voluntarily to the territorial community without altering colonial borders, while assuming special fiduciary responsibilities in relation to entities, such as East Timor, that were legally treated as "non-self-governing" as that term was understood within the U.N. system.[3]

Decolonization was understood to mean that the people of the territory were to acquire sovereign rights, and no third-party state had a legal or moral basis for interference. Such sovereign rights did not necessarily mean statehood. A people could opt for any freely chosen political arrangement, including a perpetuation of colonial rule. There were some minor and partial exceptions to this generally agreed upon pattern of confining decolonization to the colonial boundaries. A few former colonies incorporated territories beyond their boundaries, but located on their periphery. The instances of Goa and Western Sahara come to mind. In some respects, the Indonesian effort to take over East Timor resembles these cases, but with important differences as well. Unlike Goa, East Timor was not a colonial enclave caught in the throes of decolonization, whereas Western Sahara's circumstances remain relatively obscure due partly to the absence of internationally visible leadership that was important in building wide public sympathy with the plight of the East Timorese under Indonesian rule. Despite this, Morocco's continuing domination of Western Sahara is moving slowly to the top of the agenda of unresolved self-determination claims.

The special circumstances surrounding the East Timor failure to complete the process of self-determination can be briefly summarized. First of all, the East Timor claim to the right of self-determination seems clear under international law and has been accepted all along by the colonial administering party, Portugal, and even acknowledged in 1975 by Indonesian officials, virtually until the day of the invasion. Indonesia mounted some legitimating arguments to justify its use of force in the years since 1975. Indonesia insisted that a majority of the people in East Timor wanted to become part of Indonesia, thereby making annexation consistent with self-determination. Indonesia also advanced historical claims, which alleged that East Timor was an integral part of Indonesia. And finally, Jakarta contended that East Timor on its own could not be a viable state, and if it attempted to be independent it would harm itself and its neighbors. These Indonesian arguments were never viewed as persuasive by independent observers or in the international community. As such, they failed to offer a credible basis for denying the applicability of the normal outcome of decolonization, namely, national independence and sovereignty.[4]

The 1975 Indonesian invasion of East Timor flagrantly violated the most basic norm of the U.N. Charter, the rule against any international use of force that could not be justified as self-defense against a prior armed attack.[5] The United Nations, with a principal reliance on the United States, justified its support of South Korea in 1950 as a matter of coming to the assistance of a victim of aggression. Additionally, the Suez Operation of 1956 in which France and the United Kingdom joined with Israel to attack Nasser's Egypt was successfully opposed by the U.N. Security Council because of its border-crossing initiation of war. And in the recent past, the legal rationale for the 1991 Gulf War rested squarely on the unopposed assertion that Iraq's attack upon and annexation of Kuwait was aggression under the Charter, justifying all necessary force to reverse the outcome and restore Kuwaiti sovereignty. For more than twenty years the fate of East Timor resembled nothing so much as the fate of Kuwait *before* the Security Council–mandated force.[6] In many ways, East Timor's situation was far worse than that endured by Kuwait as the process of Indonesian pacification was accompanied by serious famine and many forms of brutality resulting in massive civilian casualties over the course of many years.[7]

In effect, the Indonesian actions in 1975, and subsequently, disrupted the process of decolonization in East Timor and perpetuated in a new form the status of colonial subordination. The process of decolonization is not completed until the right of self-determination is authentically and fully exercised. Portugal came to recognize this reality and accepted a special responsibility for its inability to secure political independence for East Timor in 1975. The tragedy of East Timor was to get caught in a historical vise between the disintegration of Portuguese colonialism and the expression of Indonesian expansionism. This vise was tightened by the U.S. alignment with Indonesia in a Cold War setting, which consigned the fate of East Timor to decades of geopolitical oblivion, that is, as outside the circumference of international concern. The fate of East Timor was treated in this period as a matter of indifference to centers of operative military and political power in Southeast Asia.

DISREGARDING INTERNATIONAL LAW

Given this background, how should we understand the passivity of the United Nations in the face of Indonesia's blatant and total violation of East Timor's right of self-determination? Such a violation was carried to completion, as well, by Indonesia's unprovoked initiation of a war of aggression and its clear responsibility for sustained and widespread Crimes Against Humanity, which, according to some commentators, amounted to the commission of genocide. The concept of Crimes Against Humanity was given its authoritative definition in Article 6(c) of the London Agreement of 1945, which established the Nuremberg Tribunal to prosecute surviving German military and civilian leaders as war criminals:[8]

> Crimes Against Humanity: murder, extermination, enslavement, deportation, and other inhumane acts committed against civilian populations, before or during the war; or persecutions on political, racial or religious grounds in execution of or in connection with any crime within the jurisdiction of the Tribunal, whether or not in violation of the domestic law of the country where perpetrated.

Subsequent to Nuremberg (and Tokyo) the idea of Crimes Against Humanity was broadened to drop the link with an international war and used as one basis for the recent criminal prosecutions at The Hague under U.N. authority by the International Criminal Tribunal for Rwanda, as well as being included in the statute approved in the form of the 1998 Rome Treaty to set up a permanent International Criminal Court.

A separate crime of Genocide was established by treaty in 1948 and differs from Crimes Against Humanity in that its essence requires a specific intent to eliminate a given people in whole or part. Obviously, Crimes Against Humanity encompasses and overlaps with genocide, but not the reverse.[9]

The agreed facts establish beyond any reasonable doubt that Indonesia is guilty of violating the most basic rules of international law in the course of carrying out its policy of the conquest and annexation of East Timor.[10] And yet no substantive action was taken on behalf of East Timor either within the United Nations, by Indonesia's principal ally, the United States, or by states in the region. There were two U.N. Security Council resolutions, 384 (1975) and 389 (1976), that affirmed East Timor's right of self-determination, instructed Indonesia to respect the territorial integrity of East Timor and to withdraw its military forces without delay, and reaffirmed the continuing responsibility of Portugal as the administrator of a non-self-governing territory to ensure that the right of self-determination inhering in the people of East Timor come to be properly exercised.[11] But nothing further was forthcoming from the Security Council; despite the council's authority to impose sanctions and take other enforcement action, these two resolutions represented the full extent of the council's response to the situation in East Timor.

The central explanation for this disregard of Indonesia's illegal conquest and annexation relates to the geopolitical setting in 1975. The Cold War was at its height. The United States had endured a serious defeat in Indochina and was eager to avoid any further deterioration of its strategic position in Southeast Asia. Henry Kissinger, the U.S. secretary of state, was cynically shaping American foreign policy during the Ford presidency in ultra-realist directions. From such a perspective, Indonesia was perceived as a regional ally of great strategic significance. In contrast, the prospects if East Timor became independent were for the emergence of a Fretilin-controlled government that was perceived as being "leftist." The Australian government, evidently primarily moved by its interest in Timorese oil, also seemed to believe that if Indonesia absorbed East Timor it would contribute to the stability of the region. Under these circumstances, it is hardly surprising that the United States and its regional allies in all likelihood actually welcomed Indonesia's initiative despite its illegality. The fact that Ford and Kissinger left Jakarta the day before the invasion of East Timor commenced strongly reinforces the impression of tacit assent issued by the United States in its role as "the geopolitical manager" of the region.

In general, when geopolitical factors push policy in a direction that is in conflict with international law, then the law gives way, at least *behaviorally*. As was the case here, *rhetorically*, the Indonesian invasion was censured by the General Assembly as a serious violation of the Charter, and the United States even joined in voting in favor of the first Security Council resolution adopted unanimously in 1975. Later on, directly and indirectly, the United States assisted Indonesia in muting or avoiding the further instances of censure, an approach quite opposite to that taken toward either Soviet incorporation of the Baltic countries or of its oppressive role in Eastern Europe. It should come as no surprise that governmental policymakers, of a realist cast of mind, are prone to disregard international law in the face of strong geopolitical considerations that move in a contrary direction. It was Kuwait's good luck that Washington's geopolitical analysis of the situation called for a preventive war against Iraq. The alleged concern for Kuwait's sovereignty, despite the clear indication that its style of government was highly authoritarian and not observant of human rights, provided a politically

Figure 10.1   Veronica Pereira Maia, Sydney, 1996. "I wove this Tai and wove in the names of all the victims of the massacre in Dili on 12 November 1991. When it touches on my body I am overwhelmed with sadness. I remember the way those young people lost their lives for our nation." Courtesy: Ross Bird.

necessary legal pretext for recourse to war against Iraq with the backing of the United Nations.[12]

In effect, the people of East Timor were not protected or helped despite their victimization being flagrantly at odds with the most fundamental rules of international law. The adverse geopolitical climate was too strong. In this regard, the East Timorese are not alone in the world. The Tibetans, Kurds, Palestinians, Chechins, and many other ethnic communities of distinct peoples have been denied the right of self-determination for comparable geopolitical reasons, as have virtually all indigenous peoples in the world.[13] There are a range of views among peoples subject to discrimination, including a commitment, as in the case of minorities within the United States and South China, overwhelmingly to seek redress within the system.

CLARIFYING THE POSITIVE ROLE OF INTERNATIONAL LAW

From such an experience it is tempting to draw the inference that international law is irrelevant to the exercise of the right of self-determination, and that having international law on its side was of no use to East Timor. Tempting but mistaken. The clarity of international law in relation to the claims being championed by the East Timorese was essential to their long struggle for formal acknowledgment and support, helping to keep hope alive among the constituency of dedicated activists internationally. International law was also useful in exerting pressure upon both the government of Portugal and the United Nations to act in such a manner as to uphold the norms that were unquestionably applicable. Even such supporters of Indonesia as Australia and the United States needed to tread carefully, due to the embarrassing inconsistency of their overall espousal of the rule of law and their opportunistic neglect of its implementation in relation to East Timor. In essence, international law was mainly useful in the years between 1975 and 1997 as part of a holding operation, of an insistence that the Indonesian effort to overcome East Timor's claim of sovereign rights could not be treated as a closed book.

The legal/moral argumentation on behalf of East Timor was effectively disseminated throughout the world by José Ramos-Horta and others during this long period of neglect. The recognition of the contributions by Ramos-Horta (along with Bishop Carlos Filipe Ximenes Belo) in the award of the Nobel Peace Prize in 1996 both followed from the persuasiveness of their legal/moral argument and contributed greatly to the global awareness that the people of East Timor had been illegally deprived for decades of their fundamental rights without much of an effort by the United Nations to come to their assistance. It made East Timor a symbolic issue in the years, especially since 1997, when Jakarta was seeking to reestablish its credentials as a legitimate state on the road to genuine democracy. While in Indonesia a few years ago, I recall hearing Indonesian officials referring to East Timor as "a pebble in our shoe," an oblique reference to the moral/legal weakness of the Indonesian position on this salient normative issue and yet classifying East Timor as merely a nuisance as the territory was not so important in relation to the size and strength of the country taken as a whole.

The international law circumstance also put the United Nations, the United States, and the entire Western world on the defensive with respect to East Timor, contributing to subsequent pressures that eventuated in the U.N.–monitored 1999 referendum, which validly registered the strong proindependence sentiments of the East Timorese in a manner that contrasted with the contrived results of the phony "Peoples Assembly" installed in Dili after the invasion. This normative dimension also helped ensure that East Timor was a sufficiently known reality to receive attention from the global media if tensions heightened. In many respects the Timorese cause had better prospects than did that of the Tibetans. Indonesia is economically and strategically far weaker than China, and far more vulnerable to outside pressures.

Of course, the basic change in East Timor's prospects resulted from an overall transformation of the geopolitical climate, as well as from the play of internal forces within Indonesia. In the wake of the end of the Cold War, concerns about global strategic alignment were considerably weakened. In this regard, geopolitical discipline relaxed, creating more space for normative considerations. Such an altered context was then deeply influenced by Indonesia's fall from International Monetary Fund (IMF) grace in the aftermath of the Asian financial crisis. Instead of Indonesia being seen as the darling of the second generation of Asian emerging markets, it was now being castigated as the kingpin of "crony capitalism," and its once admired and pampered leader, Suharto, was condemned as an Asian autocrat whose time of useful service to Indonesia had long passed. Confronted by these troubles, abetted by outside pressures, Indonesia did shift leaders and sought to convince its former friends and future creditors that it was once more a respectable country as assessed by the more normatively oriented geopolitics of the 1990s. To make this shift seem genuine meant adopting a more persuasive image of constitutional respectability, and there was no faster way to move in this direction than by appearing to resolve the still smoldering conflict involving East Timor by a recourse to democratic procedures. Such a mood strengthened the hand of transnational activists, but also negotiators on behalf of Portugal and the United Nations, eventuating in the agreement to hold a U.N.–monitored referendum.

But again, despite the favorable global setting, even this deferred implementation of the right of self-determination on behalf of East Timor was confronted by formidable obstacles. To begin with, it is still not clear that Jakarta ever believed that it would have to abide by principles of fairness in relation to the referendum process, and even if the Habibie leadership was prepared to accept an outcome that opted for independence, it was obvious that the military establishment, or a significant part of it, was unwilling to countenance an Indonesian withdrawal.

Furthermore, the dynamics of occupation had built up a network of collaborators, which formed the backbone of the militias that wrought havoc on the population after the East Timorese defied intimidation to vote by more than 78 percent in favor of political independence. In effect, even a geopolitical climate that supports the implementation of international law offers no assurance of compliance if there is strong and lawless opposition situated within the occupying power and its allies. In Indonesia there was also some domestic and regional anxiety that East Timor's success in establishing a state would stimulate several other secessionist movements within Indonesia to intensify their efforts, thereby subjecting the whole country to a prospect of major civil warfare and further fragmentation, if not dissolution. Such fears were not misplaced. (See Gerry van Klinken's chapter in this volume.)

Again, the main point here is to underscore the relevance of international law to the promotion of the legal rights of the people of East Timor in the far more propitious global setting of the late 1990s as a consequence of the decline of the sort of bipolar geopolitical discipline that had dominated international relations throughout the Cold War era. Additionally, Indonesia's related vulnerability to external normative criticism was relevant to the changed prospects for East Timor. At the same time, these circumstances were not sufficiently transformative to enable East Timor to move serenely toward political independence in accord with the recorded wishes of the overwhelming majority of its citizenry. Unfortunately, the implementation of legal rights was blocked by the persisting commitment of the Indonesian military to the status quo in East Timor, as well as by "the facts on the ground" created by the corrupting presence of the long "illegal" occupation of the country. Transition in East Timor was not responsibly protected by the international community until after the militia onslaught of 1999 had taken thousands of lives and terrorized virtually the whole of the population, as well as looting, vandalizing, and destroying much of what had value in an extremely poor country. Unfortunately, the result of this second cycle of Crimes Against Humanity on a massive scale is to deprive East Timor of the means of self-government for the foreseeable future, possibly making the country dependent on a long-term, postconflict U.N. presence tasked with building a viable governmental and economic infrastructure as quickly as possible. Despite the horror of this second cycle, its magnitude seems far less than the first cycle of the late 1970s that has been estimated to have resulted in the deaths of more than a quarter of the population. The information about recent killing by the militias is still sketchy but is believed to have been in the neighborhood of five thousand. Such a number still involves mass killing, and the terrorizing impact drove a high proportion of the East Timor population into hiding in the mountains where they remained for weeks. Also, this recent outrage, in contrast to 1975, was in direct response to a U.N. referendum, concentrated in a short time interval, involving reliance mainly on paramilitary forces, and carried out in the presence of a large number of international media representatives.

Mary Robinson, the U.N. High Commissioner for Human Rights, raised the question as to whether the actions of Indonesia and the paramilitary militias were not grounds for establishing a special court on the model of The Hague tribunal now dealing with crimes charged in relation to former Yugoslavia. An investigation under U.N. auspices of this second cycle of criminality has now been completed, implicating high Indonesian military officers in the militia terror that occurred in East Timor before and after the referendum. Apparently, no attention will be given to the criminality that ensued after the 1975 Indonesian invasion, which could implicate Suharto and the highest military and civilian officials in his regime. The Indonesian government also has indicated that it would investigate the events in East Timor, and although some action has been promised, the exact nature of this action is uncertain at this point. This divisive and explosive subject matter remains a major unresolved challenge for the Wahid leadership, especially given the mount that the criminality was planned and guided from Jakarta.[14]

At this writing, pressures are growing to convene a tribunal to address charges associated with Khmer Rouge rule in Cambodia in the mid-1970s, a time period roughly the same as that of the first cycle of Indonesian criminality. The difference in the international response to these two outbreaks of extreme criminality is quite striking. From a strictly international law perspective, the Indonesian behavior is in many respects a greater challenge. The invasion of East Timor was itself an instance of a Crime Against Peace, which disrupted decolonization and denied a people their right of self-determination. In contrast, the events in Cambodia were a horrifying sequel to a civil war in which there was no issue of decolonization present. Again, the difference in treatment relates, it would seem, to geopolitical factors—the ideology of the perpetrators and their relationship to the governments currently in control of world order.

A CONCLUDING NOTE

In conclusion, it is misleading to adopt a legalist view of the right of self-determination and assume that because the grounds of its invocation are present, the means for its implementation can be found. Similarly, it is a tactical error to dismiss the relevance of international law as an aspect of a resistance struggle that builds and sustains effective support among states and international organizations that constitute the formal global system, as well as among activists and non-governmental organizations, and acts as a holding pattern that is often effective in deferring indefinitely the legitimation of an essentially illegal and cruel set of circumstances. Finally, the United Nations, with the backing of the United States and regional powers, has accepted a peacekeeping challenge, which involves restoring normalcy after the militia rampage and then major help in the early phases of East Timorese state-building.

For all of their suffering, as of the end of 1999, the East Timorese are far closer to achieving their goals of political independence than are many other captive peoples in the world.[15] It was evident that the "nations" captive in the former Soviet Union could not achieve self-determination without the collapse of the Soviet state. It is evident that the Tibetans are not likely to achieve self-determination so long as the strong Chinese state remains in control of the country. And what of the Kurds, Kashmiris, and many others? What would have to change to put such peoples in a position comparable to that now at last enjoyed by East Timor? Or was the incompatibility of Indonesia's annexation with the guidelines of international law a crucial help in enabling the Timorese resistance to prevent Indonesia from ever reaching political closure on East Timor, let alone moral and legal closure? How important was the continuing Portuguese pressure on Indonesia in keeping the issue of East Timor alive, especially within U.N. circles?

Answering these questions, even provisionally, helps us grasp both the wider lessons of East Timor's final realization of self-determination and the factors that seem to make it a special case with only limited general applicability to such settings as Western Sahara, Puerto Rico, and Tibet.

NOTES

The author wishes to thank Stephen Shalom, Mark Selden, and Richard Tanter for particularly helpful editorial and substantive suggestions.

1. At that point, the Australian Minister of Foreign Affairs made the following statement: "The Government has made clear publicly its opposition to the Indonesian intervention and has made this known to the Indonesian Government. . . . [Indonesia's] control is effective and covers all major administrative centers of the country. This is a reality with which we must come to terms. Accordingly, the Government has decided that although it remains critical of the means by which integration was brought about, it would be unrealistic to refuse to recognize de facto that East Timor is part of Indonesia." As quoted in the *Judgment of the International Court of Justice in Case Concerning East Timor*, Judgment of 30 June 1995, page 97. Australia alone accorded de jure recognition to the annexation of East Timor on 18 August 1985, a move partly prompted by the then Australian government's interest in entering into negotiations with Indonesia for a deal covering oil deposits in the Timor Gap.

2. The operative international law acknowledgments were contained in the famous *Declaration on the Granting of Independence to Colonial Countries and Peoples*, U.N. General Assembly (UNGA) Res. 1514 (1960).

3. See Article 73 of the U.N. Charter specifying the responsibilities of states administering non-self-governing territories.

4. See Roger Clark's careful refutation of each of these lines of Indonesian argument in "The 'Decolonisation' of East Timor and the United Nations' Norms on Self-Determination and Aggression," in *International Law and the Question of East Timor* (London: Catholic Institute for International Relations, 1995), 65–102.

5. Articles 2(4) and 51.

6. From a legal perspective, the U.N. response was itself controversial due to its failure to seek convincingly a diplomatic solution combined with a more sustained reliance on sanctions. See Richard Falk, "Reflections on the Gulf War Experience," in *The Gulf War and the New World Order*, ed. Tareq Y. Ismael and Jacqueline S. Ismael (Gainesville, Fla.: University Press of Florida, 1994), 25–39; Farhad Malekian, *Condemning the Use of Force in the Gulf Crisis* (Uppsala, Sweden: Uppsala University, 1992).

7. Among many accounts see George Aditjondro, *In the Shadow of Mount Ramelau: The Impact of the Occupation of East Timor* (Leiden, The Netherlands: Indonesian Documentation and Information Center, 1994); Matthew Jardine, *East Timor: Genocide in Paradise* (Tucson, Ariz.: Odonian Press, 1995); "East Timor: Decolonization, Occupation and Genocide" in A. Barbedo de Magalhes, *East Timor: Land of Hope* (Oporto, Portugal: Oporto University, 1990), esp. 47–60; and Amnesty International, *Indonesia and East Timor —Power and Impunity: Human Rights under the New Order* (London: Amnesty International, 1994).

8. Note that a parallel tribunal was set up after World War II to prosecute Japanese leaders. Both tribunals have been criticized on various grounds, especially the Tokyo tribunal, as ex post facto justice and as "victors' justice." The force of this latter criticism rests on the exemption from legal scrutiny of those responsible for comparably "criminal" acts by the victorious side in the war. This line of thinking is well developed in Richard H. Minear, *Victors' Justice: The Tokyo War Crimes Tribunal* (Princeton, N.J.: Princeton University Press, 1971). With the passage of time, and the buildup of grassroots support, especially in the 1990s, the idea of criminal accountability at an international level has been much more widely accepted. See, e.g., R. Falk, "Telford Taylor and the Legacy of Nuremberg," *Columbia Journal of Transnational Law* 37, no. 3 (1999): 693–723. At the same time, much criticism has been voiced over the deliberate refusal of the occupying authorities in Bosnia to arrest such principal indicted Serbian leaders as Ratko Mladic and Radovan Karadzic. See Christopher S. Wren, "Judge Says Yugoslavia Impedes Work of War-Crimes Tribunal," *New York Times*, 9 November 1999, 7(A). The Pinochet detention in Britain, and eventual release, revealed both the widespread pressures to apply international criminal standards to alleged perpetrators of Crimes Against Humanity and Torture, and the counter-pressures associated with more traditional conceptions of territorial sovereignty.

9. For useful short accounts see the relevant entries in Roy Gutman and David Rieff, eds., *Crimes of War: What the Public Should Know* (New York: Norton, 1999), 107–8, 153–57.

10. See for example Lauri Hannikainen, "The Case of East Timor from the Perspective of *Jus Cogens*," in *International Law and the Question of East Timor*, cited in note 4 above, 103–17.

11. The General Assembly, using stronger language of censure, including "deploring" the Indonesian actions of invasion and annexation, passed a series of resolutions up until 1982. UNGA Res. 3485 (XXX) (1975), 31/53 (1976), 32/34 (1977), 33/39 (1978); 34/40 (1979); 35/27 (1980), 36/50 (1981), and 37/30 (1982). After 1982, the General Assembly retained East Timor as an item on its agenda, while deciding each year to defer consideration of any action until a subsequent session. East Timor remained listed officially throughout as a non-self-governing territory subject to chapter 9 of the Charter. The secre-

tary general continued throughout this entire period to pursue diplomatic negotiations involving Portugal, Indonesia, and East Timor, with the aim of reaching a mutually agreed upon settlement.

12. For an argument that generalizes this point see Richard Falk, "The Cruelty of Geopolitics: The Fate of Nation and State in the Middle East," *Millennium* 20 (1991): 383–94.

13. For consideration of the evolving right of self-determination, the obstacles to its realization, and the various modes of its exercise, see "The Question of Self-Determination: The Cases of East Timor, Tibet and Western Sahara," (Conference Report, Palais des Nations, United Nations, Geneva, 25–26 March 1996). For more general consideration of the various legal dimensions of the right of self-determination, see Hurst Hannum, *Autonomy, Sovereignty, and Self-Determination* (Philadelphia: University of Pennsylvania Press, rev. ed., 1996); Wolfgang Danspeckgruber, ed., *Self-Determination and Self-Administration: A Sourcebook* (Boulder, Colo.: Lynne Rienner, 1997); also useful is Thomas D. Musgrave, *Self Determination and National Minorities* (Oxford: Oxford University Press, 1997).

14. For journalistic confirmation see Rajiv Chandreskaran, "Indonesian Military Tied to Recent Timor Attacks," *Washington Post*, 20 March 2000, 11(A), 18(A).

15. However, the devastated condition of the country is such as to deprive the people of East Timor of the political, social, and economic preconditions for independence. The country is dependent for the foreseeable future on international largesse and a reconstructive and state-building process under U.N. auspices. For a skeptical view of the near-term evolution of East Timor see Seth Mydans, "Liberated East Timor Lacks Law, Order, and Much More," *New York Times*, 16 February 2000.

11

U.S. Support for the Indonesian Military: Congressional Testimony

Allan Nairn

This is a slightly edited unofficial transcript of the statement made by Allan Nairn at hearings on the Humanitarian Crisis in East Timor, held before the International Operations and Human Rights Subcommittee of the U.S. House Committee on International Relations on September 30, 1999, in Washington, D.C. Following Nairn's statement are excerpts from the discussion with committee members. Material in brackets and endnotes has been added by the editors. Thanks to David Bourchier for assistance in identifying Indonesian military officers. The text of this testimony was transcribed from an audio tape.

Allan Nairn: Today, as we're meeting here, Dili is in ruins. Half of Timor is in effect held hostage. They're finding the remains of decapitated boys, as AFP [Agence France-Presse] reported yesterday. They're finding police file photos of dead torture victims with their hands bound behind their backs. Uncounted thousands of Timorese are still in hiding and surviving on roots and leaves. And General Wiranto's militias are threatening further terror.

And yet this is a great day, because East Timor stands on the brink of freedom. It's hard to imagine, really. They said it couldn't be done.

Back in December 1975, when the Indonesian military began consulting with Washington about a possible invasion, they promised that they could crush Timor within two weeks. General Ali Murtopo came to the White House and met with General Brent Scowcroft. President Ford and Henry Kissinger went to Jakarta and sat down with Suharto. And then sixteen hours later, the invasion was underway. The paratroopers dropped from U.S. C-130s. They used new U.S. machine guns to shoot the Timorese into the sea.

In 1990, when I first went to Timor, the intelligence chief Colonel Gatot Purwanto confirmed that by that time their operation had killed a third of the original population.

On November 12, 1991, when the troops marched on the Santa Cruz cemetery, they carried U.S. M-16s. They didn't bother with warning shots. Amy Goodman and I stood between them futilely hoping to stop them from opening fire. But they opened fire systematically and they kept on shooting because, as the national commander, General [Try] Soetrisno, explained: "These Timorese are disrupters; such people must be shot." That was army policy; that is army policy.

And at no time during these years of slaughter did the U.S. government's executive branch ever decide that the time had come to stop supporting the perpetrators. President Carter and Richard Holbrooke sent in OV-10 Broncos and helicopters. Presidents Reagan, Bush, and Clinton sent in weapons, multilateral financing, and sniper trainers.

But now they say circumstances have changed. President Clinton has announced a military cutoff, and there is even a Clinton doctrine under which the United States says it will intervene to prevent mass slaughters, genocides, pogroms, and ethnic cleansings.

In recent weeks, commentators have criticized the United States for failure to intervene, for not sending in foreign troops fast enough to stop the Indonesian army's final burst of Timor terror.

But, Mr. Chairman, I want to make the point today that intervention is not the issue. The Clinton doctrine and the questions flowing from it do not apply in Timor or Indonesia because the killing is being perpetrated with the active assistance of the United States. The United States is not an observer here; it is not agonizing on the sidelines. It has instead been the principal patron of the Indonesian armed forces. The issue is not whether we should step in and play policeman to the world, but rather whether we should continue to arm, train, and finance the world's worst criminals.

I think most Americans would say no, we shouldn't do that, and I know that many in Congress from both parties would agree. But as of this moment, U.S. policy is still, the temporary cutoff notwithstanding, to restore as soon as possible its support for the Indonesian armed forces.

On March 3, 1999, Admiral Dennis Blair, the U.S. commander in chief, Pacific, told Congress that the TNI/ABRI, the Indonesian armed forces, is the main instrument for order in Indonesia. He was speaking, as he and the world knew, after twenty-four years of army terror that has claimed the lives of perhaps a million Indonesians and two hundred thousand East Timorese.

In most people's eyes, such violent behavior is the antithesis of order, but for the U.S. executive branch it has been the basis of a policy. In dozens of countries, unfortunately, the United States has chosen to use and succor killer armies. From Guatemala City to Bogota to Beijing, it has embraced the enemies of freedom.

But today in Timor we can rejoice, because for once that policy has been defeated. And in Jakarta, Surabaya, and Medan, on the streets of the fourth largest country in the world, brave Indonesian students and working people are demonstrating against the army. They demand that it get out of politics, that it dismantle its feared police state. They are risking their lives for real democracy. The United States should be on their side. But it isn't, Mr. Chairman, at least not yet.

That's why we are here today. Congress needs to act to reverse the fundamental course of U.S. policy. The bill, H.R. 2895,[1] which you and others are backing, is a good start to ending support for terror in Timor, but Congress needs to go further in at least two basic respects.

First, the cutoff should be conditioned not just on Timor issues, but also on an end to Indonesian army terror everywhere. The army should not be able to win back U.S. support by choosing new targets. Severe repression in Aceh, West Papua, and elsewhere is already underway. Congress should not be supporting it simply because the army has finished with Timor.

Second, although this cutoff bill may be the most comprehensive ever attempted, there are still many lines of support for the TNI/ABRI and the Indonesian national police that the legislation does not cover. Last year there was an uproar in Congress when it was disclosed that the Pentagon's JCET[2] program was training the army in urban warfare, psy-ops, and sniper technique. Congress, like the press and public, had thought that military training was cut off when Congress canceled Indonesia's IMET[3] training after the 1991 Dili massacre.

Today, it is again the conventional wisdom that the United States no longer trains the Indonesian military and that U.S. material support for the TNI/ABRI is now at a token level. It is indeed the case that due to public pressure, a bipartisan coalition in Congress has cut many lines of support, including bans on small arms, armored vehicles, and the use of U.S. weapons in Timor and the cancellation of deals for F-5 and F-16 fighters.

But it is also the case that contrary to Congress's understanding with the executive branch, the United States has through 1999 been intensifying its links with the TNI/ABRI, even as Timor militia terror and repression in Aceh have escalated. And it is also the case that there are many complex lines of support for Indonesia's armed forces that to this day remain largely unknown to even the most engaged members of Congress.

For the past five months I've been in Indonesia and occupied Timor trying to investigate these lines of support. It would take many hours to lay out the facts in detail, but I'll just mention a few brief examples to give an idea of the scope of the problem.

A couple of weeks ago, I reported in *The Nation* magazine on internal Pentagon cables, classified cables, that indicated that two days after the Liquiça massacre—that horrific church massacre in which the militias, backed up by uniformed *Brimob* [police mobile brigade] troops, went into the church and the rectory and hacked dozens to death—the senior U.S. uniformed officer in the Pacific, Admiral Dennis Blair, sat down with General Wiranto, the Indonesian

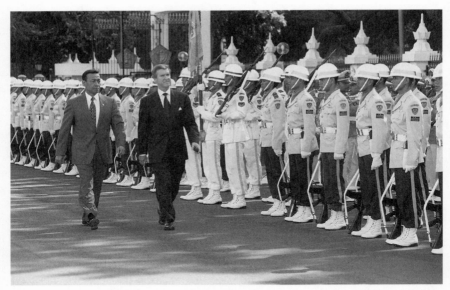

Figure 11.1   Indonesian Minister of Defense General Wiranto (left) escorts U.S. Secretary of Defense William S. Cohen (right) as he inspects the troops during an armed forces full honors ceremony welcoming Cohen to Jakarta, Indonesia, on August 1, 1998. DoD photo by Helene C. Stikkel.

commander. Blair had a mission from the State Department and others to tell Wiranto to shut the militias down.

But in fact, as the classified cable summarizing the meeting in great detail shows, Blair did the opposite. He offered Wiranto new U.S. military assistance. He offered to join Wiranto in lobbying the U.S. Congress to reverse standing U.S. policy, to get the IMET military training restored.

He offered Wiranto the first new U.S. training program for the Indonesian security forces since 1992. This was a crowd control and riot control program that was focused on *Brimob*, precisely the unit that two days before had helped stage the Liquiça massacre. He even invited Wiranto to be his personal guest at his quarters in Hawaii.

Wiranto and his people were delighted by the meeting. They took it as a green light to proceed.

I can now report to the committee, Mr. Chairman, that there was an additional meeting after the Blair-Wiranto session that had perhaps even more significant implications. This one took place on July 14 in Jakarta. It involved Admiral Archie Clemins, the commander of the U.S. Pacific Fleet. Admiral Clemins came in to make a presentation to senior ABRI leadership, including the naval leadership.

Now, at this time the militia campaign was in full swing. The Liquiça massacre had happened, the assault on Dili had happened. This was the assault in which the militias staged a rally in front of the governor's office. It was broadcast live on the official state radio station, Radio Republic Indonesia. Eurico Guterres, the militia leader, stood up and issued a public death threat against the Carrascalão family.

The militias then proceeded to trash the Carrascalão house, kill the son of Manuel Carrascalão, kill dozens of refugees who were hiding in the rear of the house, rampaged through Dili shooting people on sight—this all after a ceremony that had been presided over by the Indonesian occupation governor and General Zacky Anwar Makarim, the Indonesian military coordinator of the militia operation, and as I will discuss in a minute, a longtime protégé and trainee of U.S. intelligence.

So this was after the Dili rampage, after countless other militia killings.

And on July 14, Admiral Clemins came into Jakarta, and according to Indonesian officers who were present and according to Admiral Clemins' own presentation notes for the meeting, he offered the officers an increase, a step-up in the U.S. military relationship with Indonesia. He said reengagement is crucial to maintaining the U.S.–Indonesia relationship. He referred to the Siabu Range in Medan, where Indonesia had given the United States rights to stage air-to-ground firing exercises, and he made a politically crucial proposal. He proposed that in Surabaya, at the Indonesian naval eastern fleet headquarters, training facilities be established for the U.S. military.

Now, anyone who follows Indonesian military politics knows that there are few hotter issues than the prospect of U.S. military bases in Indonesia.

Some in the military are for it. Some are against it. It is a highly charged issue. Here Admiral Clemins was going to the military leadership and proposing what he called possible training sites to train U.S. troops directly on an ongoing permanent basis on Indonesian soil. Admiral Clemins went so far as to say that the U.S. goals for the Asia-Pacific region depend on maintaining our strategic partnership with Indonesia. This at a time when the State Department and the White House were publicly threatening to cut off the Indonesian army because of the militia terror and the terror in Aceh.

He then went on to urge the Indonesian military to, as he put it, maintain access to advanced technology. He specifically was talking about new, large-scale purchases of high-tech electronics, which would allow the Indonesian navy to integrate their command and control and surveillance facilities directly with those of the U.S. Navy. And he went on to discuss in some detail the FDNF IT21 installation. These are U.S. naval electronics that he was urging the Indonesian military to link up with. . . .

Now, as this was going on and as the militias were rampaging on the streets of Dili, the United States was continuing to ship ammunition to Indonesia. Last year [1998], Representative McKinney and the chairman and others made a special effort to try to cut off the influx of U.S. ammunition and spare parts. At the time, it did not succeed. But this year we could see the consequences.

A few weeks ago, as Dili was burning and as the U.N. had evacuated, as foreign journalists had left, I had the opportunity to be, I think, probably the last foreign journalist left on the streets of Dili. And I was walking around in the early mornings going from one abandoned house to another. You could hear the militias coming around the corners with their chopper motorcycles. They would fire into the air and honk their horns as they were about to sack and burn another house.

And you also found littering the streets, hundreds upon hundreds of shell casings. They came from two places, one from Pindad [PT Pindad: Pusat Industri AD. Army Industries Center], the Indonesian military industries, which have joint ventures with a whole list of U.S. companies. And the other from Olin Winchester of East Alton, Illinois. These cartridges had been recently shipped in to Battalion 744, one of the territorial battalions in Timor, and then issued to the militiamen. As you can see from these photos, they come in the new white Olin Winchester boxes, twenty cartridges to a box. These were among the bullets that they were using to terrorize Dili.

The units on the ground that were specifically running the militia operation included some of those most intensively trained by the United States. This includes Group 4 and Group 5 of *Kopassus, Brimob*, the *Kostrad* Infantry Units. The individual officers coordinating the militia operation, including General Zacky Makarim, Admiral Yoost Mengko, General Sjafrie Sjamsoeddin, Colonel Wioyotomo Nugroho, who was the on-the-ground coordinator for the militias in the initial months of their operation, were all graduates of U.S. IMET and intelligence training.

I'll just stop by citing one dimension that I would suggest Congress look into. Congress—many in Congress—believe that they have cut off U.S. training for the Indonesian military and police. As far as I can tell, that is not the case. There are several other training programs going on beside IMET, beside JCET.

Admiral Sudono, the longtime chief of Suharto's secret police, a man who was presented with the Legion of Merit by the U.S. Joint Chiefs of Staff, told me in a series of on-the-record interviews, that for years the CIA has been providing intelligence training to intelligence operatives from the Indonesian armed forces. He said that this training involved ten to fifteen Indonesian officers per year who would be brought over to the United States for a two- to three-month intelligence course. He said that, as he understood it, this training continues to the present.

Last year, when I was arrested by the Indonesian armed forces and interrogated, the man who was interrogating me, who identified himself as Major Dodi Rabowo [name unclear], at the end of our interrogation session, he leaned over to me and said, you know, I am a member of U.S. intelligence. I said what do you mean? What are you talking about? And he then went on to describe in detail training that he said he had received at the Ciputat police camp in Jakarta and in Quantico, Virginia. As Rabowo described it, this training involved instructors from the FBI, DEA [Drug Enforcement Administration], and CIA. And it included training in subjects such as indoor pistol technique, surveillance, and interrogation.

Over the ensuing year in speaking to many Indonesian and U.S. officials, I have finally been able to confirm all the key elements of Rabowo's story. Indeed there has been ongoing training at Quantico. Indeed the FBI to this day has its own special training program for the Indonesian police. Many are brought to the FBI Academy, others receive training on site in Indonesia, often in intelligence and weapon-handling techniques. There are several different strands of so-called anti-terrorist training.

Just one month ago, according to U.S. military sources in Jakarta, a U.S. intelligence team was due to come in and provide what they called countersurveillance training to the Indonesian security forces. The Pentagon has been providing new advanced equipment to BIA, the Indonesian military intelligence agency, including special radios for use in operations in Irian Jaya, West Papua. There's a whole strand of links involving training and material supply, and it's not even covered by the relevant legislation dealing with the Pentagon. It involves the FBI, the CIA, the DEA, Customs, and the U.S. Marshals. It's a very intricate series of connections.

According to Indonesian police documents I've seen, the recent training includes explosives and explosive countermeasures. According to a former chief of the SGI (that's the special intelligence unit in East Timor), to whom I spoke, the *Kopassus* has received training from U.S. Special Forces troops in techniques including the assembly of explosives. And what this SGI colonel claimed was torture resistance. This is—these are sessions in which he said torture techniques are discussed and practiced to a certain extent on trainees. The theory being, if you get caught by the enemy this might happen to you so you ought to know what the techniques are. He said that this training was not very impressive to the *Kopassus* since they already knew all the torture techniques. And he even gave me the names of some individual *Kopassus* officers who he said had died in training as these counter-torture techniques were practiced. But he said it was part of the curriculum that the U.S. forces had given.

I'll stop there. There's one more thing, one more interesting side note. Even as the militia terror was rising to its height, there was another strand of training going on involving what you might call localization or privatization. A number of Indonesian police and intelligence officers were being sent for training with individual U.S. police departments. One crew was just up at the New York City Police Department Police Academy just about a month and a half ago. Others—I know contacts have been made with the departments in Virginia and California as well. These training sessions are technically not under the auspices of the State Department or Pentagon, but apparently they are arranged with the help of the local CIA station in Jakarta and, they say, with approval from State Department officials in Washington.

And a related type of training is happening right now at Norwich University in Vermont where at this moment at least nine *Kopassus* special forces soldiers are being trained. This is a program that was set up with assistance from the U.S. Defense Intelligence Agency. Again, it's not technically under the current State Department or Pentagon umbrella, but it's yet another way in which the U.S. executive branch manages by hook or by crook to provide support for the Indonesian armed forces.

So the short answer to what has the U.S. role been with the Indonesian military in the months of the militia terror, is that it has been deep, it has been extensive, and many key officials have been attempting to intensify it. And I believe that should stop. And I believe that many in Congress have clearly shown the will to stop it. It's just a matter now of tracking down all these lifelines that run into Jakarta. And it takes a lot of work, but then going around and systematically cutting them off one by one, because that's the only thing that will work.

Thank you, Mr. Chairman.

EXCERPTS FROM DISCUSSION WITH COMMITTEE MEMBERS

Nairn: I think you're absolutely right, Mr. Chairman, that this is entirely controlled from the top. Two weeks ago when I was arrested by the military on the streets of Dili, I was held at the *korem* military headquarters, that's the main occupation headquarters for all of East Timor—the headquarters of General Kiki Syahnakri, the head of the Committee for the Restoration of Peace and Stability (that was the martial law authority in Timor).

And the entire back half of the base was filled with uniformed *Aitarak* militiamen, with their black *Aitarak* T-shirts and their red and white headbands. You'd see them leaving the *korem* base on their motorcycles and their trucks holding their rifles and pistols to go out and stage their attacks.

And I asked one of my interrogators there, Lieutenant Colonel Willem [probably Col. Willem Rampangilei]: "Are those *Aitarak* guys in the back there?" And he said: "Oh yes, they live here. They work out of here. We have them here so we can control them," he said. And they do indeed.

I was later brought over to Polda [regional police headquarters] for interrogation, that's the main Dili police headquarters. And at Polda it was the same story. In the operations room and the intelligence room, you'd see the uniformed *Aitarak* men going in and out. That was where they worked out of.

And then the following day when they flew me back to West Timor for further interrogation, it was on a military charter. And aside from my two military escorts, the rest of those on the plane were uniformed militias, some of whom I recognized from the streets of Dili as being some of the most threatening characters. And they had their guns, their rifles on the plane.

But these were actually all members of police intelligence. My military escorts explained to me that they were being rotated back after having served their one-year tour. These were the militiamen.

And incidentally, you know, for those who say that Wiranto does not have control, that's nonsense. The only official under the current organizational structure, the only official to whom both the military and police report is Wiranto. And there's been extensive both military and police involvement in running these militias. And only a total cutoff will send the strong message. . . . Nairn: One point I want to make about the constant Pentagon argument. The argument for training is: Well, when you train officers it gives you access to them. It teaches them good values and so on. Those arguments are summarized in this cable. This is a cable from Ambassador Roy to CINCPAC [commander in chief, Pacific].

He makes all the arguments about how when we train officers, they get good values. They rise in the ranks. And then to clinch the argument, it cites examples of the best and the brightest of the Indonesian officers who've been trained by the U.S.

These are the examples they cited. General Feisal Tanjung, who became the commander in chief of the Indonesian armed forces, one of the most notorious hardline, repressive officers; [Lieutenant] General Hendropriyono, one of the legendary authors of repression in Indonesia, who was involved in Aceh. He's the man who commanded Operation Cleanup in Jakarta prior to the '94 APEC [Asian-Pacific Economic Cooperation] summit. This was the operation in which they swept through the streets, picked up street vendors, petty criminals, prostitutes; executed many of them, according to human rights groups. Major General Sihombing, a longtime Intel man who became deputy chief of the secret police. [Major General] Agus [Wirahadikusumah] who has a less egregious human rights record than the others. His main distinction is he's bought a lot of U.S. weapons for the Indonesian military.

And then their final example of the best and the brightest was General Prabowo, the most notorious of all the Indonesian officers; also one of the most extensively U.S.–trained officers, famous for his personal participation in torture in Timor, West Papua, Aceh; for the kidnappings last year in Jakarta.

NOTES

1. The East Timor Self-Determination Act of 1999, introduced in the House of Representatives on 21 September 1999, by Rep. Patrick Kennedy, called for the imposition of an immediate suspension of all U.S. assistance to the government of Indonesia (other than humanitarian aid) until that government respects East Timor's independence and ceases its interference there. The bill was not enacted, but an amendment to the Fiscal Year 2000

Foreign Operations Appropriations Act prohibited military assistance, including military education and training, to the armed forces of Indonesia until six human rights conditions were met, including the return of East Timorese refugees from West Timor and prosecution of those responsible for human rights violations in East Timor. Despite acknowledging that the conditions had not been met, the Clinton administration resumed some military cooperation with Indonesia in the summer of 2000, claiming that the limited military-to-military relationship was not covered by the legislation.

2. Joint Combined Education and Training: a program to provide military training for foreign military officers on foreign soil.

3. International Military Education and Training: U.S. Pentagon program for training foreign military officers in the United States.

12

East Timor and Asian Security

Wade Huntley and Peter Hayes

The crisis in East Timor, sparked by the August 30, 1999, vote for independence and culminating in the introduction of the U.N.–sanctioned International Force for East Timor (InterFET), is not simply the latest chapter in East Timor's tragic history. The bloodshed and turmoil in East Timor have cast in stark relief the utter inadequacy of existing Asia-Pacific security arrangements to cope with regional crises, let alone enduring challenges, and highlight vital questions concerning the relationship of international security and human rights in the post–Cold War world.

U.S. RESPONSIBILITY

Although important questions remain concerning lines of authority in East Timor and in Indonesia, there is little doubt now that primary responsibility for the killings of innocent civilians in East Timor in the wake of the referendum must be borne by the Indonesian military and the militia forces it sanctioned and supported. Nevertheless, to fully appreciate the nature of the international reaction to the crisis, it is also vital to emphasize the history of international culpability in Indonesian repression in East Timor.

The principal bearer of such broader responsibility is the United States, the dominant power in the region, that for decades has consistently prioritized its perceived national interest in resisting popular activism and preserving stability in Indonesia. Following this approach, the United States turned a blind eye to the massacre of Indonesians in 1965–66, signaling its willingness to tolerate the Indonesian military's gross abuse of international human rights standards. Accordingly, the United States tacitly accepted and surreptitiously supported Indonesia's 1975 invasion of East Timor following the end of Portuguese colonial rule. Although not explicitly condoning the invasion, Washington worked behind the scenes to subvert any meaningful U.N. efforts to halt Indonesian bloodletting in the territory. Subsequent to this de facto validation of the invasion, the United States not only willingly overlooked a quarter-century of harsh Indonesian rule, but also effectively abetted this repression by helping arm and train Indonesian forces and by resisting efforts to focus international concern on the plight of East Timor's people. U.S. reluctance to support U.N. preparations to prevent postreferendum violence is only the most recent example of this complicity.

As the postreferendum crisis unfolded, many U.S. commentators stressed Indonesia's strategic importance to U.S. national interests. Yet many frequently cited factors, such as the strategic importance of Indonesian-controlled sea-lanes, oil in the region, and the position of Indonesia as a middle-ranking power in the region, are simply artifice. For example, arguments based on the importance of the Malacca and/or Lombok Straits ignore the relative ease and small cost of using alternate sea lanes around Australia should turmoil in Indonesia lead to the closing of these routes.[1] Reliance on such justifications worked only to undermine U.S. credibility among the Timorese and their supporters elsewhere in the region.

Some arguments as to the need for U.S. caution in approaching this crisis do, however, have validity. In particular, there is a basis for the assertion that the United States has lost some of its capacity to exercise leverage over the players in Indonesia and East Timor, despite the apparent increase of its strategic capabilities. For example, long-standing intimate relations between U.S. and Indonesian armed forces have waned of late. Although the Indonesian military continues to regard this relationship as symbolically important, its practical value has diminished. Ironically, each severed tie (such as the cessation of joint training exercises one week before the referendum) left one less tie that the United States could *threaten* to cut to coerce behavior it desired. Thus, the Clinton administration's suspension of all military contact with Indonesia (eventually exercised over Pentagon objections) may have had much less impact than many asserted on Jakarta's final decision to pull out its troops from East Timor and allow in the peacekeeping force.

Indonesia is dependent upon the United States and Japan for over $1 billion per month in credit from the International Monetary Fund (IMF), World Bank, and Asian Development Bank issued after the 1997 Asian financial crisis. This circumstance provided the United States and Japan with considerable leverage. However, this leverage was not easy to utilize as a policy instrument. The Indonesian military, directly responsible for the violent suppression of East Timor, would have been among the least affected segments of Indonesian society by a cutoff of this support. During the killing in September, therefore, neither the threat nor the implementation of an aid cutoff was as coercive of Indonesia's military leadership as many predicted. Indeed, wholesale economic sanctions would have punished the country's civilian population for the actions of its military, regardless of the attitude most Indonesian citizens held on those actions. In the longer run, wielding this powerful but crude weapon risked undermining Indonesian economic recovery, increasing poverty, bankruptcy, and social stress, and making it even more difficult for the Indonesian political elite to accept moves toward democracy. This reality continues to reduce rather than expand American power over the Indonesian military's behavior throughout Indonesia's far-flung provinces.

Despite these limitations on its power, however, events have demonstrated that when it elects to do so, the United States sets the tone for the course of events in Indonesia and elsewhere in the region. Although initially reluctant to directly intervene in East Timor, President Clinton was forced to focus on the crisis at the 1999 Asia-Pacific Economic Co-operation meeting in New Zealand, at which time Australia and other states held their strongest leverage on the United States to support an international peacekeeping force. Even in acquiescing to pressure from both domestic and international opinion, the Clinton administration issued only tepid criticism of Indonesian complicity in pre- and postreferendum violence. Nevertheless, following Clinton's direct criticisms, Indonesia quickly accepted an international force for East Timor, demonstrating its continuing sensitivity to U.S. pressure. The international presence that subsequently took shape under U.N. mandate—including Australian and then Philippine leadership, troops from these countries and other U.S. allies (Korea, Jordan, etc.), an offer of Chinese police, and a humanitarian deployment of the Japanese Air Self-Defense Force in West Timor—certainly bears a U.S. stamp of approval.

Two conclusions follow from these observations. First, opportunities have always existed for judicious and targeted action in support of the people of East Timor. For this reason, justifications of inaction on grounds that inadequate means of influence existed were simply specious.

Second, the United States remained central to the outcome of the crisis. To be sure, Australia took considerable initiative in calling for the referendum and subsequently in proposing and leading InterFET. However, as we show below, it did so self-consciously as a deputy of U.S. power. The evident continuing centrality of the United States to the outcome of the crisis exposed the inability of other states in the region to act in concert to play this role.

What has happened—and what will occur—in East Timor will have lasting effects on the course of security structures in the East Asia and Pacific region. The course of events is likely to raise the acceptable performance standard for Asian militaries with respect to gross violations of human rights. In this regard, developments have added to the post-Kosovo precedents concerning justifications for humanitarian intervention and hence are already globally relevant.

The absence of a preexisting regional security apparatus capable of reacting quickly and effectively to the emerging crisis has already imposed costs on all the relevant actors, including the United States, Indonesia, and especially the people of East Timor. The ad-hoc cobbling together of the Australia-led multinational force, while a significant first in achieving broad regional commitment of personnel and funds, has not rectified this shortcoming.

GLOBAL TRANSFORMATION AND SECURITY ISSUES

The end of the Cold War transformed a global security system that had evolved into a tightly managed and relatively stable bipolar structure. With the collapse of the former Soviet Union, the heavy-handed management of "spheres of influence" by both Cold War superpowers receded. Although this reduction in superpower meddling in some cases facilitated regional accommodation (as exemplified by Vietnamese entry into the Association of Southeast Asian Nations [ASEAN]), in many other cases regional and local conflicts suppressed by the superpowers smoldered with hostility or erupted into open warfare. At the same time, proliferation of advanced military technologies has accelerated in the post–Cold War period, evinced most strikingly in the 1998 nuclear tests by India and Pakistan. Thus, the end of the global superpower Cold War has left in its wake the very real prospect of many states acquiring nuclear arms in the next ten to twenty years, with the consequent emergence of numerous "regional cold wars" in which specific volatile conflicts (such as those around Kashmir or the Taiwan straits) come under the shadow of potential nuclear confrontation.

At the same time, with tensions with Russia reduced, the United States no longer faces the deterring power of Russian nuclear weapons in peripheral zones, whether adjacent to or distant from Russian shores. It also finds itself less challenged and therefore with more available, deployable, and usable conventional forces than in past decades. Consequently, the United States is both less inhibited about intervening militarily in such zones than it was during the Cold War and more ambivalent about being spread thin or lost in the unruly frontiers of violence erupting around the world—as occurred most memorably (for Americans) in Somalia. To respond to this new multi-layered set of security challenges, the United States has developed an array of new conventional weapons of unprecedented accuracy and lethality, while at the same time attempting to squeeze extra military power out of nuclear weapons—traditionally reserved for strictly nuclear contingencies—by expanding the scope of possible targets of nuclear attack to include non-nuclear weapons, and non-nuclear-armed adversaries.[2] This shift has been matched by the exterminist logic that now informs Russian nuclear doctrine, as evidenced by their abandonment of their no-first-use commitment of previous decades.

The U.S. security agenda is still topped by traditional concerns, such as countering familiar global and regional challenges to U.S. power from Russia, China, regional non-status-quo states (such as Iraq and Iran), and states proliferating weapons of mass destruction (such as North Korea). However, this agenda is now crowded by contending demands for attention in Washington by "non-traditional" security concerns, including protection of human rights, environmental security, illegal migrants, refugees, "failed states," narcotics and criminal networks, urban warfare and subnational terrorism, and "asymmetric warfare" including cyberwars.[3] In addition, old ideologies and institutions from the Cold War live on, making it hard for American decision-makers to abandon archaic organizational operating procedures or rules of thumb when confronted with new types of crises. This U.S. inability as yet to give sufficient attention and clear thinking to the new security problems it faces in the post–Cold War era, combined with the reduced constraints on U.S. military intervention, have produced—unsurprisingly—U.S. military interventions that appear inconsistent, incoherent, and unpredictable on both realist and humanitarian grounds. East Timor was to prove no exception to this trend.

COLLECTIVE REGIONAL SECURITY—ASEAN AND THE UNITED NATIONS

As the violence in East Timor unfolded in the hours and days immediately following the referendum vote, it became apparent that forceful and speedy intervention to stop the killing was absolutely urgent. However, there was no international consensus on its form or on how to implement it.

At the time, some argued that first responsibility properly belonged to the ASEAN member states, and the ASEAN Regional Forum (ARF). Walden Bello, for example, called upon ASEAN to move "immediately" to form the core of a U.N. peacekeeping mission.[4] Viewing U.S. and Australian complicity with past repression of East Timor as too great a stain to be whitewashed, Bello asserted, "All commitments of armed peacekeepers to East Timor must be done under the mandate of the United Nations and ASEAN."

Although the force ultimately deployed received a U.N. mandate, the ASEAN states—as a group or, for the most part, individually—proved incapable of taking on meaningful leadership roles. As Richard Tanter argued at the onset of the crisis, the ARF "has made no contribution to resolving the East Timor conflict in the past, and has little to offer now."[5] Unlike Europe with its tried and tested institutions for conflict avoidance and resolution, he argued, the ARF has never addressed the violation of human rights as an interstate agenda item. Instead, the ARF and ASEAN set precedents earlier in relation to Burma that kept the standards of respect for human rights low rather than pushing them toward international norms. The non-governmental Council for Security Cooperation in the Asia Pacific that parallels the ARF also has failed to address these issues. Thus, the region lacks basic institutions and procedures to address systematic governmental human rights abuses, especially when they arise in connection with "internal security" problems.

Subsequent events proved the accuracy of Tanter's diagnosis. As days passed, initiative to form a peacekeeping force fell by default to Australia and, behind it, the United States. Despite Indonesia's expressed desire for more active involvement by ASEAN states—that is, neighbors other than Australia—those states proved fractious and contentious. Malaysia, despite its active role in past U.N. peacekeeping operations, reacted ambivalently as the crisis unfolded and ultimately bowed out of InterFET's first phase of deployment in a pique after U.N. secretary general Kofi Annan offered Thailand the role of second-in-command behind Australia. Thailand's own involvement has been a source of domestic tension, pitting its activist foreign minister Surin Pitsuwan against more traditional military and defense elites, and thus muddling somewhat the signal sent by Thailand's involvement. Although the Philippines made a substantial troop commitment to InterFET, it too blurred its message by joining China in opposing the U.N. Human Rights Commission vote to conduct an international inquiry into the East Timor situation.

In sum, ASEAN member states, individually and collectively, reacted to the crisis with contradiction and paralysis. A principal source of these vacillating postures was the prevailing norm among these states proscribing "interference in the internal affairs of other member states." Inaction and inertia were reinforced by the weakness of pre-existing mechanisms for policy coordination and joint action. Additionally, all these states—like the United States—have been historically very reluctant to endanger vital economic, political, and security relations with large, oil-rich, and militarily powerful Indonesia for the sake of opposing human rights abuses in small and poor East Timor. To what extent this failure of ASEAN states to respond in a united fashion reveals the underlying inherently weak regionalism (originating during the Vietnam War and focusing on "internal security" in subsequent decades), and to what extent it revealed the cleavages within ASEAN reflecting member states' external great power relationships, remain subjects for future debate. Undeniably, ASEAN nations joined the U.N. Transitional Administration in East Timor (UNTAET) only when more powerful players had already made clear that Indonesian rule in East Timor would have to come to an end.

The prospective consequences of ASEAN inaction are sweeping. The call to place an effective international peacekeeping force in East Timor presented the ARF with an opportunity to establish a role for itself in resolving security dilemmas and other tensions in the region. The inaction of the ARF effectively ceded this leadership opportunity to the United States, Australia, other allies, and the large powers at the United Nations. Moreover, this inability also ended any notion that the ARF has political leadership in regional security dialogues, in relation either to Southeast Asia or to the Asia-Pacific region as a whole. In short, the opportunity for the ARF to function as the fulcrum for regional security coordination and dialogue was squandered, and it is unlikely that the ARF or related nascent regional institutions will play any major role in security deliberations or outcomes in the near future. With no other meaningful autonomous security institutions on the horizon, the path is clear for big powers to continue to contend for hegemony in the region.

HEGEMONIC REGIONAL SECURITY—THE ROLE OF AUSTRALIA

In addition to the U.S. role in the East Timor crisis, the role taken up by Australia also compels attention. In particular, the crisis presented an opportunity for Australian prime minister John Howard to redefine Australia's historic approach to Indonesian and regional relations in ways that will have significant impact on Australia's foreign policy and on regional security relations for years to come.

Ever since the fall of Singapore to Japan in 1942 demonstrated the limits of British security guarantees, Australia has faced a tension between its Western origins and its Asian geography. In foreign policy, this tension has meant seeking to balance ongoing links to Britain and the United States, on the one hand, and developing links to immediate neighbors, on the other. In this context, Australia's relations with Indonesia—with its large population and abundant resources—has been a central challenge to Australian policymakers.

After the pro-Western Suharto regime took power in the mid-1960s, Australian policymakers worked (with varying success) to maintain close ties to the regime, helping ameliorate Australia's underlying foreign policy tension at least with respect to Indonesia. In this context, Indonesia's occupation and repressive rule of East Timor was an unwelcome irritation. Although the Whitlam government condemned the invasion and Australia became home to many East Timorese independence activists, policymakers then and after retained their perception of the importance of sustaining close ties to Jakarta.

Beginning in 1983, the Labor governments of Bob Hawke and Paul Keating increased efforts to improve Indonesia-Australia ties and sought specifically to build ties to the Indonesian military. These efforts, together with Australian goals of tapping Timor Gap oil, in 1985 led Australia to become the only nation to formally recognize East Timor's incorporation within Indonesia, followed by the December 1995 signing of the Canberra-Jakarta "Agreement on Maintaining Security" (AMS). The AMS, negotiated in secret and insulated from parliamentary oversight, sparked controversy. Supporters heralded the agreement for strengthening Australia's relationship to its most powerful neighbor, with beneficial effects for relations throughout the Asian region. Critics—including opposition leader John Howard—condemned wording in the AMS widely understood to oblige Australia to refrain from pressuring Indonesia on East Timor and other irredentist issues.

Within months of reaching the AMS accord, Australia's Labor Party lost power in national elections, and Liberal Party leader John Howard became prime minister. Although initially the new government affirmed support for the AMS, rising turmoil in Indonesia—the impact of the Asian financial crisis and the sub-

Figure 12.1   Street demonstration, Melbourne, 1996. Courtesy: Ross Bird.

sequent fall of the Suharto regime—eroded perceptions of Indonesia's powerful position, engendering instead the specter of a disintegrating or "Balkanizing" region and raising questions as to the wisdom of emphasizing close ties to Jakarta.[6] Thus, the crisis brewing in East Timor presented Howard with a welcome opportunity for a dramatic break from his predecessors' approaches to relations with Indonesia.

With Indonesian president B. J. Habibie inching toward concessions on East Timor, the Howard government decided to press the issue. On January 12, 1999, the Australian government proclaimed support for autonomy and an eventual vote on self-determination in East Timor, abrogating the implicit proscription entailed by the AMS.[7] Only fifteen days later, Habibie made his historic announcement that the East Timorese would be allowed to vote to choose, in effect, between autonomy and independence. The Indonesian military's direct responsibility for the subsequent violence in East Timor demonstrated its rejection of Habibie's acquiescence to East Timorese self-determination. Hence, the Howard government's decision to pressure Habibie on East Timor has met with criticism for failing to anticipate—and perhaps even facilitating—the Indonesian military's predictable response. However, the Howard government's motivations for pressing the issue at this time reached beyond East Timor itself. The deteriorating situation in East Timor also offered the Howard government an opportunity to put into action its pro-Western vision of Australia's future regional role, by adopting a more forceful position toward Indonesia and positioning Australia to play a prominent role in resolving the situation.

As violence in East Timor spread, and as previously cultivated ties to the Indonesian military proved ineffective as a tool to induce its restraint, Australia became an early and active advocate of U.N. intervention. In the wake of the August 30 proindependence vote, the murderous rampage of Indonesian-backed prointegrationist militias made immediate action paramount. In this context, with no coherent regional security structure in place to offer credible alternative authority, and the United States holding back from taking the initiative, the U.N. Security Council approved the formation of InterFET under Australian leadership.

The Howard government's view of Australia's role in InterFET became clear with its September enunciation of a new strategic doctrine. Howard's vision would have Australia not only adopt a more "active" role in Asian security matters, but do so as a "deputy" to the United States and a broader agenda of Western-oriented interests. The approach, quickly dubbed the "Howard Doctrine," clearly casts Australia's InterFET role not as a unique necessity, but as a model for the future. The doctrinal shift was accompanied by predictable calls for substantial increases in Australian defense spending to match the new activist role.

Some commentators have remarked that the "Howard Doctrine" represents a dramatic new orientation in Australia's approach to regional security relations. This observation holds only in regard to the extent to which the approach dispenses with efforts to accommodate Indonesia. In terms of the projected affinity with the United States, the approach taps a deep vein of thinking that has existed in Australia since the end of World War II. As the Cold War dawned, Australian defense planners sought specific security guarantees from the United States. Because the 1951 treaty between Australia, New Zealand, and the United States (ANZUS) only partly satisfied these aims, many analysts have since avowed that Australian "loyalty" to the United States, both in the Asia Pacific and elsewhere in the world, would cement an affinity of interests that would secure U.S. support in time of crisis. Howard's offer to have Australia act as "deputy" in the region (while the United States acts, presumably, as "sheriff" to the world) is simply the latest incarnation of this long-standing ambition among Australia's most pro-Western defense thinkers, reflected, for example, in Australia's military support for the United States in Vietnam.

The Howard Doctrine, then, is an effort to take advantage of the crisis in East Timor to move away from reliance on collective security mechanisms and adopt a stronger military posture within the framework of American power and priorities. As a security policy for Australia, the deepest flaw in this approach remains what it has always been: U.S. and Australian interests are not always convergent and are not made more convergent merely by Australian fidelity. In 1984, the United States collided head-on with Australia over the U.S. desire to conduct MX missile tests in the Tasman Sea in direct contradiction to Australian government policy opposing first-strike weapons. In that instance, the controversy unleashed over these tests caused the United States to cancel them. However, within two years, when New Zealand's antinuclear policy threatened U.S. nuclear weapons posture throughout the Asia Pacific, Pentagon decision-makers swiftly jettisoned New Zealand as an ANZUS partner, sweeping aside decades of its alliance loyalty. Today, the Howard Doctrine rests on the assumption that the United States will not subject Australia to a similar fate.

Such an assumption is enormously risky. Anti-Australian sentiment and violence has emerged throughout Indonesia, and relations with Australia's other northern neighbors have suffered due to the correct perception that Australia has backed away from its commitment to integrate with Asia as enunciated by the Keating Labor government. Even though InterFET has now handed security responsibilities to UNTAET, East Timor continues to pose dangers for Australia. Military leaders in Jakarta might still respond to their loss of East Timor by provoking instability there and on the Irian Jaya–Papua New Guinea border— Australia's worst military nightmare. In such a deteriorating relationship, the United States would have some very difficult choices to make between Jakarta and Canberra. There is no guarantee that the sheriff would support the deputy. Hence, for Australia, the East Timor situation is extremely delicate and dangerous.

Conversely, successful cooperation between the Indonesian military and UNTAET's forces to disband militias and repatriate refugees from West Timor could allow Australia the option of reconstructing its relationship with Jakarta in more positive ways. Such success would also work to reinforce the Howard Doctrine's premise of a de facto division of labor between Australia and the United States, wherein Australia would lead interventions into small hot spots threatening regional instability, while the United States would involve itself supportively and less overtly. Developing such a relationship might also help Australia push the United States to pay its U.N. dues, still in massive arrears and threatening the United Nations with bankruptcy. The InterFET intervention in East Timor gave Australia rare leverage on the United States, and if the operation is ultimately successful, Australia will have earned much political capital in Washington.

Nevertheless, even this more successful realization of the Howard Doctrine bodes ill for broader regional security outlooks. The deputization of Australia will do little to relieve the onus of U.S. hegemony that tends to follow from unilateral American military responses to regional security turmoil, whether in relation to Iran, Iraq, Korea, Afghanistan, or Taiwan, to mention just some of the important cases. Instead, an aggressive proxy relationship of this nature is likely to aggravate Australia's relations with its immediate neighbors for years to come and undermine efforts to build genuine collective security mechanisms in the region. Only if Australia can parlay its self-defined role as U.S. deputy into a lever capable of inducing greater active U.S. support for building such mechanisms—a very big "if"—will the Howard Doctrine prove to be a positive contribution to regional peace and security.

CONCLUSION: THE IMPERATIVE OF INTERVENTION

The high visibility Indonesian reign of terror over the people of East Timor, and Indonesia's direct flouting of the U.N.–sponsored referendum, provided strong justification for forceful and immediate action, and for the eventual constitution of InterFET. The imperative of intervention, in terms of the threat to human life and the social fabric of East Timor, was clear.

The potency of this imperative reveals how, in the post–Cold War era, international politics can no longer be easily segregated into high and low spheres, within the former of which only "hard interests" are relevant. Today, overt violations of the human and civil rights of individuals and groups at every level of political organization have become a vital international security issue throughout the world. Balancing justifications for humanitarian international action and respect for national sovereignty now presents the most vexing questions for contemporary international law and for national, regional, and global policy.

The United States, by virtue of its economic, political, and military predominance, will inevitably continue to play a leading role in setting the tone and terms by which critical precedents will be set and international norms will be forged. The United States will set this tone either by its action or by its inaction. For all its choices, the one choice that the United States does not have is to refrain from choosing.

The political clarity of contemporary humanitarian imperatives, in the face of traditional appeals to national interest, highlights an important emerging new feature of international relations: the pivotal role that can be played by civil society armed with new technologies of communication.[8] The presence of non-Indonesian witnesses to events in East Timor, including journalists, activist groups, U.N. officials, and other international citizens, made it impossible to conceal the massacres being directed from Jakarta. Access by independent eyewitnesses to instantaneous communication media—cell phones, satellite transmissions, Internet-based networking—made it possible to generate widespread public awareness and conviction in "realtime": that is, while such awareness could still make a difference. Appeals to abstract conceptions of security could not stand up to the force of sheer recognition of the underlying human realities. Public opinion forced the hands of the leaders of the great powers, who would have preferred to turn a blind eye to these realities and walk away from their consequences. Public opinion also had its impact on the political imperatives driving the leaders of medium and small powers such as Australia, but only belatedly and in a way that led to a militarized rearguard action attempting to retrieve a situation already out of control.

In this sense, the crisis in East Timor is the archetype of the future. As international crises rooted in humanitarian concerns increasingly arise, the potential grows for concerned individuals to play ever-greater roles in bringing brutal realities to international attention. For those committed both to expanded definitions of human rights and an end to violence, the challenge is to devise solutions that will replace hegemonic unilateralism with cooperative efforts to build peace and justice led by regional groups and the United Nations.

Meanwhile, capable powers must be prepared to react very rapidly in ways that maximize international support if they are to satisfy both the humanitarian imperatives and security challenges such crises will pose. The United States, in particular, can no longer simply trade off its commitment to promoting human rights for maintenance of its own security. As noted above, arguments concerning the supremacy of U.S. national interests over human rights have historically often been shallow, specious, and deceitful. At the same time, the limited efficacy of precipitous unilateral U.S. actions should caution against a wholesale embrace of overarching humanitarian imperatives as a singular precept of U.S. foreign policy. If the United States is to exercise effective leadership, it will need not only to avoid trite "realist" excuses for inaction, but also withstand emotive pressure to act solely on grounds of human rights concerns. Neither "realist" definitions of national security nor humanitarian imperatives alone are sufficient guides to the complex realities and choices of the post–Cold War world. Rather, these priorities are now inextricable elements of a common problem.

This new intertwining of security and human rights concerns is evident in the case of East Timor and will be the case often in the future. The United States must be prepared to be effective and responsible in its inevitable leadership role as future international crises based on humanitarian concerns arise—as they inevitably will. Only careful and fully considered approaches that eschew both "realist" and "liberal" unilateralist impulses, and that maximize support by regional and global partners, are likely to produce timely and effective action that satisfies both the humanitarian and security imperatives posed by such crises. Unfortunately, tens of thousands of East Timorese have had to pay with their lives for this lesson to be learned.[9]

NOTES

Lyuba Zarsky, Tim Savage, and Jason Hunter contributed indispensably to the conception and argument of this article.

1. John Noer and David Gregory, *Chokepoints: Maritime Economic Concerns in Southeast Asia* (Washington, D.C.: Center for Naval Analyses, National Defense University Press, 1996.)

2. See H. Kristensen, *U.S. Strategic Nuclear Reform in the 1990s,* Nautilus Institute Nuclear Policy Project Paper, <http://www.nautilus.org/nukepolicy/USA/StratRef.html>, March 2000.

3. See D. Held, A. McGrew, D. Goldblatt, J. Perraton, "The Expanding Reach of Organized Violence," in *Global Transformations, Politics, Economics and Culture* (Stanford, Calif.: Stanford University Press, 1999), 87–148.

4. See Walden Bello, "East Timor: An ASEAN-U.N. Solution," NAPSNet Special Report 10, 10 September 1999 <http://www.nautilus.org/napsnet/sr/East_Timor/index.-html>.

5. Richard Tanter, "The East Timor Disaster," NAPSNet Special Report 1, 7 September 1999 <http://www.nautilus.org/napsnet/sr/East_Timor/index.html>.

6. James Cotton, "East Timor and Australia: Twenty-five Years of the Policy Debate," NAPSNet Special Report 18, 21 September 1999 <http://www.nautilus.org/napsnet/sr/East Timor/index.html>.

7. This announcement included the revelation that Howard had written to Habibie on 19 December 1998, urging support for this course of action.

8. See the essays online at <http://www.infoaxioms.org>, a study site maintained by the Nautilus Institute on the impact of new information technology on U.S. foreign policy making.

9. The Nautilus Institute has responded to the urgent crisis in East Timor by compiling unique assessments and analyses by key experts from throughout the world, in an effort to promote and broaden debate over appropriate responses to the crisis. Many of these analyses were produced specifically for the Nautilus Institute. Between September 7 and October 25, 1999, the Nautilus Institute distributed over a dozen analyses, press releases, and media overviews through the Northeast Asia Peace and Security Network (NAPSNet); links to this material can be found online at <http://www.nautilus.org/napsnet/sr/East_Timor/index.html>. The institute will continue to solicit and disseminate analyses and sponsor related activities as long as the crisis continues. We welcome all responses to this endeavor.

Part IV

East Timor and Indonesia

13

East Timor and the Crisis of the Indonesian Intelligence State

Richard Tanter

Hours before the People's Consultative Assembly (MPR) elected Abdurrahman Wahid as Indonesia's fourth president on October 20, 1999, it voted to revoke East Timor's constitutional status as the twenty-seventh province of Indonesia. The coincidence of these two events—the formal acknowledgment of the end of the murderous folly of Indonesia's colonial project in East Timor, and the formal end of the New Order after the first fair elections in more than four decades—provides a fitting symbol of the close connection between East Timor and the crisis of the Indonesian state.

The two events were closely related: B. J. Habibie's responsibility for the "loss" of East Timor in the eyes of most MPR members rendered him finally unelectable, whatever other liabilities may have made him unpalatable to Indonesian power brokers and voters. Habibie's extraordinary decision in January 1999 to recognize the possibility of self-determination was the turning point in the gathering momentum propelling East Timor toward independence. Whether Habibie believed a ballot would safely yield a clear majority for Indonesia, whether he bowed to the pressures of Indonesia's international financial donors, or whether he believed it was time to cut the country's losses in a hopeless and debilitating cause and allow the East Timorese a path to independence, is not clear. What is clear is that Habibie's use of his limited personal authority broke the stalemate that had long prevailed in East Timor. Indonesia could not defeat Timorese nationalism, but neither had the East Timorese resistance found means to defeat the colonial invaders.

Indonesia's colonization of East Timor, throughout its quarter century history, was always an expression of the fundamental character of New Order Indonesia under President Suharto. Three aspects of the regime's character are particularly important in explaining Indonesia's long hold on East Timor.

- The dominance of the militarized Indonesian state by intelligence organizations whose normal operating procedures included planned terror, murder, and intimidation of differing population groups, large and small, and political surveillance of virtually the entire population
- A rentier political economy in which the bulk of state revenues for three decades was derived from oil tax revenues and foreign aid
- The legitimation, together with financial and military support for the regime, by the United States and other powers

This chapter begins by asking how Indonesia was able to sustain its illegal invasion of East Timor for almost a quarter of a century in the face of a multitude of U.N. condemnations; and how Suharto was able to rule Indonesia for more three decades without significant domestic legitimacy and with reliance on massive state violence towards the Indonesian citizenry. This discussion concentrates on the political and economic characteristics of the Indonesian rentier-militarist state that made Suharto's rule viable, and outlines the connections between the erosion of those characteristics, the fall of Suharto, and the collapse of Jakarta's rule in East Timor. The chapter next sketches the role of Indonesian intelligence organizations and special forces in the last phase of Indonesia's occupation of East Timor; it then outlines the role of surveillance and terror in New Order Indonesia and introduces the institutions that make up the Indonesian intelligence state. Finally, it briefly assesses the possible future of the Indonesian intelligence state under the Wahid administration.

THE END OF THE EAST TIMOR OPERATION

The worldwide reaction to the massive killings in East Timor following the U.N.–directed ballot on August 30, 1999, building on pressures on Indonesia throughout the preceding year to end its military occupation of East Timor, severely limited the options of the Indonesian military and state leaders.

The Indonesian military and political presence in East Timor had been changing in character for some years, partly in response to a shift in the locus of East Timorese resistance from guerrilla activities in the mountains to urban protests by younger people, particularly educated youth. A long-term policy of using East Timorese to fight East Timorese had led to the expansion of a confusing array of uniformed civilian auxiliary "self-defense forces," popularly called militia.[1] But the most important Indonesian military development in the last years of the East Timor occupation was a shift to a far greater reliance on the use of nonregular troops.[2]

Figure 13.1   Indonesian soldiers and Timorese dancer on the parade ground in the front of the governor's residence in Dili. Courtesy: Steve Cox.

Special Forces (*Kopassus*) units, together with various thugs (*preman*) and black-clothed goons, sometimes from the armed forces, sometimes not ("ninjas"), operated both overtly and covertly, emphasizing the combination of terror and tactical intelligence drawn from a network of military surveillance and spies penetrating most of the society. Some of the militia groupings operating in 1999 had their roots as far back as the early 1980s, but most seem to have been constructed in the last two years of Indonesian rule.[3]

In late 1998 and early 1999, the number of militia groups, and the pace and scale of terrorist militia activities supported by the Indonesian military, increased considerably. These groups were in some cases simply a re-formation under a new name of preexisting groups under their old leadership, but many were new. Large numbers of weapons were provided from sources within the Indonesian military (TNI), and militia members were offered payment to participate. Young men who did not accept an invitation to join were often subject to violent intimidation.[4]

This was the background to the last phase of Indonesian rule in East Timor, headed by Major General Zacky Anwar Makarim, which began immediately after Habibie's January 27 announcement of a referendum.[5] Anwar's appointment by Wiranto as security advisor to the Indonesian team preparing for the Popular Consultation and responsible for liaising with UNAMET shocked many U.N. officials, who were already well aware of the weaknesses of the May 5 Agreements between Portugal, Indonesia, and the United Nations. Anwar, an old East Timor intelligence hand in the Indonesian military, had been head of army intelligence at the time of the Santa Cruz massacre, and until three weeks before Habibie's announcement had been head of the Armed Forces Intelligence Agency (BIA/ *Bais*).[6] However, the United Nations was effectively powerless to deal with the problem. While no longer formally holding an intelligence position, Anwar's role as the principal coordinator of the unfolding program of terror was unchanged.[7]

The Indonesian Commission of Inquiry into Violations of Human Rights in East Timor (KPP-HAM) had no doubt that the long-term campaign against independence from the time of Habibie's announcement in January constituted deliberate crimes against humanity that "included systematic and mass murder; extensive destruction; enslavement; forced deportations and displacement; and other inhumane acts committed against the civilian population." These crimes, the commission concluded, were planned and carried out by the Indonesian military and police forces, together with the militia forces they created and controlled.[8]

Many of the details of the 1999 Indonesian campaign led by the intelligence agencies against East Timorese independence remain unclear, but the broad outlines and the roles of the major players are now known. The most difficult aspect to grasp is the rationale for the final wave of terror that followed the announcement on September 4 of the results of the Popular Consultation. To many observers, it seemed to have no rational purpose whatsoever, yet there was a purpose to all of the violence. The basis of the intelligence plan was at all times to maintain Indonesian rule by one of three strategies. The first strategy was to prevent the Popular Consultation from taking place. Should that strategy fail, the second was to use terror to ensure that the Popular Consultation resulted in a vote for integration. And finally, in the event of a decisive vote for independence, the strategy was to nullify the effects of the vote by creating a civil war situation characterized by mass evacuation and street fighting that would both call the fairness of the ballot into question and dampen the ardor of the United Nations to intervene more effectively. This Indonesian intelligence plan came remarkably close to success.

OBJECTIVES OF PREBALLOT VIOLENCE

Before the referendum, orchestrated violence could contribute in a number of ways to the Indonesian objective of either preventing the ballot from taking place, or, failing that, terrorizing the population to assure majority support for integration. First, the militia could be used to establish in the minds of outside observers the idea that there were two roughly balanced political forces inside East Timor, pro- and anti-Indonesian. This would suggest a "civil war" situation rather than overwhelmingly popular resistance to colonial invasion. Second, violence would create an atmosphere inimical to the execution of the plan for a U.N. ballot, and subsequently give grounds for its delay.

Third, and most important, violence could directly and indirectly destroy the political base of support for the independence option. Known proindependence East Timorese were attacked, tortured, and killed in large numbers between Habibie's announcement and the U.N. ballot. The fear generated by these usually-public murders was then amplified by apparently random killings of ordinary East Timorese, especially those who refused to indicate their support for autonomy by displaying Indonesian flags.

OBJECTIVES OF THE POSTBALLOT VIOLENCE

The negotiations leading to the May 5 Agreements jolted the Indonesian side into planning on the assumption that the ballot would at some stage go ahead and that there might be a negative result. Documentary evidence remains contested, but at least two documents from this period indicate the scale of planning for such an outcome: the so-called Garnadi report to Coordinating Minister of Politics and Security, Feisal Tanjung,[9] and a May 5 order from the army chief of staff to the Dili commander.[10] Both documents recommended mass evacuations, destruction of facilities in the wake of the withdrawal, and "repressive/coercive measures." In the event of a vote for independence, other documents indicate that a month before the ballot, Indonesian police in East Timor were preparing for the voluntary and forced evacuation of hundreds of thousands of East Timorese to West Timor.[11]

After the announcement of the results of the U.N. ballot, steps were taken to allow Indonesia to ignore its commitments under the May 5 Agreements to assure a transition to independence. In addition to isolating East Timor by intimidating U.N. staff and foreign media into evacuating, the postballot violence had three main components.

First, following on from the preballot phase, was the organized killing of those capable of providing political and moral leadership in an independent East Timor, including key activists of the National Council of Timorese Resistance (CNRT) and Catholic religious leaders and intellectuals. This continued in East Timor until the arrival of InterFET forces in September.[12]

The second component was the massive forced relocation of at least a major part of the East Timorese population—to "buffer zones" in western East Timor, over the border into West Timor, and even to other parts of Indonesia.[13] Indiscriminate violence was used to terrorize people to leave their homes. At least 250,000 eventually crossed the border to West Timor, mostly unwillingly, to face, in Amnesty International's words in December 1999, "continued risk of threats, intimidation, harassment, extortion, and in some cases, unlawful killing, 'disappearance,' and sexual violence."[14] The implementation of the intelligence plan involved a large-scale coordinated operation by all elements of the Indonesian armed forces.[15]

The third dimension of the postvote operation was the looting and plundering by the militias and TNI forces of anything moveable and the destruction of what remained. Apart from personal enrichment of the looters themselves and their TNI and militia commanders, the motive seems to have been to destroy the very economic foundations of East Timor society. If East Timor was to be left, it would be left with nothing. The looting was an apparently planned combination of removal of valuable capital items and saleable household goods, and wanton vandalism. As one Australian military observer remarked in the town of Suai, "They even ring-barked the trees."

The Indonesian operation in East Timor ended as it began twenty-four years earlier: a tactically competent and strategically bungled terror operation directed by a coven of secretive military intelligence and special forces officers separated for operational purposes from the normal armed forces hierarchy.[16] Tactically, Anwar's operation was appallingly successful: unknown numbers of local proindependence leaders were killed.[17] The loss of so many people with unusual skills of leadership, in a small population that had already lost a quarter of its number to earlier waves of Indonesian aggression, will be very hard to overcome; and the legacy of destruction will pose formidable obstacles to an independent East Timor.

Yet strategically, Anwar's operation turned out to provide the route—at immense cost in human lives to be sure, but nevertheless the route—to independence. Once the CNRT leadership took the painful but essential decision to sit on their hands during the Indonesian terror after the ballot and avoid clashes with the militia and TNI forces, Anwar's objective of portraying the postballot violence in the world media as yet another regrettable civil war in a distant and unimportant country was doomed to fail. In an appalling but quite real sense, the creatures of the Indonesian intelligence state were the agents of East Timorese freedom.

THE INDONESIAN INTELLIGENCE STATE: THREE DECADES OF TERROR AND SURVEILLANCE

The sheer brazenness of the East Timor killing must have brought back to consciousness the great trauma that swept Indonesia in 1965 to 1966. In fact, horrific and distinctive in execution though it was, the level of terror in East Timor in 1999 was not out of the ordinary in Suharto's New Order Indonesia. Three types of terror have been crucial to establishing and maintaining military control of Indonesia since 1965.[18]

First, Suharto's rule was founded on the great killings of 1965 to 1966—the *constitutive terror* of the New Order. Army soldiers, and mainly-Islamic anticommunist groups aided and encouraged by the army killed, between five hundred and eight hundred thousand (and possibly more) in a ten month period following the coup and countercoup of September 30–October 1. With the aid, complicity, and congratulations of Western governments, the Army led a systematic and largely unhidden campaign to kill hundreds of thousands of defenseless alleged communists and Chinese Indonesians. The Communist Party was destroyed, and Sukarno's power shattered. Suharto and his generals came to power; and they, together with their domestic and foreign commercial partners, became incredibly rich. Periodically reminding the population of the "events of 1965," or lamenting the "possibility of a repeat of 1965," has been an extremely effective military tactic, particularly in combination with the repression of the trauma. Until the very last years of Suharto, public discussion of the killings was impossible—the topic was literally unspeakable. It was as if citizens of Germany East and West had been unable to speak of the Holocaust from 1945 until the 1990s, and then only with great caution.[19]

Second, after the worst of the constitutive terror edged back from daily consciousness by the late 1960s, *intermittent targeted terror operations in the center* were important and effective tools of control by the military. After the complete liquidation of the left by 1968, the targets of terror shifted: at different times they became Islamic groups disenchanted with the earthly paradise produced by Islamic cooperation in 1965 to 1966; radical students; criminal gang leaders out of favor with army bosses (the *petrus* killings[20]); and, as industrialization progressed, labor activists organizing outside the stultifying framework of government-controlled unions. While the destruction of particular immediate targets was always the primary goal, an important secondary function was the revivifying of the underlying sense of generalized terror deriving from 1965 to 1966.[21] For example, when military intelligence decided, with President Suharto's explicit support, to break the growing power of uncooperative gang bosses in the cities of Java by simply using military special forces and police to assassinate several thousand alleged criminals in 1983 to 1985, the bodies of the bullet-ridden dead were laid out in public places, or near the homes and workplaces of prominent opponents of the regime.[22]

Third, the standard response to discontent with Jakarta's rule on the edges of the archipelago has been terror: *peripheral terror*. The final phase of the terror in East Timor differed from that of the preceding twenty-four years only in its intensity in a very short time frame, and in the attention given it by the rest of the world. In Aceh and Irian Jaya, militarized responses to local grievances for comparable periods have by and large gone unnoticed. Military control of the media until the last years of the New Order meant that these matters were unreportable in Indonesia. In addition, the very vagueness of people's awareness of "troubles" in the peripheries contributed to the general sense of low-level terror that characterized the population as a whole through most of the Suharto period.[23]

Figure 13.2   This photo of a young boy lighting a candle over unmarked graves on Mount Matebian became the symbol of the Oan Kiak Trust in 1995, which now funds the education of more than 150 East Timorese orphans. The trust was a cooperative venture between elements of the Australian rock industry, the Timorese Association in Victoria, and the estate of Captain Col Doig, a 2/2nd Australian commando from western Australia who served in Timor during World War II. Courtesy: Ross Bird.

The key institutional apparatus in all of this was the large and well funded network of military and nominally civilian intelligence organizations that make up the Indonesian intelligence state, which was very little affected by the mild and limited democratizing moves of 1998 to 1999, and which remained in place at the beginning of the Wahid presidency.[24] As head of military intelligence, Major General Zacky Anwar Makarim and his successor controlled a network of surveillance that reached down from TNI headquarters in Jakarta, through every layer of military administration to every village and city neighborhood in the country. The surveillance apparatus was and remains geared to providing a fine-grained observation of the nation as a whole according to need.

Coupled to the surveillance capacities of BIA/*Bais*, every regional military command, and every layer beneath it, has an intelligence section that not only coordinates surveillance requirements but has a capacity and a mandate to take whatever actions are deemed necessary. Special forces such as the *Kopassus* red berets have their own teams and networks and can co-opt regional military command resources. The intelligence task forces that have terrorized the East Timorese have their parallels in every other area of Indonesia of concern to the military.

Beyond the military intelligence hierarchy under *Bais* control, nominally civilian organizations such as Bakin (the State Intelligence Coordinating Agency) or the intelligence division of the attorney general's department or the intelligence division of the highly militarized national police all play a key part in the maintenance of the system of surveillance and repression. Three decades of a legal system under military direction and a cowed and co-opted legislature provide the last elements of the picture.

THE POLITICAL ECONOMY OF THE RENTIER-MILITARIST STATE

Looking back at the horrors of Suharto's rule from 1966 to 1998, and the occupation of East Timor from 1975 to 1999, it may be hard to imagine how the East Timorese endured so long. How was it possible for the Indonesian state to exercise such extraordinary violence towards the people of East Timor and their own people for such a long period of time? The argument that follows here focuses on one particular aspect of the New Order's political economy: the rentier-militarist state and its external preconditions.[25] In the case of Indonesian politics in the New Order period, external strategic and economic factors interacted to set the limits of possibility of domestic politics. This was true both in allowing Suharto and the armed forces to rule the country for more than thirty years and in framing the manner in which Suharto lost power.

New Order Indonesia was essentially a rentier economy in two quite distinct senses: one domesticly and one externally oriented. First, its domestic political economy was dominated by the allocation of government-controlled economic resources largely on the basis of direct and indirect access to government officials who were mostly senior military officers. In this domestic sense of rentier economy, the dominant factor in capital accumulation came not from productive investment (manufactures, increased agricultural productivity, value-added processing of minerals and other natural resources, etc.), but from appropriation of a portion of the economic surplus by a group of rentiers. Army officers used military resources for private benefit; state officials "rented" the prerogatives of office to private partners; privileged individuals derived income from monopoly control over the imports of particular goods or services or from monopolistic license to exploit natural resources; and so on.[26] Of course, without the unprecedented mobilization of state violence available to the Suharto government, the domestic rentier economy would not have been sustainable.

The second rentier characteristic of New Order Indonesia, and the one that was the prerequisite of Suharto's long power and decline, was Indonesia's location in the international division of labor. New Order Indonesia was a rentier state in this *externally oriented* sense insofar as the great bulk of both national income and state revenue for all but the first few years of the New Order period was derived from oil tax revenues and foreign aid. "For all practical purposes one can consider the oil revenues almost as a free gift from nature or as a grant from foreign sources."[27] Foreign aid is also, for the most part, a "rent" in much the same way: a rental payment to the recipient country for a political service based on its political or geo-strategic value to the donor country.[28]

This was the key to Suharto's political longevity. A government that can expand its activities without resorting to heavy taxation acquires an independence from the people seldom found in other countries. In political terms, the power of government to bribe pressure groups or coerce dissidents will be greater than otherwise. The peculiar quality of rentier-militarist regimes, understood in this externally oriented sense, is their relative capacity to ignore, or at least postpone, cultivation of domestic support and the class compromises that that process requires. The legitimation that finally mattered in New Order Indonesia was that of the army as the dominant power center, and then the opinion of state managers in Washington and Tokyo.

EAST TIMOR AND THE UNDERMINING OF RENTIER-MILITARIZATION

By the same token, rentier-militarization as a form of state power is highly vulnerable. Not only does the stoppage of external rents severely damage finances, but it almost immediately provokes a systemic political crisis. By the early 1990s at least, very important elements of the external supports for the rentier-militarist state were in disarray. The interests of the United States had changed in two ways in relation to Indonesia. On the one hand, the end of the Cold War meant that the United States no longer felt preoccupied with a global struggle to contain communism in the shape of the Soviet Union and China, nor imperiled by popu-

lar movements elsewhere. Communism was a nonexistent political force in Indonesia after the late 1960s. On the other hand, the U.S. strategic economic preoc-
cupation from the Reagan administration onwards with establishing and
expanding a framework for highly mobile U.S. capital and unrestricted investment rights lowered the U.S. tolerance for the baroque patronage structure that it
had allowed to develop around President Suharto in Indonesia. Through means
both direct and indirect, the United States sought a dismantling of much of the
domestic aspects of the rentier state (e.g. through deregulation of import controls
and regularization of financial institutions) and encouraged the foundation of an
alternative—and more familiar—pattern of capital accumulation rooted in
export-oriented industrialization with considerably expanded foreign investment.[29]

The "successes" of rentier-militarization transformed Indonesian society in
complex ways and in part generated social forces inimical to its continuation.
This was evident in 1999 in the complexity of sources of support for political
parties other than the ruling *Golkar* party. Not only were there television images
of young stockbrokers seen demonstrating for Megawati Sukarnoputri, but Abdurrahman Wahid's Party of National Awakening (PKB) was clearly drawing a
considerable amount of its support from nominally "conservative" but economically distressed Islamic voters who were responding to Wahid's message of social
justice.

Yet Indonesia's economic growth was built on institutional sand. The currency
crises of 1998 and their fiscal consequences burst upon the New Order state like
a tidal wave, taking Suharto with it. Foreign aid at levels unprecedented even
under the New Order was required to maintain the Indonesian state in temporary
solvency and to prevent complete social and political breakdown. More than $40
billion in foreign loans coordinated by the International Monetary Fund (IMF)
through 1998 to 1999 brought direct, detailed, and stringent conditions on Indonesian budgetary and financial policy—with devastating economic, social, and
political effects.

Finally, it was precisely the dependence of the New Order on external legitimation and external sources of state revenue that ultimately undermined the autonomy of the military in East Timor. This applied both to the decision to allow
self-determination in East Timor and then crucially in ending the terror of September 1999. During the 1990s East Timor had turned Indonesia into something
approaching a pariah state. The key institutional shift—Habibie's announcement
that he would consider a ballot for independence—did not flow from personal
fickleness or idiosyncratic motives. The United States had shifted its position on
East Timor some time previously, viewing Indonesia's involvement in East
Timor as an expensive mistake in which the United States had no strategic
stake.[30] Coordinating Minister for Economic Affairs Ginanjar Kartasasmita, attending an economic summit in Switzerland with key rich nations at the time of
Habibie's "shock" announcement, made clear the crucial background. East
Timor, he said, had simply become too expensive for Indonesia. The major credi-

tors of the New Order, led by the United States and Japan, simply were no longer prepared to support Indonesia over East Timor either financially or politically. The collapse in external preconditions for rentier-militarization did not determine the outcome of the issue, but it did set the limits of possibility.

This erosion of the external preconditions of rentier-militarization also determined the final ending of the militia terror in East Timor immediately following the August 30 ballot. There were, in practical terms, no domestic Indonesian political forces willing and able to bring the terror under control. Habibie was quite without authority vis-a-vis the military. The terror was only stopped in response to remarkably blunt public threats from President Clinton and Secretary of Defense William Cohen to suspend IMF and other loans to Indonesia immediately, unless Indonesia agreed to accept the admission of foreign peacekeeping forces.[31] To be sure, Clinton only acted after considerable and costly delay, in the face of unexpected global mass media attention and mobilization of public opinion in the United States. Yet it was the peculiar character of Indonesia's political economy that made the threat to the world's fourth largest country credible and effective and opened the last door for East Timor's independence.

THE INDONESIAN INTELLIGENCE STATE UNDER AN ELECTED PRESIDENT

With an astonishingly small number of honorable exceptions (such as courageous but small groups like KIPER and Solidamor), Indonesian political groups and intellectuals remained unsympathetic toward East Timor independence until the very end. Intellectuals were by and large paralyzed by the nationalism that saturates Indonesian political thinking. The basic fact of Indonesian colonial occupation was simply unrecognized. The colonial project was often dismissed or justified by saying that even if there were gross abuses of human rights in East Timor, they were nothing different from what was happening elsewhere in the nation. "First democracy, then Timor." Moral questions aside, the issue of Indonesian militarization and the Timor colonial project were seen as having nothing to do with each other.

Yet there is a sense in which East Timor brought down the New Order. Indonesia's semipariah status over East Timor greatly magnified the degree of dependence on creditors when the currency crisis arrived. Habibie's final failure to receive a vote of approbation in the MPR on October 20 because of his Timor policy put an end to the plan, in place from the day of Suharto's resignation in 1998, to continue the New Order structure in a slightly refurbished guise. The very visibility of the postballot violence in Timor placed the election of a new president and the construction of a new cabinet in an entirely different framework from what could otherwise have been expected. This was particularly so outside the country, but also to a surprising degree within Indonesia itself.

The key questions now are first whether the Indonesian domestic intelligence apparatus will survive the change of presidency; and second, if it does, whether its capacities will be diminished.

The most urgent requirement is obvious from the East Timor experience: an end to the use of large-scale planned killing, violent intimidation, and invasive surveillance as a normal tool of Indonesian politics.

Serious reform of the Indonesian intelligence state to achieve such an end would involve substantial positive steps, including: drastic revision of the new National Security Law passed (but not signed into law) in the last days of Habibie's presidency; repudiation of the armed forces' self-proclaimed political role;[32] abolition of the military's role in supervision of civil administration at all levels, in practice as well as in theory; abolition of the army's territorial commands, and withdrawal of territorial forces from policing activities and surveillance of local populations; abolition of the armed forces and army Territorial Affairs staff; complete separation of the national police from the Ministry of Defense and Security; constitutional revision to ensure permanent subordination of the armed forces to elected civilian leadership; reevaluation of the military legal code, and strict application of provisions bearing on illegal activities involving violence towards civilians, including prosecution under military law of officers failing to control subordinates; increasing the powers and resources of the National Human Rights Commission; upgrading of the autonomy and capacities of the judicial system to implement the law; severing of nonformal links between the attorney-general's department and the military (e.g. military intelligence training of civil servants in intelligence affairs); and legislation to ensure parliamentary oversight of military activities and budgetary procedures in general, and the activities of military and civilian intelligence agencies in particular.

The willingness and ability of the new Indonesian president and parliament to pursue such reforms remains to be seen. But the power of the intelligence state has already been diminished, for at least four reasons.

Despite the considerable remaining privatized and extrabudgetary financial resources available to the Indonesian military, the combination of economic regularization and the economic crisis of recent years have cut into the money needed for unaudited and unsupervised black operations. As the social effects of the economic crisis deepen, the demands on government resources will be greater and the available resources even smaller.

Furthermore, a key resource for effective terror is public belief in the omnipresence and omniscience of the intelligence organizations. Powerful as they may be, this is not the case in Indonesia following the democracy movement and fall of Suharto in 1998 to 1999. The beginnings of scrutiny of the military in general that has come with the surge in press and civil freedoms in the past years has somewhat diminished the sense of omnipotence of the intelligence apparatus. Indonesia is far from a democratic society, but it has moved well beyond the repression at the height of the New Order.

The military—and intelligence organizations in particular—rarely acted alone in their political interventions. Often they worked with or through various political organizations and community groups, many of which later came to resent the way they had been used. The allied or manipulated groups varied over time and according to need. For example, in the early New Order period, anti-Sukarno student groups, and Chinese and Catholic groups in addition to the huge Islamic organizations, played a key role in breaking the power of Sukarno and the Left. These groups provided considerable resources—material, moral, and political—to sustain and cloak black operations. None of these groupings is willing or able to provide such resources now. Indonesian society today, after more than thirty years of rapid capitalist transformation, is of course very different from what it was in 1965, but the slow decline of the New Order was characterized by an ebbing in the political resources available to President Suharto, and in a comparable though lesser fashion, the intelligence organizations.

Finally, the military itself is not a monolithic organization with an unchanging organizational mission and political character. Most analyses of the last years of the Suharto period concentrated on perceived "nationalist" or pro-Suharto factions as against those of a more seriously Islamic persuasion, and that hardy perennial of Indonesian military analysis: vague assertions of differences amongst the generations of military academy classes.

Two considerations deriving from the military's stated mission may decide the future of the intelligence state, though in opposite directions. On the one hand, the Indonesian military, for all its five decades of domestic preoccupations, is also an outward-looking military organization charged with the defense of the republic against external as well as internal threats. The strategic environment of East and Southeast Asia is becoming considerably more unstable than it has been for many years. In particular, the Indonesian military is concerned with the continuing low-level/high-stakes conflict over the oil-rich Spratley Islands group. This is especially the case given the regional escalation in sophisticated (and expensive) weapons platforms and C^3I capacities over the past decade. The demand to meet potential external threats creates a degree of professional pressure for regularization of military organizational procedures. This is hardly a democratizing pressure in itself, and the professionalization of intelligence organizations under Murdani did nothing to diminish their capacity for brutality.[33] Yet it is also true that the Indonesian intelligence state was structured first and foremost around the army's dominance of the state, and in particular by the system of comprehensive surveillance and capacity to intervene in the community that was inherent in the army's territorial command system.

The primary object of the intelligence apparatus's attention in recent years, East Timor and Aceh apart, has been control of labor organization in what had been, until the currency and financial crisis, the rapidly expanding industrial sector. Sooner or later, the social effects of the economic and fiscal crisis will confront the new government of Indonesia. A Wahid presidency, hostage to some unknown degree to the military and laboring under the restraints of enormous debt and IMF–approved budgets, will almost certainly face growing social unrest. A civilian leadership does not by itself diminish the likelihood of militarized responses to domestic social and political crisis—and that has been the specialty of the Indonesian intelligence state. But if the early reforms of the military initiated by President Wahid can be sustained and built upon, and the rule of law buttressed, it may be that a democratic Indonesia could respond to social crisis without terror.

NOTES

I am grateful to David Bourchier, Angus McIntyre, Mark Selden, Steve Shalom, Sylvia Tiwon, and Gerry van Klinken for helpful comments on earlier drafts.

1. These included *Wanra (Perlawanan Rakyat,* People's Resistance), *Ratih (Rakyat Terlatih,* Trained Populace), and *Kamra (Keamanan Rakyat,* People's Security). These militia units were not unique to East Timor, but developed a special significance there in the colonial context. See Robert Lowry, *The Armed Forces of Indonesia* (Sydney: Allen and Unwin, 1997), 110–12.

2. Douglas Kammen, "Notes on the Transformation of the East Timor Military Command and Its Implications for Indonesia," *Indonesia,* 67 (April 1999): 75.

3. See Peter Bartu and Helene van Klinken in this book, and the annotated listing of militia groups active in mid-1999 in East Timor International Support Center, *Indonesia's Death Squads: Getting Away With Murder—A Chronology of Indonesian Military Sponsored Paramilitary and Militia Atrocities in East Timor from November 1998 to May 1999* (Darwin: ETISC Occasional Paper No. 2, May 1999), 9–11.

4. See for example, Marian Wilkinson, "Justice Must Be Done," *Sydney Morning Herald,* 29 January 2000; Lindsay Murdoch, "Soares Sanctioned Murder: Militia Chief," *Sydney Morning Herald,* 11 February 2000.

5. This very brief account of BIA and *Kopassus* activities in 1998 to 1999 draws on three important sources: "Indonesia's Dirty War in East Timor, *Tapol Bulletin,* 7 June 1999, <http://www.gn.apc.org/tapol>; East Timor Observatory, *Operasi Sapu Jagad —Indonesian Military's Plan to Disrupt Independence,* Comissno para os Direitos do Pauve Maubere, Ref: FA 10-1999/10/21eng, 28 October 1999; and the reports of the East Timor International Support Center (ETISC), including *Indonesia's Death Squads,* and *The Systematic Annihilation of the East Timorese Nation* (Darwin: ETSIC Occasional Paper No. 3, 15 September 1999), <http://www.easttimor.com/downloads/paper_3.doc>. *Operasi Sapu Jagad* (Operation Clean Sweep) was the name apparently given to at least the first part of the 1999 operation.

6. Somewhat confusingly, Anwar's successor as head of BIA, Major General Tyasno Sudarto, changed the organization's name to *Bais* (Strategic Intelligence Agency). This was almost the same as its original name under its founder, Benny Murdani, when the organization was called *Bais* ABRI.

7. Anwar was appointed formally as head of security for the Indonesian liaison team with UNAMET at a time when his military role was unclear. He was removed as head of

Bais on 5 January 1999, and Habibie's announcement was three weeks later, on 27 January. (*Korem 164/Wira Dharma*).

8. "Executive Summary of Report on Human Rights Violations in East Timor," Commission for Human Rights Violation in East Timor (KPP-HAM) established by the National Human Rights Commission (Komnasham), 22 September 1999, <http://www.east-timor.com/archives/1465.htm>.

9. The "Garnadi report" was a memorandum (Number: M.53/Tim P4-OKTT/7/1999) written on 3 July 1999 by retired Brigadier General H.R. Garnadi, Secretary of P4OKP, Assistant Coordinating Minister I/Home Affairs, with the heading: "Subject: General Assessment if Option I loses." Although the authenticity of the document was challenged, the KPP-HAM accepted its authenticity. See "Team: Document on Timor Burning Valid," *Indonesian Observer*, 29 December 1999, and "Former Minister Rejects E. Timor Carnage Plan," *Indonesian Observer*, 14 January 2000.

10. See Richard Lloyd Parry, "How Jakarta's Generals Planned the Campaign of Terror in East Timor," *The Independent*, 5 February 2000, 15.

11. Parry, "How Jakarta's Generals Planned."

12. See the important chronological documentation of militia and TNI killings from late 1998 to September 1999 published by the Darwin-based ETISC, available at <http://www.easttimor.com/etisc_documents/etisc_documents.htm>. For details of the deaths of priests and nuns in Dili and Suai after the U.N. ballot, see ETISC, *Systematic Annihilation of the East Timorese Nation*.

13. Letter from NGOs (nongovernmental organizations) to President Clinton, 27 January 2000, <http://www.etan.org/news/2000a/01ngo.htm>.

14. Amnesty International, "No End to the Crisis for East Timorese Refugees," Report—ASA 21/208/99, December 1999, <http://www.amnesty.org/ailib/aipub/1999/ASA/32120899.htm>

15. Indonesian police and TNI plans included the evacuation of pro-Indonesian Timorese—especially those who had worked for or with the Indonesian government and the military, and their families. The proportions of "willing" and "coerced" evacuees is unclear, but in January, foreign observers in camps in West Timor estimated that roughly one-third of the refugees in these camps at that time were reluctant to return because of fears arising from their Indonesian government connections in the past.

16. Zacky Anwar, the director of terror operations in East Timor in 1999, in fact combined special forces and intelligence backgrounds in a way characteristic of many of those in senior positions in East Timor in the 1990s. Graduating from the ABRI Military Academy in 1971, Anwar served as an intelligence officer of RPKAD/Kopassandha (two Special Forces precursors of *Kopassus*), including at least three operations in Irian Jaya against the OPM (*Organisasi Papua Merdeka*, Free Papua Movement). Six years with *Kopassus* in East Timor were followed by increasingly senior appointments in intelligence staff positions throughout the 1990s. Other officers with long Timor experience, with comparable backgrounds, especially in *Kopassus* intelligence roles, involved in the last phases of the East Timor operations include Brigadier General Mahidi Simbolon, chief of staff of *Kodam* (Regional Command) IX/Udayana, which controlled East Timor; Brigadier General Amirul Isnaeni, Deputy Martial Law Commander East Timor; and Major General Sjafrie Sjamsoeddin, long-time associate of Anwar's, sent to East Timor immediately following the August 30 ballot.

17. See discussion in Tanter, Selden, and Shalom, "East Timor Faces the Future," in this volume.

18. See Richard Tanter, "The Totalitarian Ambition: The Indonesian Intelligence and Security Apparatus," in *State and Society in Contemporary Indonesia*, ed. Arief Budiman (Clayton, Victoria: Centre of Southeast Asian Studies, Monash University, 1991), 215–88, and Richard Tanter, "Intelligence Agencies and Third World Militarization: A Case Study of Indonesia," Ph.D. dissertation, Monash University, 1992.

19. See Robert Cribb, ed., *The Indonesian Killings of 1965–66: Studies from Java and Bali* (Clayton, Victoria: Centre of Southeast Asian Studies, Monash University, 1990), especially Cribb's introduction.

20. On the *petrus* killings see John Pemberton, *On the Subject of "Java,"* (Ithaca, N.Y.: Cornell University Press, 1994), 311–18; James T. Siegel, *A New Criminal Type in Jakarta: Counter-Revolution Today* (Durham, N.C.: Duke University Press, 1998); and Joshua Barker, "State of Fear: Controlling the Criminal Contagion in Suharto's New Order," *Indonesia*, 66 (1998). The term *petrus* was an acronym from the Indonesian words for "mysterious killers" *(penembak misterius)* or "mysterious killings *(penembakan misterius).* In his memoirs, Suharto proudly acknowledged responsibility for the campaign: *Soeharto: Pikiran, Ucapan, dan Tindakan Saya—Otobiografi*, seperti dipaparkan kepada *G.Dwipayana and Ramadan K.H.* (Jakarta: Citra Lamtoro Gung Persada, 1989), 389–91.

21. Van Klinken notes that the military has been quite open about the use of "menacing enemy images." Asked in March 1996 about mysterious "organizations without form" *(organisasi tanpa bentuk: OTB)*, thought likely to be intelligence provocation fronts, Lieutenant General Syarwan Hamid, newly appointed ABRI chief of social and political affairs, commented: "That in fact is our method of building up security. With a small capability, we hope our security efforts can be preventive and early. That is the most effective way to build stability. We spread vigilance, if necessary to every layer of society so they, too, are careful. . . . How many soldiers do you have? Just five hundred thousand people. Yet we have a territory that stretches from Sabang to Merauke. That's from Portugal to the middle of the Soviet Union. The budget for security per square kilometer in Indonesia is extremely low. With that we have to build security using effective methods. Society must participate." *(Gatra, 30 March 1996), in Gerry van Klinken, "Will the Next Indonesian Succession Be Violent?" Australian Journal of International Affairs 11, no. 3 (1997): 359.

22. Tanter, *Intelligence Agencies*, chapters 11–12.

23. On Aceh, see Gerry van Klinken's chapter in this volume, and Sylvia Tiwon, "From East Timor to Aceh: The Disintegration of Indonesia?" *Bulletin of Concerned Asian Scholars* 32, nos. 1–2 (January–June 2000): 97–104.

24. Tanter, *Intelligence Agencies,* provides an account of the history of New Order intelligence agencies to the late 1980s. The editors of *Indonesia* highlight two aspects of a subsequent shift: "In the days of Benny Murdani, his powerful *Bais* ABRI (Armed Forces Strategic Intelligence Agency) had within it a special directorate for Timor affairs. This directorate was eliminated in the course of Suharto's replacement of *Bais* by the much weaker contemporary BIA, and his purge of Murdani loyalists. In the absence of an East Timor directorate, control of East Timor affairs fell almost completely into the Old Timor Hands of Prabowo's *Kopassus* clique." "Current Data on the Indonesian Military Elite: January 1, 1998–January 31, 1999," *Indonesia*, 67 (April 1999), 142. However, note that

Zacky Anwar Makarim came to BIA following a substantial career in RPKAD/*Kopassus* operations. In other words, the division between "intelligence" and "special forces" at a general level may be misleading on occasion.

25. Since this argument is to a degree intentionally one-sided, it must always be borne in mind that there is a great deal more left unsaid. The erosion through the late 1980s and 1990s of external support for Indonesian rentier-militarization created the possibility that domestic social forces in opposition to President Suharto could have their full effect. That complex story of transformation in Indonesian domestic politics, including conflicts over economic policy, and conflict within the armed forces and the state bureaucracy, the effects of class transformation, the intersection of religion and class issues, and long-standing center-regional tensions remains to be told.

26. See Richard Robison, *Indonesia: The Rise of Capital* (Sydney: Allen and Unwin/ASAA, 1986).

27. H. Mahdavy, "The Patterns and Problems of Economic Development in Rentier States," in *Studies in the Economic History of the Middle East*, ed. M. A. Cooke (London: Oxford University Press, 1970), 428–29.

28. For more than a quarter of a century the essential pattern was that either oil or aid or both were the national economic base. The yield from corporate taxes on oil rose from 55 percent of central government domestic revenues in 1974 to a high of 71 percent in 1981 before falling to 40 percent between 1986 and 1988. Foreign aid was vital in the first years of the New Order, then fell away somewhat as large oil revenues came on stream, but rose again slowly in the late 1970s and early 1980s. The necessity for foreign aid returned with a vengeance as oil revenues collapsed and debt repayments escalated in the mid-1980s. Aid dependence diminished somewhat in the early 1990s amidst much talk of "Asian dragons," and after the currency crisis of 1998 dependence on foreign aid returned in even more urgent form. See Tanter, "Oil, IGGI and U.S. Hegemony," in Jeffrey Winters, *Power in Motion: Capital Mobility and the Indonesian State* (Ithaca, N.Y.: Cornell University Press, 1996), 98.

29. See in particular the argument in Winters, *Power in Motion*, 142–91.

30. In the early years of the Indonesian invasion the United States saw three direct threats to its interests from an independent East Timor. The first was the possibility that a left-wing Fretilin government would become a "Cuba of the South Pacific." The second was a belief that an independent and radical East Timor would lead to instability in Indonesia especially by providing an alternative model of development. The third perceived risk was that a leftist-controlled East Timor might threaten the U.S. navy's ability to send its submarine forces through the deep Ombai-Wetar Straits north of East Timor. The first fear was always unfounded and based on a Cold War misreading of the character of Fretilin. The second fear was overtaken by the clear fact that it was the invasion of East Timor itself that was destabilizing Indonesia, turning it into a diplomatic near-pariah. The third fear may well have been replaced by Indonesia's insistence that under the legal concepts developed from the Third U.N. Conference on the Law of the Sea, which ended in 1982, Indonesia as an archipelagic state held sovereign right to all "internal waters," including the Ombai-Wetar Straits. In 1988, Indonesia asserted these rights by closing the Sunda and Lombok Straits for a period of days, pointedly demonstrating that other possible submarine routes from the Pacific to the Indian Ocean were no longer to be considered the high seas (Michael Leifer "Indonesia Waives the Rules," *Far Eastern Economic Review*, 5 January 1989).

31. Wade Huntley and Peter Hayes argue that the use of this public and crude financial pressure demonstrated the extent to which the United States had lost influence over the Indonesian military. See Huntley and Hayes in this volume.

32. Major General Agus Wirahadikusumah, assistant for planning to the commander of the armed forces, called for the abolition of the armed forces' dual function, as a step towards reform of the military leadership. See TNI Watch, "Tantangan TNI, cabut dwifungsi," *Xpos*, No.39/II, 31 October–6 November 1999. <http://apchr/murdoch.edu.au/minihub/siarlist/msg04022>. Wirahadikusumah was subsequently appointed by President Wahid to be commander of the Army Strategic Reserve (*Kostrad*).

33. Moreover, highly technically trained naval and air force officers have demonstrated their willingness to use terror for domestic political purposes under other dictatorships— such as in Argentina in the 1970s and 1980s.

14

Big States and Little Independence Movements

Gerry van Klinken

What does the sudden independence of East Timor from Indonesia, won by a combination of global and local forces, tell us about the future of the big postcolonial state of Indonesia? For that matter, we might ask what it tells us about the future of any big postcolonial state (Sudan, Nigeria, Congo), or of imperial states such as the former Soviet Union.

States can be centralist or federalist, or something in between. They can also be democratic or nondemocratic, or something in between. These two simple axes mark out a field upon which we can plot all the states in the world. Rudolph Rummel has shown that one corner of this field, namely the centralist, nondemocratic state, is highly dangerous to its own citizens.[1] The concentrated but unaccountable power that the elites of such states wield has led to death on a scale that far exceeds all domestic or foreign casualties of war in the twentieth century.

For historical reasons, Indonesia became precisely such a centralist, nondemocratic state. But I argue that the independence of East Timor in 1999 is a sign that Indonesia may be about to move (or be moved by forces beyond its control) out of that dangerous corner towards a constellation of dispersed power. The move along the democratic axis has been widely discussed, the move away from centralism much less so. Our inquiry into this latter shift is fraught with difficulties, but it should start from the realization that the centralist, nondemocratic state failed Indonesia's people. A distinct weakening of the center since the resignation of President Suharto in May 1998 provided the opportunity for a broad range of elites to highlight those failings in increasingly urgent ways.

THE COLONIAL LEGACY

Like most postcolonial countries, Indonesia was a state before it was a nation. On December 27, 1949, the newly ascendant Indonesian elite won full control over a state whose territory had been carved out by Dutch imperialism in the last half of the nineteenth century. Unlike say China, Japan, or Korea, which have long statist traditions, the Indonesian state had no historical legitimation of any depth. Much as Sukarno tried to invent a legitimation for it drawn from geography, from shared hopes, or sometimes from the problematic precedent of the premodern trading empires of Majapahit (Java) and Sriwijaya (Sumatra), the Indonesian state remained uncomfortably tied to the alien project of extraction and imperial competition that gave rise to it and defined its borders.

Dutch colonial officials did make some efforts to establish a federal structure during the 1920s and 1930s. They often explained their efforts in the democratizing language that suited the new "ethical" policy towards the natives. But in reality they intended to seize the opportunity to extend centralized bureaucratic rule into the remotest regions.[2] When the Japanese invaded in 1942, the Netherlands Indies was still a centralized, autocratic colonial state.

Those few Indonesians, all from outside the central island of Java, who did support federalist ideas, did so in the conviction that political movements achieve their greatest power not from the "artificial" constructs of socialism or Indonesian nationalism, but from historically rooted identity markers—ethnicity, religion, and tradition.

The 1945 constitution establishes the "unitary" nature of the Republic of Indonesia in its first clause. A late Dutch attempt to impose a federative form on the embryonic republic only made those Indonesians with the greatest say even more determined to defend the unitary form.[3]

Nevertheless, many regional elites had supported the Dutch federal idea in 1949. Arthur Schiller even called the short-lived federal constitution of that year "wholly an Indonesian document."[4] Moreover, the regional revolts of 1956 to 1957 led to a law in 1957 that granted extensive autonomy to restive regions, albeit within the context of the unitary state. An autonomy deal in 1959 did much to ameliorate demands in Aceh, and it still provides the model today for how to deal with provincial unrest. But these concessions were short-lived, as central power regrouped in subsequent years, and the bold experiments of regional autonomy, and for that matter federalism, were gradually withdrawn.[5]

Indonesians in the 1950s not only challenged the centralist aspect of the state they inherited from their colonial masters, but also its nondemocratic aspect. The 1945 constitution had been drafted under a Japanese colonial regime experiencing its death throes, but the 1950 constitution was a liberal document that consciously aimed to move the state away from its Dutch and Japanese colonial origins. Full parliamentary accountability was its central feature. A remarkably free election was held in 1955. However, this experiment failed as well. In 1959, with approval from a military growing impatient with the slow pace of democratic negotiation, President Sukarno restored the "revolutionary" 1945 constitution. Herbert Feith disconsolately summed up the period by entitling his classic study *The Decline of Constitutional Democracy in Indonesia.*[6]

Making concessions to the regions was depicted in the national discourse as a regrettable administrative necessity, in conflict with the centralizing task of "nation-building." While stimulating loyalty to the new state, nation-building completed the colonial emasculation of the once independent social orders between the central state and the individual. It systematically discouraged regional languages, which thus failed to modernize and went into steady decline in the mass media and the schools, if less so in daily life. Throughout the archipelago it co-opted community and religious leaders for the central state. If this was true in the 1950s, it became even more so thereafter.

Late in 1965 the military began actively to seek allies for a short cut to "stability." From this point on, state terror took the place of debate. State-backed militias slaughtered perhaps a half-million people on the grounds that the victims had "betrayed" the state by allegedly backing a supposedly communist coup attempt on September 30, 1965.[7] One and a half million others were arrested, tens of thousands of them with the intention that they never be released. Most of those who survived were freed due to international pressure in 1979, but a few languished in prison until just after Suharto resigned in 1998.

Another two hundred thousand died as part of the purely imperial project of annexing East Timor. Life in the capital, meanwhile, went on as if nothing untoward had occurred.

The final proof, if more was needed, of the callous violence of which the centralist nondemocratic state was capable was the expulsion from their homes by state-backed militias in September 1999 of half a million East Timorese for having wanted out from the Indonesian state that had imposed a reign of terror since 1975.

Such mass slaughter, imprisonment, and terror ought to cast a shadow, not so much over Indonesian society (for being fractious), but over the centralist, nondemocratic state that is its ultimate perpetrator. These horrors take a prominent place on a long list of atrocities committed by such states against their own citizens in the twentieth century.[8]

The creators of Suharto's regime hoped that growth produced by a capitalist economy would reduce demand for political participation, particularly among crucial elites. They were right, because it did for several decades. But when economic growth suddenly plummeted below zero in early 1998, a political crisis ensued that soon brought down Suharto as well. As its political environment suddenly thawed after being frozen for over three decades, Indonesia fell into a turmoil that remains far from resolved.

The Indonesia of 1999 resembles the Indonesia of 1957, when disempowered regions also confronted a centralizing state after a much-anticipated election. As then, so today many hope to reconstruct a democratic culture that is open to negotiation even on the possibility of radically new state arrangements. But others—including the military men who planned the scorched earth destruction of East

Timor after the U.N. ballot—find in this talk of popular empowerment only con-firmation of their deepest fears.

We should place developments in East Timor in the context of an Indonesian state that is tainted by colonial-style repression of the regions by a powerful cen-ter, which has until recently been democratically deficient, and which is now in crisis.

EAST TIMOR AS A CASE OF SECESSION

In a moment I shall argue that the East Timor case from the perspective of the Indonesian state has some characteristics of a secessionist movement. But of course in both historical and legal terms it never belonged to Indonesia at all, and resistance is more properly described as a nationalist reaction to an illegal occupation. International law, and the U.N. consensus, understands East Timor in these terms, and this formed the basis for a strong international campaign for independence. Belatedly, even governments that had welcomed the "integration" of East Timor into Indonesia and asked the United Nations to recognize it too, have been assuming this view.[9] No matter how belated, every government that agrees to uphold the resolutions of the United Nations deserves a round of ap-plause. Indeed, even if it bears partial responsibility for failing to act in ways to stop or mitigate the death, destruction, and forced migration of 1999, the United Nations has been East Timor's savior.

However, the fact that the multinational force went into East Timor only after receiving an "invitation" from the Indonesian government reminds us of an im-portant blind spot in the U.N. worldview. The organization is predicated on the sovereignty of its member states, no matter how cruel those states may be towards their own citizens. The United Nations, therefore (notwithstanding chapter 7 of its charter), has great difficulty tracing problems to a crisis within the state itself.

Even the decolonization agenda, as important as it is for the United Nations, and which benefitted East Timor because it was a Portuguese colony, is hedged about by state-centered limitations. The most important of these is the successor state principle, in which borders once established by the Western colonial powers can never be changed, no matter how reasonable the case for change.

Legally therefore, East Timor is not a case of secession and has nothing to say about the Indonesian state because it never belonged to Indonesia. But sociologi-cally, it shares some characteristics with secessionist movements of the kind seen in several places around Indonesia.[10] The resistance contained both a nationalist aspect, which was at first directed against the Portuguese and which carried on when denied by Indonesia, as well as a politics of resentment, which it shared with many other regional movements around Indonesia. If East Timorese had improved their lives following the 1975 invasion then, in spite of the many dead, we might have seen the resistance decay slowly as the horrors receded into historical memory. Far from fading, however, the resistance grew ever stronger, especially in recent years. This demonstrates that much of its energy had contemporary roots.

Prominent among the constantly refreshed contemporary grievances channeled into the resistance movement was frustration with the (largely unplanned) inundation by aggressive small entrepreneurs from southern Sulawesi, not just in Dili but throughout East Timor. Another was the difficulty educated young East Timorese experienced gaining access to jobs in the civil service, the major employer in this impoverished territory.

One reason for the Indonesian decision to "open up" East Timor early in 1989 (for the first time since the invasion) was to attract private investors. Few came. East Timor always remained the poorest province in Indonesia on many social indicators. Jakarta did throw bucket loads of "development" money at East Timor, but much of it fell into the hands of newcomer contractors, who bounced it straight back to their head offices in Surabaya and Jakarta. Oil exploration activity in the Timor Sea benefited West Timor a little, but East Timor not at all.

East Timor's Carrascalão family are substantial landowners. They have a history of collaboration with Jakarta. Mario Carrascalão was the governor between 1982 and 1992. His brother Manuel was a provincial parliamentarian. Both had assisted the Indonesian invasion force in 1975. When both began to show increasingly open sympathies with the independence cause from about the mid-1990s, Jakarta should have seen it as a threatening omen. By 1999, with the national economy in tatters, almost no elite East Timorese still believed they could get a better deal with Indonesia.

Such grievances are not unique to East Timor. They are widely shared around the periphery of the Indonesian archipelago, where economies often have an extractive, frontier-colonial character with profits siphoned off to interests elsewhere.

Aceh at the western tip of the archipelago also has a lively secessionist movement. Legitimated by the argument that the Dutch should not have annexed the Acehnese sultanate by their 1873 invasion, the movement is fueled by the economic inequalities flaunted by Mobil's gigantic liquid natural gas plant at Lhokseumawe that it opened in the 1970s.[11] At the eastern end of the country, West Papua/Irian Jaya has a movement legitimated by complaints that the 1969 U.N. ballot integrating it with Indonesia was unfair, and fueled by the way non-Papuans dominate every aspect of the economy.[12] In both areas the military has multiplied popular anger by the brutality it practices with impunity.

In Riau province in Sumatra, another major oil-producing area, students have launched an entirely peaceful campaign for the people of the province to get a vastly increased slice of the royalties.[13] Two other major arenas of conflict are not essentially secessionist, but they too can be traced to failures on the part of the state. In West Kalimantan, violence within society may be related to state-protected land grabs by large plantation companies.[14] In Ambon (Maluku) it can be traced to state-protected corruption in making civil service appointments.[15] (We return to Aceh and Maluku below).

One notable feature of the June 7, 1999, election result is that the protest vote against *Golkar*, the Suharto-era establishment party, was strong in the heartlands, but *Golkar* retained areas of dominance in the outer regions.[16] This result reflected a pattern long understood by the colonial Dutch and Japanese, who often felt compelled to make political concessions to the populism of densely populated Java but were generally able to run an unencumbered autocratic regime in the outer islands. Urban elites in the outer regions are generally more dependent than those in Java on employment in the civil service. *Golkar* did well in those provinces where that dependency is highest. But these are also the provinces where poverty is highest. While urban elites may have genuinely preferred the certainties of *Golkar*, it is difficult to believe that the poor felt the same way.[17]

Of such considerations are "balkanization" fears born. They are the result of a state that concentrates unaccountable power in the hands of a privileged elite in the capital city.

NATIONAL ELITES ARE PART OF THE PROBLEM

The military is not alone in treating people as subjects rather than as citizens. Key nonmilitary elites in Jakarta too illustrate the failure of the centralist, nondemocratic state in their response to unrest in East Timor. The most striking difference between the views on East Timor of Indonesia's foreign minister and of international observers lay in the explanation each gave for the violence on the ground. The international community was moved by the view that the East Timorese were united in a legitimate nationalist rejection of a brutal, alien regime. Foreign Minister Ali Alatas, on the contrary, insisted that this was a fractious society pretty evenly divided between those who favored integration with Indonesia and those who rejected it. This image of a primitive realm where life is nasty, brutish, and short often includes a racial element. The East Timorese resistance, Jakarta's policy makers often say, is led by a mestizo elite that had it good under the Portuguese, whereas indigenous Timorese felt liberated by joining Indonesia.[18]

The Jakartan view, official but I suspect widely shared in elite circles, that the natives need not empowerment but a firm guiding hand is not directed only at East Timor. The rash of unrest around the archipelago that has accompanied the weakening of central government authority since late 1996, but especially the resurgence of regional demands following the resignation of President Suharto in May 1998, mainly elicited anxious talk of "disintegrasi" in the mainstream national discourse.

The strongest example of the lack of empathy for humanitarian problems in the regions even among nongovernment elites was their overwhelmingly negative reaction to the result of the U.N. ballot in East Timor that was announced on September 4, 1999. Joining a flood of wounded nationalist comment in the mainstream dailies, even Democracy Forum, a respected group of intellectuals that did sterling work opposing Suharto, said that President Habibie had undone all Indonesian "sacrifices" for East Timor in the past with a hasty and pragmatic decision to let it go.[19]

Elite reactions to other regional problems were equally uncomprehending. At its national congress held in February 2000, the National Mandate Party (PAN), the only party that had said during the election campaign that it was open to the idea of federalism, failed to even mention the word in its resolutions—it was evidently too costly to do so. The other major political parties, including those that were to provide the president and vice president, had at election time accused PAN of abetting "national disintegration" by its openness to federalist ideas. At the same time the lively debate about federalism on the Jakarta seminar circuit in late 1998 had a year later all but died.

Not merely political parties hold strongly to centralist views, but cultural figures as well. Goenawan Mohamad, Indonesia's most prominent journalist, widely respected as a poet and a man of moral sensitivity, told a seminar in December 1999 that he doubted if an independent Aceh would be more democratic, because it did not have good "human resources."[20] He seemed to be echoing the widespread elite fear of anarchy in the regions should the center weaken.

THERE IS LIFE IN THE REGIONS

If Durkheim and his followers describe collective violence in the pathological language of "breakdown," it is also possible to take the view that it might instead represent "politics by other means." Under conditions of severe repression, resistance has the capacity to provide the basis for new socio-political opportunities—it can lay the groundwork for a more just and stable order. Thus one person's breakdown is another's fresh start. Secessionist movements are peculiarly liable to be presented either in the language of breakdown (by the central elite) or of new opportunities (by the secessionists and their sympathizers).

Contrary to the view long promoted by Jakarta that, left to themselves, the East Timorese are hopelessly fractious, we have many reasons to think of the victory of the local in East Timor as a victory not for chaos but for a new order. Especially in view of the intimidation practiced against them by anti-independence forces, the 78.5 percent of East Timorese who voted for independence showed extraordinary unanimity about their desired future. Through twenty-four years of resistance, the guerrilla army Falintil too has shown discipline and has rarely descended to violence against civilians. These are good omens for a peaceful future.

The East Timorese resistance has consciously steered away from propounding ethnic or religious stereotypes to mobilize support. The Catholic hierarchy has mostly kept itself out of the political movement, allowing the latter to develop along secular, pragmatic lines. While it remains to be seen how the resistance will transform itself into an effective government, there are indications that it is laying the appropriate foundations both among the people of East Timor and the states with whom it will need to interact.

Casting our eyes around the archipelago we soon discover more instances of conflicts that are described by the Jakarta elite in terms of breakdown, but are seen locally as hopeful and credible struggles for a better future. It is still difficult for us to understand these local movements well since, even today, their hopes and complaints are kept largely hidden by a mainstream media that so much shares the centralist ideology that it literally cannot understand what it hears. While some, such as the Acehnese and West Papuans, are secessionist in nature, all want to reclaim local government, long hijacked by the interests of big capital and a brutal military, for the local community.

Everywhere local communities are forcing fresh negotiations with large mining companies or paper pulp mills that had raped the local environment with impunity throughout the Suharto years. The protests that stopped the giant Indorayon pulp mill in North Sumatra, and the quieter renegotiation for compensation being conducted with Rio Tinto (gold, East Kalimantan) and Inco (nickel, Sulawesi), are three important examples of an entirely responsible local assertiveness. Similarly, the "anticorruption" protests that forced hundreds of local government officers throughout the country to resign in 1998 show us, not the forces of anarchy and breakdown, but local communities that seek to protect legitimate interests.

If they are permitted to develop, these local forces can restore order at a level of the state that has been dysfunctional for a long time. If they are repressed, they may explode and end in a worse fate for Indonesia.

I have portrayed the alternatives to unitary centralism as potentially viable because much of the evidence suggests this, and because the orthodox view has too arbitrarily and for too long ruled them out of order. However, I am keenly aware of counterexamples in which national or elite views of the inescapably chaotic state of society in the regions seem all too realistic.

Local movements around the archipelago often have a xenophobic aspect, directed at "foreigners" who may have lived in the area for generations and who are just as poor as the "core" group. Ethnic and religious intolerance is an important mark of the intense Acehnese, Dayak (West Kalimantan), and West Papuan feeling that has exploded over the last year or two. (Mind you, the locals think they are purifying and strengthening the community—the exact opposite of social breakdown. Achmad Kandang, an armed guerrilla leader, for example, is a hero in Aceh because young people are turning away from gambling and going back to prayer, as his father proudly told one interviewer.) Remarkably, such intolerance has not been prominent in East Timor.

We do not need to romanticize these local movements. The Free Aceh Movement, GAM, portrays its struggle in frankly racist (anti-Javanese) and authoritarian terms.[21] Not content to expel thousands of Javanese transmigrants from the territory, it drove some hundred thousand fellow Acehnese civilians from their homes in the months around the June 1999 national election, hoping to attract the attention of the U.N. High Commissioner for Refugees.[22] Many hundreds have died in neighbor-kill-neighbor ethnic conflicts in West Kalimantan in 1997 and Ambon in 1999. The Free Papua Movement has repeatedly taken Javanese transmigrants or civil servants hostage, sometimes with fatal results, simply because they are non-Papuan.

Presumably because of their infancy, regional movements sometimes make religious appeals that exclude adherents of other faiths, an approach that does not augur well for practical politics. Several influential West Papuan figures (for example the late Thomas Wainggai) have adopted a millennialist Christian ideology. Unlike the East Timorese and the Acehnese, the West Papuan movement has only an embryonic party structure and relies to an extent on Christian clerical leadership.

Then there is the possibility that, even if Indonesia does not break up into independent smaller units, the vertical dispersion of the state's powers will produce a local "bossism" similar to that described for the Philippines by John Sidel.[23]

However, media commentary too often fails to recognize that local xenophobia is never the only factor at work. Over against it we usually find an admirable pragmatism practiced by many local political players. Aceh, for example, has lately forced itself onto the attention of Jakarta less by any action of the xenophobic and uncompromising GAM, than by a variety of urban coalitions that are often quite critical of GAM. They are promoting an East Timor–style referendum, something that GAM initially viewed as unnecessary. Their efforts resulted in apparent approval of the idea from the leaders of four major national political parties on September 15, 1999.[24]

Similarly responsible activism is seen in West Papua, where the coalition Foreri has sponsored round-table discussions about alternatives. President Habibie met one hundred Papuan delegates on February 26, 1999, though without immediate result.

The evident failure of the centralist, nondemocratic state in Indonesia is spurring action not only along the democratizing axis but also along the decentralizing one. This second dimension of reform merits as much sympathetic attention from the international community as the first one. The reconstruction of local political life in Indonesia will be a huge task. Although there is a danger such sympathy will be viewed by national elites as sponsoring the breakup of Indonesia, its aim should be to transform the centralist postcolonial Indonesian state and make it functional rather than to destroy it.

TWO CASE STUDIES: ACEH AND MALUKU

It may be helpful to briefly highlight two areas of regional Indonesian conflict besides East Timor and to ask: Is it possible to discern signs of resurgent local political community in the midst of those conflicts, and what might their shape be?

While the Indonesian discourse on more dispersed forms of state power has a long history, the popular protests against the central state's past military brutality that emerged in Aceh soon after Suharto resigned in 1998 gave it an urgency it had not had since the 1950s. For the first time in decades a political party—PAN—put forward federalism as a practical option for Indonesia in January 1999. PAN did not dominate the June 1999 polls (winning 7 percent of seats, it ranked last among the big five parties), but President Abdurrahman Wahid in October 1999 was also responding to the political crisis in Aceh when he created the new post of State Minister for Regional Autonomy. He filled it with U.S.–educated Ryaas Rasyid, previously director general for regional autonomy within the Home Affairs Department. President Wahid initially told the Acehnese he agreed to their demand for a referendum on the constitutional future of the territory.

These gains were by no means uncontested. In Jakarta before the June election, PAN's proposals were rejected by the Indonesian Democratic Party of Struggle (PDI-P), the party that was to gain the largest number of votes. More ominously, they were repeatedly rejected by the still very powerful military. According to rumor, Ryaas Rasyid was by February 2000 about to resign because he felt frustrated at his lack of clout. The president has retracted his support for a referendum in Aceh. The existing decentralization/deconcentration program within the Home Affairs Department concentrates on the local regency (*kabupaten*), not the provincial level, and will thus not satisfy political aspirations. In other words, Jakarta's capacity to undertake meaningful decentralizing reform remains in doubt.

Inertia in Jakarta will by default lend events on the ground in Aceh a momentum of their own. As in Chechnya, another case that can be read as a popular revolt against an internal colonialism maintained by a crumbling postauthoritarian state, that momentum oscillates between a de facto central government vacuum and military attempts to reassert central government authority. Newspaper reports in northern Sumatra (of which Aceh forms the northern tip) have since late 1999 described the virtual disappearance of an Indonesian government presence outside the main towns. In most rural areas civil servants have fled after intimidation by GAM militants, leaving GAM (or sometimes criminal bands claiming GAM's badge) free to collect revolutionary taxes and administer rough justice unimpeded. While the military restrained itself on Jakarta's orders, Aceh experienced something approaching de facto federal statehood (federal because it lacked any international recognition). Such de facto federalism may become an Indonesian pattern while the center remains weak.

However, there are indications that the Indonesian armed forces (TNI) in Aceh may be about to imitate the Russian assault on Chechnya that began in late 1999. Throughout 1999 the TNI launched sporadic raids on what it considered guerrilla bases, often accompanied by the human rights abuse typical of a counterinsurgency campaign. They may yet increase the intensity and return Aceh to the dark days of 1989 to 1992.

In an attempt to divine the strength of Acehnese demand for more self-determination, Ed Aspinall identifies four political forces in Aceh.[25] The most hopeful for those looking for signs of healthy local political life is a vibrant new civil society led by students, urban intellectuals, nongovernment organizations, and the press. This group dominated the political agenda in 1999 with its nonviolent demand for a referendum. It could well continue to set the tone if Jakarta showed a willingness to deal with it in political ways.

The second group is the Acehnese political and business elite. These have generally done well out of the centralist arrangement. Aspinall thinks that even now they still consider themselves part of a greater Indonesian national elite. The third group, itself heterogeneous, consists of Islamic leaders. Some elements support the republican emphasis on the civil society movement, while others are less concerned with statehood issues than with a stricter social morality.

Since colonial days, Jakarta has always worked hard to co-opt the business, political, and religious elites for its centralist project. This way they did not have to deal directly with the grievances of the population, whose interests were often opposed to those of the elites, for example on land ownership issues, labor importation, or the environment. The Wahid government is making it increasingly clear that it is not about to abandon this tactic, despite the great cost in human lives.

Fourth is the armed wing of GAM, which remains in great need of further study. Like Falintil in East Timor, it may consist of some hundreds of armed militants. But it does not enjoy the almost universal local support Falintil did. The civil society movement in particular quietly expresses disapproval of its tactics of expelling transmigrants on ethnic grounds, of removing Acehnese peasants from their homes for political purposes, of sabotaging local government and schools, and of threatening dissidents. GAM's main figurehead leader is the reclusive Hasan di Tiro, a shadowy former Indonesian diplomat with oil interests who lives in exile in Sweden.[26] Some of his loyalists say they want Di Tiro to lead a revived sultanate, presumably on the Brunei model.

If Jakarta reverts to a repressive approach, or even if it stalls on democratic and above all constitutional reform, the promising tone set by Aceh's civil society movement could well be drowned in a cacophony of violence in which GAM militants will become the key role models for Aceh's young people.[27]

One of the least addressed yet no doubt most important subtexts of the Aceh conflict is control over the considerable riches of Mobil Oil's Arun natural gas field at Lhokseumawe.[28] GAM has been careful to avoid sabotaging its plant, although it has kept up pressure with several minor incidents. Jakarta has recognized the importance of this subtext by making provision in its new laws on regional autonomy for returning a substantial proportion of oil, gas, and timber revenues to those regions that possess them.

One of the most difficult ethical issues facing proponents of self-determination for Indonesia's natural resource-rich regions is deciding at what point valid local control over resources that chance to be there becomes an act of deprivation against the economic needs of overpopulated parts of Indonesia elsewhere. The other side of the coin of the embryonic regional autonomy laws is that resource-poor regions stand to lose the subsidies they once enjoyed from the center. However, the enclave nature of the Arun gas field has left Aceh below the national average on several welfare indicators, so plainly the just level of local allocation in a resource-rich region has not yet been reached in Aceh.[29]

If Aceh is a fairly clear case of a demand for local self-determination directed against the state, the Maluku (Moluccas) conflict that broke out in January 1999 was not directed against the state but occurred between groups claiming to represent different religions. Despite remnants of the 1950 South Moluccan independence movement being active from their base in the Netherlands, neither secessionism nor even federalism are strong themes in the discourse around the bloody Christian vs. Muslim civil war that broke out in Ambon, capital of the archipelagic province of Maluku, on Idul Fitri, January 19, 1999. Yet the conflict is intimately related to a failure of the centralist state.

Much Indonesian opinion acknowledges that at the heart of the Maluku conflict is a corrupt, clientelist system for distributing access to bureaucratic power. Much of the largely agricultural- and fisheries-based Maluku was never deeply touched by the centralizing Suharto regime. But the situation is different in the far-flung province's few urban areas. A substantial proportion of its population in the towns is dependent on employment in the civil service, or on government contracts or handouts.[30] This in turn helps to preserve a mercantilist and absolutist mindset among the provincial elite that has declined in Java, where it is possible to become wealthy outside the state. Just as European rulers of the seventeenth century believed that control of wealth was their preserve, and that they could exercise it by controlling territory and the population that inhabits it, so control over the bureaucracy is seen in Maluku as the key to wealth. Once having captured the bureaucracy, the aim is to control territory and population, which accounts in part for the transmigration program and now for the huge refugee movements. Thus the key scarce resource is not money as such but the top layer within the provincial bureaucracy.

However, recruitment to the bureaucracy is not transparent. It occurs via clientelist networks that tend to wear religious identifiers and that have very long vertical extensions—from presidential courtiers in Jakarta to street thugs in the province. Under Suharto, the deals held up. Once he was gone, the highly personalized system collapsed into mutual suspicion and then open warfare. Ambonese Christians used to control the bureaucracy in the colonial time, and they still occupy its lower reaches. But the top levels were increasingly closed to them in the later years of the Suharto regime. The selective misery that the economic crisis of 1998 imposed on low ranking civil servants, and the failure of the clientelist deals made under Suharto, may have led the Protestant elite to strike first.

The general population was easily drawn into the conflict by the "consociational"[31] nature of Maluku's polity, in which people from different religious communities live side by side but almost never take part in intercommunal voluntary associations.

The conflict escalated when fighting spread from around Ambon in the south to Halmahera in the north of the province in October 1999. There, too, rival elites had grown increasingly anxious in the wake of Suharto's resignation and the accompanying economic crisis. Plans to divide the province of Maluku into two provinces heightened anxiety over who should control its northern half. No serious analysis of the northern Maluku conflict has yet appeared. When it does it will show the amazing resilience of clientelist loyalty to two sultans—those of Ternate and Tidore.

These two figures, each living on a tiny island within sight of the other offshore from Halmahera, seemed to have lost their influence under Suharto. But it is a characteristic of clientelist systems that political manipulation behind the scenes is more important than the formalities of power, which are a mere charade. When the flow of patronage was thrown into crisis by the sudden resignation of Suharto, the formal institutions had nothing to offer and so the "real" power that had been hidden became disturbingly visible. Each of these sultans mobilized their dependent followers with the memory of hundreds of years of conflict over territory and their populations. Altogether several thousand are thought to have died in Maluku in 1999.

Local political life in Maluku is clearly in desperate straits. Just how we evaluate prospects for the future will depend on the outcome of a debate on the nature of the current conflict. In his magisterial literature review on analyses of ethnic conflict in Southeast Asia, David Brown[32] separates "primordialists," who feel ethnicity is real and original, from "situationalists," who believe it is constructed as part of a conflict whose core issue lies elsewhere.

Primordialists (who seem to dominate recent foreign press commentary on Indonesia) see in Maluku the reason why Suharto was right and nothing other than a centralized, nondemocratic state can ever work in a society as fissiparous as Indonesia's. Certainly the depth of feeling in Maluku over religion makes primordialism an attractive explanation.

However, if the situationalists are right, as most scholars of ethnic conflict generally hold today, then the unstable clientelism that characterizes Maluku's bureaucracy, and perhaps even its consociational polity, may be products of a dependency created by the centralist state, rather than "natural" givens that preclude a more empowering alternative.

PROSPECTS

At the end of the nineteenth century, the Netherlands Indies grew into a large colonial state when the Western powers carved up much of the world among them. The thousands of lives lost to establish the colony of the Netherlands East Indies, particularly in Aceh, made no dent on that great power agreement. Similarly, during the long Cold War, particularly after 1965, Indonesia was an important Western ally, and the atrocities the state committed to maintain itself drew little international action. But the Cold War ended in 1991. While the United States is not at all interested in promoting the breakup of Indonesia, its diplomacy on East Timor culminating in 1999 marks a huge reduction in its tolerance of brutality by client states in remote places, no matter that this is the world's fourth largest nation.

U.S. president Bill Clinton declared after the war in Kosovo, "Whether you live in Africa, in Central Europe or anywhere else, if someone intends to commit massive crimes against innocent civilians, he should know that, to the limit of our capacities, we will prevent it." Clinton may have been rhetorical, cynical, or genuine, but his statement will not be reassuring to leaders of states inhabiting the dangerous corner of Rummel's field of modern states.

The rise of the local does not have to portend the breakup of Indonesia. More likely, in the short term at least, is that it will signify a dispersal of power from the center to the regions as community movements adopt state-forming strategies. Even if Aceh does eventually split off, the same need for local empowerment will still have to be dealt with in other places.

Two indications that Indonesian central state actors appear ready to make substantial concessions to local demands for more control could already be seen in the last Suharto-era parliament, elected in May 1997. It continued to produce legislation for sixteen months after Suharto resigned. Among the results were a law giving provinces greater authority to choose their own governor (law no. 22/1999), one returning a large percentage of locally raised primary resources revenues to the provinces (law no. 25/1999), and one that affirms Islamic syariah law in the "special" province of Aceh. These laws still await implementing regulations.

However, the counterindications are also strong. Most of them are connected with the military. It is establishing new garrison commands in "difficult" areas around the country.[33] Its abominable behavior in East Timor after the ballot was widely interpreted as a warning of what systematic terror the state might unleash on any other people contemplating secession.

Federalism has been spoken of in more practical terms than ever before, but it has almost no support within the Wahid government, which remains Java-dominated. Indeed the idea faces serious conceptual difficulties. Federalism normally brings together previously separate entities. There are few examples of unitary countries loosening up into a federation—Germany is one, the devolution of the United Kingdom may be another.

These contradictory movements at various levels of Indonesia's state and society probably mean that nothing will be resolved quickly or cleanly. But the extreme violence that the centralist, autocratic state has shown once more it is prepared to commit against entire local populations should inspire us to support those trying to reconstruct it for more human ends. Or else we may condemn Indonesia to a fate beyond anyone's control.

NOTES

Profuse thanks to Richard Tanter, Mark Selden, and Steve Shalom for helpful, detailed criticism of earlier drafts.

1. Rudolph J. Rummel, *Power Kills: Democracy as a Method of Nonviolence* (New Brunswick, N.J.: Transaction, 1997).

2. Local municipal councils were established by a 1903 law on decentralization, but rather than empowering local communities they became vehicles to facilitate the tasks of the central government more effectively. Similarly, the 1922 Administrative Reform Law provided for the creation of provinces, but it was backed by conservative figures mainly interested in improving government control in the regions while keeping popular demands in check.

3. A. Schiller, *The Formation of Federal Indonesia, 1945–1949* (The Hague/Bandung: Van Hoeve, 1955).

4. Schiller, *Formation of Federal Indonesia*, 62.

5. J.D. Legge, *Central Authority and Regional Autonomy in Indonesia* (Ithaca, N.Y.: Cornell University Press, 1961).

6. Herbert Feith, *The Decline of Constitutional Democracy in Indonesia* (Ithaca, N.Y.: Cornell University Press, 1962).

7. Robert Cribb, ed., *The Indonesian Killings of 1965–1966: Studies from Java and Bali* (Clayton, Victoria: Center of Southeast Asian Studies, Monash University, 1990), 12, lists estimates of between 78,000 and two million killed.

8. Of course democratic, federalist states also claim victims, especially through warfare, but if we accept Rummel's research, their number falls below those who die within states in the dangerous corner of centralist dictatorship.

9. When asked what made East Timor different from other independence movements around Indonesia, Australian foreign minister Alexander Downer told ABC Radio on 29 September 1999: "Back in 1975 Indonesia invaded East Timor. The East Timorese people wanted their independence. The United Nations had never acknowledged East Timor's

incorporation into Indonesia. Circumstances in other parts of Indonesia are entirely different. They go back to the Dutch colonial rule and the creation of modern Indonesia out of that." Australian recognition of integration had been emphatic and bipartisan for over twenty years. President Habibie himself told journalists that he woke up one morning and thought: 'Hey, why the hell is East Timor with us . . . it doesn't belong to our declared territory as of independence' " (*Sydney Morning Herald*, 24 May 1999). An important reason for Indonesian military anger with Australia over leading the multinational force in East Timor is its sense of betrayal over this long-standing recognition. The pressing question in Indonesia's armed forces headquarters could well be: "Which province will they target next?"

10. Gerry van Klinken, "The Contemporary Roots of East Timorese Resistance, and Prospects for Peace," *Antara Kita* (bulletin of the U.S.–based Indonesian Studies Committee), no.43 (October 1995).

11. Tim Kell, *The Roots of Acehnese Rebellion, 1989–1992* (Ithaca, N.Y.: Cornell Modern Indonesia Project, 1995).

12. Robin Osborne, *Indonesia's Secret War: The Guerilla Struggle in Irian Jaya* (Sydney: Allen & Unwin, 1985). A new edition is in preparation.

13. Freek Colombijn, "A Peaceful Road to Freedom," *Inside Indonesia*, no. 60 (October–December 1999): 19.

14. *Communal Violence in West Kalimantan* (New York: Human Rights Watch Asia, December 1997).

15. Human Rights Watch Asia, *The Violence in Ambon*, [accessed March 1999] <http://www.hrw.org/hrw/reports/1999/ambon/>; Gerry van Klinken, "What Caused the Ambon Violence?" *Inside Indonesia*, no. 60 (October–December 1999): 15–16.

16. Gerry van Klinken, "Democracy, the Regions and Indonesia's Future," in *Pemilu: The 1999 Indonesian Election*, ed. Susan Blackburn (Melbourne: Monash Asia Institute, 1999), 23–27.

17. Some social indicators for the provinces can be found in Hal Hill, *The Indonesian Economy since 1966* (New York: Cambridge University Press, 1996), 218–25. My calculations show a correlation between the proportion of parliamentary seats won in the June 1999 election by *Golkar* and the proportion of the nonagricultural working population employed in the civil service as an astonishingly high +0.60. For the oppositionist PDI-P that figure is −0.20.

18. For example, one strain in the campaign against former Indonesian governor of East Timor, Mario Carrascalão, when he declared his support for an independent East Timor early in 1999, was that he was an opportunist whose mixed blood left him without attachment to any land ("Berliku talak tiga Timor Leste," *Ummat*, 15 February 1999).

19. Gerry van Klinken, "What Jakarta's Papers Say about East Timor" *The Age* (Melbourne), 8 September 1999. There were some noble exceptions to the nationalist outcry.

20. "Indonesia Needs a Lesson from Russia," *The Nation* (Bangkok), 19 December 1999.

21. Vanessa Johanson, "The Sultan Will Be Dr. Hasan Tiro," *Inside Indonesia*, no. 60 (October–December 1999): 10.

22. Margot Cohen, "Captives of the Cause," *Far Eastern Economic Review*, 2 September 1999.

23. For example John T. Sidel, "Philippine Politics in Town, District, and Province:

Bossism in Cavite and Cebu," *Journal of Asian Studies* 56, no. 4 (November 1997): 947–66.

24. Leaders of PKB, PAN, *Partai Keadilan*, and an Islamic party, *Partai Persatuan Pembangunan*—among them Abdurrahman Wahid and Amien Rais—together with Aceh governor Syamsuddin Mahmud, unveiled a billboard demanding a referendum at a mosque in Aceh (*Serambi*, 16 September 1999).

25. Ed Aspinall, "Whither Aceh?" *Inside Indonesia*, no. 62 (April–June 2000): 6–7.

26. For his own account of the three years in which he led an armed movement in Aceh (1976–79) see Tengku Hasan di Tiro, *The Price of Freedom: The Unfinished Diary of Tengku Hasan di Tiro* (Ontario, Can.: Open Press, 1984).

27. This argument is drawn from Anthony Reid, "Which Way Aceh?" *Far Eastern Economic Review*, 16 March 2000.

28. By the end of the 1980s Aceh contributed 30 percent of the country's oil and gas exports, and by the early 1990s Indonesia, largely thanks to Aceh, was the world's largest liquified natural gas (LNG) supplier, at 40 percent of world supply. Virtually all the revenues accrue to the central government, to the state-owned oil company Pertamina, and to foreign contractors (Kell, *Roots of Acehnese Rebellion*, 13–16). The onshore Arun field initially contained 14 trillion cubic feet of gas and 712 million barrels of condensate (Reuters, 13 July 1993). Exports are now in decline as reserves are being depleted. 24.5 million cubic meters of LNG were exported in 1999, but this is expected to decrease to 15 million cubic meters in 2000, while condensate exports will go down from 42,000 barrels a day to 30,000 barrels a day (*Jakarta Post,* 13 November 1999).

29. Only 3.0 percent of the population spent more than Rp 60,000 a month in 1990, the lowest in Sumatra, and less than half the national average of 7.1 percent. The percentage employed in agriculture was 66 percent in 1990 and had declined by only 16.5 percent over the previous two decades, compared to respective national averages of 50 percent and 24.7 percent (Hill, *Indonesian Economy since 1966*, 220–23).

30. My own calculations based on Central Bureau of Statistics data for 1990 show that 28.1 percent of the nonagriculturally employed working population (which should approximate to the urban population) are civil servants, compared to 11.3 percent for the national average. Central disbursements make up 19.4 percent of Gross Regional Domestic Product, more than twice the national average of 7.8 percent (Colin Barlow and Joan Hardjono [eds], *Indonesia Assessment 1995: Development in Eastern Indonesia* [Canberra: RSPAS, ANU, 1996], 6).

31. See Arend Lijphart, *Democracy in Plural Societies* (New Haven, Conn: Yale University Press, 1977).

32. David Brown, *The State and Ethnic Politics in Southeast Asia* (New York: Routledge, 1994).

33. Indonesia's armed forces exercise their political influence largely through a "territorial" garrison command system that covers the entire country. In 1983 the number of such commands was reduced from seventeen to ten, but the military announced in April 1999 that, for reasons of national security in the face of social unrest, this reduction was to be reversed gradually. A new command was established in Maluku in May 1999, but cabinet ministers both under Habibie and under Abdurrahman Wahid have resisted the establishment of a new command in Aceh.

Part V

The Future of East Timor

15

The Transition of a Small War-Torn Economy into a New Nation: Economic Reconstruction of East Timor

João Mariano Saldanha

This chapter provides an overview of East Timor's economy during the transition toward independence under U.N. administration and a glimpse of future prospects. East Timor's development must begin by confronting the legacy of destruction conducted by pro-Indonesian militias backed by their military masters following the independence vote in August 1999.

First the basic conditions of East Timor, especially the characteristics of a small war-torn country, are presented. The role of the United Nations Transitional Administration in East Timor (UNTAET), and its interaction with the main East Timorese political force in administering the transition toward independence, is addressed next, followed by the major economic policies in fiscal, monetary, production, and trade areas.

BASIC CONDITIONS

A Small Country

With a population of eight hundred thousand, East Timor is a small country with the potential advantage of social cohesiveness allowing rapid adjustment to external change and with opportunities to reap the benefits of international trade. Despite a small domestic market and limited natural resources, land, capital, and labor, small countries not only have development potential, but many have achieved higher per capita income than their larger counterparts. There is no significant difference in growth performance between large and small states.[1]

A Poor Country

After more than four hundred years of Portuguese colonial rule and the destructive, but also dynamic, impact of Indonesian invasion and occupation, the East Timor economy is predominantly agrarian, fragile, and dependent on Indonesia. As summarized in a recent review by the World Bank–led Joint Assessment Mission (JAM) in East Timor:

> Prior to the conflict, East Timor was primarily an agricultural economy, with a single significant export (coffee) and approximately 90 percent of the population living in rural areas. The territory was one of the poorest areas in Southeast Asia, with an estimated GDP [Gross Domestic Product] per capita of $431 in 1996, and 30 percent of households—or double the average for Indonesia—living below the poverty line. Although official recorded investment per capita ran at approximately double the Indonesian average, access to economic infrastructure and basic social services was lower than any Indonesian province. East Timor was heavily dependent on external transfers, with approximately 85 percent of recurrent and capital expenditure coming from Indonesia.[2]

A War-Torn Economy

A war-torn economy is typically characterized by falling GDP, internally displaced people and cross-border refugees, gaps in infrastructure, high inflation, weak fiscal and financial systems, fragile or collapsed institutions such as statistical and welfare services, disrupted property rights, and shattered trust.[3] This description fits contemporary East Timor well. The recent World Bank–led assessment mission estimates that the effects of postreferendum destruction left East Timor with:

1. Virtually every piece of equipment and remaining physical infrastructure of the modern sector destroyed;
2. Administrative structures, including revenue and budget functions, eliminated;
3. Substantial population, approximately 350,000, displaced;
4. GDP decline of approximately 40–45 percent in 1999;
5. Price spirals during the same period particularly for imported goods: seven times for cooking oil, five times for salt, six times for canned milk, and ten times for laundry soap.[4]

To this we must add the massive destruction of urban housing and rampant unemployment, the latter affecting 80 to 90 percent of the urban population according to estimates of February 2000.

The response of the National Council of Timorese Resistance (CNRT) has been to declare 2000 the year of emergency and to target solving the humanitar-

Figure 15.1   Two girls plant rice at Ainaro, 1998. "Around the edge of the rice field the Timorese build a small mud wall. Then they fill the field with water and put the buffalo in. The buffalo roam all over, softening the land and killing the grass, which then rots and fertilizes. The rice seeds are thrown, but when they are about 20 cm they are pulled out, and then the buffalo are put back into the field to re-trample the grass. Then the rice is replanted, but this time in the proper order. You see, the rice has children—there is the main stalk and there are smaller ones at the side, and these smaller ones are called 'children.' Planting in the proper order gives better children."—Alfredo Pires. Courtesy: Ross Bird.

ian crisis as the top priority, referring to the provision of food, shelter, and security, the repair of infrastructure from electricity to water to roads, and restoring local government, education, and health care. These will provide the foundations for the reconstruction and development to follow.

A New State

East Timor as the first newly independent nation of the millennium has the opportunity to get the basics right from the very beginning, avoiding the mistakes committed by newly independent countries in Africa and elsewhere.[5] The challenges include designing a competitive and inclusive political system, setting up key economic institutions free of corruption, taking effective emergency measures to feed and house the population, and undertaking sound economic policies for long-term development. This situation calls for leadership vision and maintaining good relations between the East Timorese people and the U.N. team on the one hand, and international donors on the other.

As a new nation, East Timor has the chance to carry out radical reforms and to introduce measures that would be difficult under normal circumstances. However, this requires simultaneously tackling issues ranging from institution building and resettlement of internally displaced people and refugees across the border, to jump-starting the economy and creating jobs.

INSTITUTION BUILDING, RECONSTRUCTION, AND DEVELOPMENT UNDER U.N. AUTHORITY

Before independence, East Timor will be guided by the U.N. Transitional Authority on East Timor (UNTAET).[6] UNTAET has moved quickly to set up a National Consultative Commission (NCC), the main policy-making body of the transitional administration that is comprised of East Timorese, especially CNRT and Church representatives, and U.N. officials and experts. In its turn, NCC has established a Judicial Commission, Civil Service Commission, Central Fiscal Agency, and Payment Bureau.

One area critical to institutional formation and development is the transformation of the civil service. UNTAET, working through the NCC and the World Bank, has proposed reducing the number of civil servants in the new administration from 28,000 to 12,000 people. Already in 1994, salaries for the then 24,570 civil servants consumed $11 million of the East Timor budget.[7] While it is essential to bring the size of the administration under control, the issues of government employment are socially explosive. In January 2000, 7,000 people showed up when UNTAET announced that it would fill 1,500 civil service positions. Recruitment was disrupted when recruiters belatedly announced that English and Portuguese language skills were requirements.

CNRT has called on East Timorese professionals to return and contribute to national development. If significant numbers of the twenty to thirty thousand expatriate East Timorese currently in Australia, Portugal, Macau, and elsewhere return, they are likely to fill many vacated positions in both the public and private sectors. There should then be little difficulty in filling civil service positions with qualified personnel. The private sector poses more difficult problems at a time when business initiatives are just beginning while government priorities, incentives, and access to credit remain uncertain. Some expatriates have responded positively, but others await clarification concerning their roles in the reconstruction process. In September 1999 the World Bank provided a three week crash course in international economics to a small group of East Timorese economists.[8] The dozen East Timorese technical experts recruited by the bank together with international experts to conduct the Joint Assessment Mission (JAM) on East Timor provide evidence of the existence of important, if scarce, Timorese expertise.

By World Bank estimates of November 1999, reconstruction in the wake of the wave of destruction following the independence ballot will cost approximately $230 million, with humanitarian relief for food, shelter, and transportation for refugees an additional $200 million.[9] Although pledges of funds were made in early fall 1999, it was not until the completion of World Bank president James Wolfensohn's visit on February 22, 2000, that the first World Bank funds became available in the form of a $7 million grant for an initial six month period to support a Community Empowerment and Local Governance project that will eventually receive $21.5 million. The World Bank has linked its funds with political reconstruction. Following election of local councils, communities are to receive $15,000 each to support locally determined projects. Additional funding is provided by the Japanese government ($1.5 million) and the Asian Development Bank ($1 million).[10] UNTAET's capacity building activities require partnership with CNRT to mobilize East Timorese professionals to serve their country. This process sends a clear message to the East Timorese and the international community alike that UNTAET is preparing the East Timorese to run their own country within two to three years.[11] The process is, however, a sensitive one. Already by spring 2000 demonstrations driven by the lack of jobs, high wage differentials, and slow pace of reconstruction had begun. Protesters in Dili called attention to job scarcity while U.N. officials drove luxury cars and lived aboard ships converted into hotels.[12]

East Timorese who work with and for UNTAET have voiced grievances ranging from the failure of the U.N. administration to consult and involve CNRT and local people in critical decisions to the fact that nearly all responsible positions have been filled by international staff, to anger over the fact that Timorese are underpaid while their international counterparts earn very high salaries. At the same time, wages are many times higher for East Timorese recruited by international agencies compared to those working in the domestic sector; roughly five times for drivers (from the equivalent of $40 to $227 per month according to UNAMET guidelines) and about ten times in the case of cleaners and messengers (from about $15–20 to $175). The danger goes beyond resentment of the two-tier structure. There is also a risk that the international presence will drive up wages to levels that deter prospective businesses that might consider investing in East Timor.

The imbalances and the contradictory effects of the international presence have been well described in the JAM Macroeconomic Team Report:

> East Timor's post-violence economy displays significant structural imbalances: retail prices and local wage structures have been highly distorted by the massive presence of the U.N. administration and international NGOs [nongovernmental organizations], while nearly all wage-earning Timorese have lost their previous employment and incomes. An ad hoc comparison of prices in the Dili market reveals two- or three-fold increases in prices of locally produced meat between August and October 1999.[13]

At the same time, CNRT needs to solve several internal problems if it is to provide effective developmental leadership. These include resolving factional disputes, eliminating business conflicts of interest, and overcoming the maneuvering for power that can undermine rational decision-making and block development.

THE MACROECONOMY

This section provides an overview of the economy during the reconstruction period with an eye to its potential. Major macroeconomic issues are fiscal, monetary, trade, and production policies.

Fiscal Issues and International Grants

In response to the postreferendum destruction and dislocation, leaving government fiscal institutions in shambles, UNTAET proposed a Central Fiscal Agency as the embryo of the Ministry of Finance in an independent East Timor. This agency will set up the revenue system, introduce budgeting, and seek foreign aid to support recurrent expenditures and reconstruction efforts.

The initial reaction of the international community to the destruction in East Timor was to offer substantial aid. At the Tokyo Donor Conference on East Timor in December 1999, donor countries pledged $520 million including $86 million for humanitarian assistance, $86 million for governance and capacity building, and $262 million for reconstruction and development.[14] Both the allocations and the sequence seem appropriate for rebuilding the war-torn economy.

The Cambodian and other international experiences provide painful lessons on postwar reconstruction for East Timor including the necessity both to activate the economy and to set the stage for long-term development. Cambodia's reconstruction failures under the U.N. Transitional Authority in Cambodia were in part due to lack of coordination among donors from different regions.[15] The specific donor pledges of reconstruction and development aid for such things as infrastructure, agriculture, health, education, and macroeconomics seem appropriate both to immediate reconstruction and long-term development. There seems to be a consensus among the East Timorese, UNTAET, the World Bank, the Asian Development Bank, the International Monetary Fund, and the international community generally on these priorities.

The international pledges are encouraging, but it is essential that the East Timorese move vigorously to secure local revenue sources for long-term development and even for the short term. Pledges do not automatically translate into disbursements. Disbursement rates can be as low as 6 percent, as in Cambodia, or at best 40 percent, as in Palestine.[16] In Kosovo, the ratio of disbursement to pledged international aid was around 25 percent.

Regardless of the ability to tap international aid, it is essential that the East Timorese develop effective programs to raise domestic revenues. Estimates by the International Monetary Fund (IMF) and the World Bank suggest that in fiscal year 2000 alone, East Timor can raise $15 million from internal revenue sources.[17] Saldanha and Da Costa identified five autonomous East Timorese revenue sources: revenues from natural resources, particularly oil and gas; income and property taxes; agricultural exports, especially coffee, livestock, and sugar; remittances from abroad; and profits from state-owned enterprises. Additional sources of revenue are from indirect taxes, such as excise tax, sales tax, and import duty.[18] The National Consultative Council (NCC) with the advice of the IMF promulgated laws on levying taxes in February 2000. An import duty of 5 percent was introduced across the board with additional sales taxes of 15 percent on items such as cars, mobile phones, and perfumes. An excise tax has been set at $1.5/liter for alcoholic beverages, $15/kg for tobacco and cigarettes, and 5 cents/liter for fuel.

The NCC will also levy taxes on exports, especially coffee beans, at 5 percent. This decision was hotly debated within the NCC amidst pressures from the IMF.[19] I believe that it is premature to levy export fees on coffee, because it may discourage attempts to expand production as well as diversification away from exporting only coffee beans. It is not too late to put on hold implementation of export fees.

The danger exists that as soon as the U.N. leaves, revenues will drop, particularly revenues from demand-driven consumption by UNTAET personnel, such as liquor and cigarettes. However, with the increase of economic activities led by the private sector, these revenues can increase. The challenge is to provide incentives to the private sector to develop.

Royalties associated with fishing activities in international waters near East Timor are another source of revenue. There have long been reports that Japanese and Taiwanese fishermen have illegally operated trawlers here and in eastern Indonesian waters, but no effort has been made to assure revenue sharing with East Timor. One of the immediate tasks of UNTAET is to conduct this negotiation with the fishermen or their respective governments.

Monetary Issues

Under Indonesian occupation, East Timor was incorporated into Indonesian monetary and financial policy. The rupiah was the currency and the Bank of Indonesia (the central bank) operated a branch in East Timor to oversee banking and financial activities. East Timor faces the task of building infrastructure and recruiting personnel to staff a monetary regime following the Indonesian departure.

The arrival of the International Force on East Timor (InterFET) on September 20, 1999, marked the resumption of economic activities in the territory following the Indonesian rampage and withdrawal. Four major currencies, namely the U.S.

dollar, Australian dollar, Portuguese escudo, and Indonesian rupiah, as well as the Thai baht and Filipino peso, have been circulating locally. The U.S. and Australian dollars, in addition to smaller amounts of the baht and peso, enter the economy through InterFET, UNTAET, and humanitarian agencies, while the escudo circulates through payment of pensions to former Portuguese employees.

In late January 2000, UNTAET began to tackle the currency problem by establishing a payment bureau, a licensing currency exchange bureau, and most importantly by adopting the U.S. dollar as the legal tender of East Timor for the transition period. These measures provide a framework for monetary and financial operations. Two international banks, Banco National Ultramarino of Portugal and Westpac of Australia, have operated in Dili since late 1999, primarily to pay pensions and UNTAET personnel salaries respectively.

While other policies were readily accepted, dollarization came as a surprise because CNRT leaders had stated publicly that they would adopt the escudo as the currency for East Timor given the historical links with Portugal. The IMF, however, gave priority to economic and technical over political and historical factors. Technical considerations include the stability of the dollar, its convertibility, and the fact that East Timor's exports and international aid are denominated in dollars. Moreover, the escudo is heading for extinction since Portugal adopted the euro as its currency. If East Timor adopts the escudo it would require two transitions, i.e. from multiple currencies to the escudo and then to the euro. The unanimous decision of the NCC to adopt the dollar solves the short-term problem of multiple currencies in East Timor.

Dollarizing East Timor means, however, that the Transitional Administration will not be able to finance government budget deficits by printing currency, bailing out domestic banks, or earning income generated from printing money. On the other hand, dollarization could assure East Timor low inflation and low interest rates given the combination of U.S. economic boom with low inflation that has continued for a decade.

Nevertheless, it will take time to fully dollarize the East Timor economy. There is a lag in conversion as well as a substantial nonmonetized or subsistence sector of the economy that remained significant during the Indonesian occupation and was strengthened by the destruction of the modern and urban sector following August 30, 1999.

The competitiveness of international banking in East Timor could be enhanced if an American bank such as Citicorp, Chase, or Bank of America, or another, such as the Grameen Bank, in addition to an Indonesian bank, also operated in East Timor. The Indonesian bank would provide an opportunity for East Timorese to access their savings in eight banks that previously operated in East Timor. Most importantly, the presence of an Indonesian bank would help to revive trade between East Timor and Indonesia.

In the longer term, it may be possible to establish a currency board that issues domestic currency 100 percent backed by the U.S. dollar. The domestic currency would be fully convertible, again assuring the prospect of low inflation and monetary stability. Problems, however, include raising sufficient hard currency reserves to back the entire monetary base. Potential sources of hard currency for East Timor include exports of oil and coffee, foreign aid (especially grants), tourism, and East Timorese savings in Indonesian banks.[20] In the short run, it is best to give time to the dollarization process and gauge its effect on economic performance before attempting to replace it with a currency board or other arrangements.

Production

All productive activities, notably those in the modern sector, were halted by the postreferendum Indonesian rampage. Business and trade did not resume until December 1999 and only then because UNTAET and InterFET provided modest stimuli to the local economy. The effects of these stimuli are, however, small and contradictory because the demand for consumption from these institutions and their personnel centers on imported goods rather than on local products. The UNTAET and InterFET troops and staff are comprised overwhelmingly of foreigners who do not spend their salaries in East Timor. Ultimately, the economy must find ways to raise the productivity of labor and land as well as the efficiency of other sectors from manufacturing to trade.

Significant productive potential lies in the agricultural sector from which almost 80 percent of the population derive their income and livelihood. Agriculture should be the first priority in economic development of East Timor, not only to provide food security, but also to provide the foundations for long-term development, including exports. Agriculture has strong linkages with nonagricultural sectors through providing labor and raw materials for industry, food for agricultural and industrial workers, markets for industrial output, and foreign exchange needed to import capital.[21]

During the Indonesian period, one third of GDP came from agriculture, especially food crops (rice and corn) and tree crops (coffee and coconut), and agriculture was the main source of export earnings. Moreover, while agriculture suffered far less than nonagricultural sectors such as construction and trade during the militia- and military-led destruction, the November 1999 World Bank assessment made clear the seriousness of the immediate problems:

> . . . many regions are experiencing labor shortages due to population displacement, together with lack of access to seeds and tools. . . . The major impediment to rice cultivation is the lack of traction, due to killing of cattle and water buffalo and destruction of tractors. It is estimated that production of rice will reach 58–70 percent of 1999 levels in the year 2000, with other staple food crops ranging from 60–75 percent of 1999 levels.[22]

The current UNTAET reconstruction and development budget is devoted exclusively to promoting the agricultural sector without reference to commercialization or modernization. Another key missing element in the agricultural reconstruction budget is infrastructure such as irrigation. Each of these is critical if the domestic economy is to be restored, and if East Timor is to develop significant agricultural exports.

There is also untapped potential in the agricultural sector. Besides food and tree crops, with its vast southern rangeland, East Timor has the capacity and experience to produce livestock for export.

A critical question pivots on the resolution of land ownership issues, particularly with respect to coffee plantations, a key to East Timor's export prospects. While 30,000 of the 50,000 hectares of coffee plantations are held by smallholders, 15,000 hectares formerly in the hands of the Portuguese government company SAPT (*Socieda de Agricola Patria e Trabalho*) were taken over by the Indonesian government, and 5,000 hectares are in the hands of large private holdings (fazendas). Whether these large holdings will be distributed to farmers, sold to corporate interests, or run as government enterprises remains unclear.

This raises the bigger issue of land reform in East Timor. The legacy of Portuguese and Indonesian land laws is not encouraging. The Portuguese government recognized communal land ownership rights but made no serious attempt to title communal lands. While Indonesian law allowed communal land ownership, in many cases the government declared communal lands to be state land and transferred ownership rights to powerful business interests, including members of the Suharto family.

Any attempt toward land reform by a new government, especially during the transition process, must begin by sensitively assessing communal land ownership patterns before attempting to title land. This is a politically sensitive and economically and administratively demanding task.

While identifying communal land is relative easy, titling could create huge political and economic problems. First, there must be strong political support for this process. Since communal lands from generation to generation were maintained through verbal communication, it is difficult to prove who holds legal ownership to the land. What is certain is that there will be multiple claims on lands across East Timor. This is likely to provoke political crisis and raise prospects of revolt if not implemented sensitively. However, conducting land reform in the transition period is an advantage because this period can be viewed as part of the process of breaking with the past and starting afresh. In my view, despite potential opposition, it would be appropriate to begin land reform immediately. However, neither UNTAET nor CNRT has provided clear indication of their thinking on land policy. One difficult problem centers on supporting this program financially since the program will create strong budgetary pressures.

Solution of land ownership problems is essential to East Timor's economic and social future. Sensitive issues will include both disputed land titles related to the period of Indonesian rule and questions of rights to land cultivated without title. The creation of clear-cut ownership rights, if impartially enforced, will provide security for East Timorese cultivators and stimulate economic growth.[23] The establishment of transparent mechanisms for resolving disputes is also essential.

One key to the economic future is investment in small and medium scale industries. This can raise productivity and exports. Investment policy should encourage the growth of such enterprises, including the allocation of credit from funds provided by public commercial banks. To stimulate competition and efficiency, interest rates should follow market rates.

Another important source of revenues is the Timor Gap Oil Field. A February 23, 2000, agreement signed by UNTAET on behalf of East Timor with a consortium of six American, Japanese, and Australian oil companies provides for a $1.4 billion investment in gas recycling. The agreement, which specifies training and employment of East Timorese, is the largest investment ever made in East Timor. Drilling is not, however, expected to begin before 2004.[24]

Trade

If East Timor can overcome problems that are the legacy of colonialism and war, it can reap the benefits of international trade. East Timor has limited capacity to produce consumer goods and capital goods. To enjoy the gains of international trade it needs to specialize in areas of comparative advantage.

This requires agricultural commercialization, crop diversification, expansion of coffee exports, and improvement of livestock production. Diversification of coffee exports through powdered coffee production is one promising avenue. Powdered coffee has been produced by several East Timorese companies. They require technical and financial assistance to become competitive exporters. The American-based National Cooperative Business Association is active in production and marketing of coffee. But locally-owned companies need to participate.

Tourism is another potential source of foreign exchange. Compared to coffee and livestock, tourism could become a quick earner of foreign exchange. East Timor's independence after a widely publicized struggle will make it attractive to certain kinds of tourists, especially backpackers, eco-tourists, and others who are prepared to rough it. Such a course, rather than one that sought to construct five star hotels, would be feasible. This sector has been completely neglected by UNTAET.

Craft industries such as traditional clothing could also earn foreign exchange. Livestock, coffee, tourism, and crafts all are small to medium scale industries in which East Timorese can actively participate in finance, production, and trade.

At the heart of trade lies the marketing issues that link the domestic and international market and provide signals concerning the shortage of goods and services. Technical assistance is needed in production, manufacturing, and marketing for small and medium enterprises.

The above modernization and export agenda need not be undertaken under a protective trade regime (quotas and tariffs). Trade should be promoted to encourage competition. Although this makes domestic industry vulnerable to external competitors, a comprehensive trade and investment package will stimulate the growth of domestic industries while promoting efficiency by allowing competition.

Saldanha and Da Costa[25] have stressed the importance for East Timor of expanded regional trade with neighboring countries, especially Australia and Indonesia. It will be important for East Timor to negotiate preferential treatment of its exports with its immediate neighbors—Australia, Indonesia, New Zealand, and Papua New Guinea—within the framework of expanded trade with these countries. Using Portugal as its entry point, East Timor can also negotiate preferential treatment of its goods and services in the European Union. East Timor should also seek preferential treatment in U.S. markets.

CONCLUSION

The basic conditions of East Timor as a small, devastated nation in transition to independence under the guidance of the international community provide unique opportunities. However, they also pose enormous challenges ranging from institution building to restarting the economy, and from controlling inflation to technical assistance.

On the economic side, four areas deserve special attention. First, in the fiscal area, there is a need to raise internal revenues so as to avoid creating a new culture of dependence. Second, in the monetary area, dollarization is a way to combat inflation and promote macroeconomic stability for the short term. But to promote growth and sustainability in the longer term, dollarization should be reviewed in light of the need to attract foreign investment. The third area is production. This chapter has emphasized agricultural production. Fourth, as a small country, East Timor needs to engage in trade like its counterparts around the world. Priorities here include raising the productivity of agriculture for exports, strengthening the production and processing of coffee and coconut, and securing appropriate technology to raise corn production for commercial purposes. In addition, East Timor must make effective use of Timor Gap oil revenues, a potential discussed in the concluding chapter. Along with agriculture, tourism can play an important role in sustaining the economic growth of East Timor in the long term.

NOTES

I have benefited from discussions with Ross Garnaut, Peter Gajewsky, Hal Hill, Ross McLeod, Chris Manning, and Peter Timmer, as well as from their comments on earlier drafts of this chapter. Thanks are also due to the participants of Conferences at Instituto de Estudos Altos Militares (IEAM), Lisbon, Portugal; University of Western Sidney, Sidney, Australia; Ministry of Youth, Lisbon, and Institute of Economics, University of Oslo. My special thanks to the editors, especially Mark Selden, who helped improve the presentation substantially. All errors are mine.

1. See William Easterly and Aart Kraay, "Small States, Small Problems?" The World Bank, 1999; A. D. Knox, "Some Economic Problems of Small Countries," in *Problems of Smaller Territories*, ed. Burton Benedict (London: The University of London, 1967); Boris Blazic-Metzner and Helen Hughes, "Growth Experience of Small Economies," in *Problems and Policies in Small Economies*, ed. B. Jalan (London: Croom Helm, 1982); and P. J. Lloyd and R. M. Sundrum, "Characteristics of Small Economies," in *Problems and Policies in Small Economies*. I follow Easterly and Kraay in defining countries with population less than one million as small countries.

2. World Bank, "East Timor, Building a Nation: A Framework for Reconstruction and Development," Joint Assessment Mission Macroeconomics Background Paper, November 1999.

3. Jonathan Haughton, "The Reconstruction of War-Torn Economies," Technical Paper, CAER-HIID, 1998.

4. World Bank, "East Timor, Building a Nation," November 1999.

5. William Easterly and Ross Levine, "Africa's Growth Tragedy: Policies and Ethnic Divisions," *Quarterly Journal of Economics* 112 (1997): 1201–50; Shepard Forman, "Yale University Panel on East Timor," November 1999; Peter Timmer, "Question for the United Nations Team Managing East Timor," Unpublished mimeo, IR/PS, University of California, San Diego, 1999.

6. For some early advice to UNTAET, see Forman, "Yale University Panel on East Timor," November 1999; Timmer, "Question for the United Nations Team."

7. João M. Saldanha and Helder Da Costa, "Economic Viability of East Timor Revisited," Working Paper No. 1, The East Timor Study Group, San Diego, 1999.

8. Michael Casey, "New Economy Has Meaning in East Timor," *Asian Wall Street Journal*, 7 October 1999.

9. *Sydney Morning Herald*, 19 November 1999.

10. The World Bank, "Rebuilding East Timor at the Local Level," 22 February 2000.

11. ABC Radio, accessed 4 January 2000. "Yale University Panel on East Timor."

12. Australian Associated Press, 5 January 2000.

13. World Bank, "East Timor, Building a Nation," November 1999.

14. World Bank, "Report of the Joint Assessment Mission in East Timor," December 1999.

15. Janet E. Heininger, *Peacekeeping in Transition: The United Nations in Cambodia* (New York: Twenty Century Fund Press, 1994), 55–59.

16. Haughton, "Reconstruction"; Heininger, *Peacekeeping in Transition*, 59–61; Ali Khadr, "Donor Assistance," in *Development Under Adversity: The Palestinian Economy in Transition*, ed. Ishac Diwan and Radwan A. Shaban (Washington, D.C.: The World Bank, 1999), 147.

17. United Nations and the World Bank, "Overview of External Financing Requirements for East Timor," December 1999.

18. Saldanha and da Costa, "Economic Viability of East Timor Revisited." On Timor Gap oil, see Tanter, Selden, and Shalom, "East Timor Faces the Future," in this volume.

19. "Timor Ire at Coffee Tax," *Sydney Morning Herald*, 29 February 2000.

20. Richard Abrahams and Herman Cortes-Douglas, "Introduction of a New National Currency: Policy, Institutional, and Technical Issues," IMF Working Paper, 1993; Jeffrey A. Frankel, "No Single Currency Regime is Right for All Countries or at All Times," NBER Working Paper Series #7338, 1999; Monetary Affairs Staff Team, "The Design of a Minimal Monetary and Exchange Structure for Countries in Post-Chaos/Post-Conflict Situations," The IMF, Monetary and Exchange Department, 1995; John Williamson, *What Role for the Currency Boards?* (Washington, D.C.: Institute of International Economics, 1995); and Athil Ghosh, et al., "Currency Boards: The Ultimate Fix?" IMF Working Paper, 1998.

21. Bruce Johnston and John Mellor, "The Role of Agriculture in Economic Development," *American Economic Review* 51, no. 4 (1961): 566–93; Erh-Cheng Hwa, "The Contribution of Agriculture to Economic Growth: Some Empirical Evidence," *World Development* 16, no. 11 (1988): 1329–39; Steven Block and C. Peter Timmer, "Agriculture and Economic Growth: Conceptual Issues and the Kenyan Experience," Development Discussion Paper No. 498, HIID, Harvard University, 1994.

22. World Bank, "East Timor, Building a Nation," November 1999.

23. Yoram Barzel, *Economic Analysis of Property Rights* (New York: Cambridge University Press, 1997); Mancur Olson, *Power and Prosperity: Outgrowing Communists and Capitalists Dictatorships* (New York: Basic Books, 2000); and Douglass North, *Institutions, Institutional Change and Economic Performance* (New York: Cambridge University Press, 1992).

24. "Australia, U.N. Mission in East Timor Sign $1.4 Billion Gas Exploration Accord," U.N. Newsservice, 23 February 2000; "East Timor: First Natural Gas Profits Only After 2004," Lusa, 28 February 2000; "New Oil and Gas Pact Agreed to by Australia and E Timor," Australian Associated Press, 28 February 2000.

25. C. Peter Timmer, Walter Falcon, and Scott R. Pearson, *Food Policy Analysis* (Baltimore: Johns Hopkins University Press, 1983). "Economic Viability of East Timor Revisited."

16

East Timor Faces the Future

Richard Tanter, Mark Selden, and Stephen R. Shalom

The long struggle for East Timorese independence, the five-hundred-year *funu*,[1] has been won. The painful residues of colonialism and war will long scar East Timorese society and culture, but for the people of East Timor, the taste of freedom is in the air. This chapter surveys the most important problems facing East Timor in its trajectory from Indonesian colony to U.N. temporary protectorate to full independence, assesses the first year of post-Indonesian rule, and examines some of the choices for, and conflicts likely to emerge in, the transition era.

TOWARD AN EAST TIMORESE STATE

On October 20, 1999, Indonesia formally acknowledged the end of its colonial rule by an act of the Indonesian People's Consultative Assembly (MPR) accepting the outcome of the referendum on independence and revoking East Timor's status as Indonesia's twenty-seventh province.

The United Nations, which operated initially through UNAMET (United Nations Assistance Mission in East Timor) and the Security Council–approved peacekeeping force, the International Force in East Timor (InterFET), established a United Nations Transitional Administration in East Timor (UNTAET). Security Council resolution 1272 of October 25, 1999, created UNTAET and gave it the following mandate:

    (a) To provide security and maintain law and order throughout the territory of East Timor;
    (b) To establish an effective administration;

243

(c) To assist in the development of civil and social services;
(d) To ensure the coordination and delivery of humanitarian assistance, reha-
    bilitation and development assistance;
(e) To support capacity-building for self-government;
(f) To assist in the establishment of conditions for sustainable development.

UNTAET is expected to remain in control of East Timorese affairs for two to three years, possibly longer, as a governing authority whose formidable objective is to make itself redundant. Its mission is to prepare the people of East Timor for independence after five hundred years of Portuguese colonialism followed by a quarter century of Indonesian conquest and devastation. UNTAET's other tasks—providing the security required to restore the war-shattered social and economic life of East Timor, protecting East Timor against threats of direct or indirect Indonesian military intervention or sabotage, assisting hundreds of thousands of refugees as they resettle, furnishing administrative and financial support, and initiating reconstruction—are subsumed within this larger mission.

Among the critical issues confronting the UNTAET interim administration is its relationship to the umbrella organization of the East Timorese resistance, the National Council of Timorese Resistance (CNRT), and to the people of East Timor more generally.

Article 1 of Security Council resolution 1272 states that UNTAET "will be endowed with overall responsibility for the administration of East Timor and will be empowered to exercise all legislative and executive authority, including the administration of justice." In article 8 the council called on UNTAET

> to consult and cooperate closely with the East Timorese people in order to carry out its mandate effectively with a view to the development of local democratic institutions, including an independent East Timorese human rights institution, and the transfer to these institutions of its administrative and public service functions.

UNTAET, charged with governing the territory, in December 1999 established a fifteen-member National Consultative Council (NCC) to advise the Transitional Administrator on all matters of policy. The council, dominated by CNRT, was intended to be "the primary mechanism through which the representatives of the people of East Timor shall actively participate in the decision making process during the period of the United Nations Transitional Administration in East Timor, and through which the views, concerns, traditions and interests of the East Timorese people will be represented."[2] The council in turn established sectoral committees dealing with specific issues.

Two months later, the Transitional Administrator reported to the Security Council:

> Through the NCC and its sectoral committees, UNTAET has set about building the regulatory framework necessary to underpin the administration of East Timor in all

areas, including the economy, local governance, justice, public and civil services. In addition to the first regulation, which defined the legal framework applicable in East Timor during the transitional period, and the second, which established the National Consultative Council, regulations have been enacted to establish the Transitional Judicial Service Commission, a Central Fiscal Authority, the Public Services Commission and a Central Payment Office. Regulations concerning the registration of commercial enterprises, the use of currencies, the new legal tender, and the licensing of foreign exchange bureaus have also been passed.[3]

Within a few months, the National Consultative Council was judged to be too small and insufficiently representative, and in July 2000 UNTAET replaced it with a National Council with thirty-three appointed members.[4] At the same time, UNTAET reorganized itself, creating eight portfolios comprising a cabinet chaired by the Special Representative of the U.N. secretary general: internal administration, infrastructure, economic affairs, social affairs, finance, justice, police and emergency services, and political affairs. The first four of these ministerial positions have been given to East Timorese, the other four to senior UNTAET staff members.[5]

In building a transitional state structure, UNTAET's logical partner is CNRT, which led the struggle for independence that culminated in the August 1999 referendum. (Indeed, in that referendum, which offered such powerful testimony to the unity of the East Timorese people, the symbol of CNRT was used on the ballots to represent the option of independence.)

In the first months of U.N. authority, however, CNRT officials complained about inadequate administrative involvement of the East Timorese, noting that "there seems to be a neo-colonialist attitude." Mario Carrascalão, vice president of CNRT, declared, "We need the United Nations to help create conditions in which life is possible, a democracy, and not deal with the people as if it were a dictatorship."[6] While Carrascalão subsequently defended the preliminary views of the World Bank assessment team of which he was a senior member, CNRT leader Xanana Gusmão expressed disquiet at the aggressiveness of external policy formulation, and at the failure of the World Bank and the United Nations to heed the wishes of the people of East Timor.[7]

While Security Council resolution 1272 calls for preparation in self-government and democratic local institutions, the real prospects for democracy in East Timor will ultimately depend heavily on the political practice of CNRT. One important positive indicator in this regard is the "Magna Carta concerning Freedoms, Rights, Duties and Guarantees for the People of East Timor" adopted at the East Timorese National Convention in the Diaspora, in Peniche, Portugal, on April 25, 1998.[8] The document displays CNRT's impressive commitment to building an East Timor that will be a model of social democratic constitutional democracy with strong protection for human rights. Another positive indicator is the responsible leadership provided by CNRT in the face of Jakarta's attempted sabotage of the referendum and the killings, expulsions, and destruction orchestrated by the Indonesian military prior to and especially following the balloting. Nevertheless, it is important to recognize the domestic and international pressures, and the historical residues of colonialism, that have so often led postcolonial governments in the periphery to choose authoritarian options limiting popular sovereignty.

Important issues face CNRT itself, aside from improving relations with its recent external enemies and establishing its position vis-à-vis UNTAET. CNRT is a broad front of political parties and individuals that united in the independence struggle. Important differences of opinion within CNRT and beyond in the wider East Timorese society, whose diaspora has now spread through several countries, will inevitably come to the fore in the postindependence era. The East Timorese today are comprised of communities and individuals with diverse resources and historical experiences. CNRT worked throughout the 1990s to build a structure that combined a capacity for effective decision-making with a respect for and acknowledgment of the diversity within the pro-self-determination forces in East Timorese communities around the world. CNRT devoted considerable efforts to reconciling differences of opinion and overcoming lingering antipathies from earlier days to build the broadest possible unity in the run up to the independence election.[9] Equally in the last years of Indonesian rule, CNRT consolidated a complex two-way flow of information and decision-making structures reaching from Cipinang Prison in Jakarta where Gusmão was confined, to East Timor and beyond to CNRT external leadership and the ever-increasing numbers of impressive activists and intellectuals emerging from East Timorese diaspora communities around the world.

It is hardly surprising that, in the absence of the common colonial enemy, challenges to CNRT leadership would arise. One challenge to the assumption of CNRT as the natural representative of East Timorese quickly emerged from younger East Timorese political activists and community group representatives. Members of CNRT's National Political Commission were criticized by activists in the urban-based resistance movement who felt excluded from the UNTAET–sponsored consultative process dominated by older CNRT elites.[10]

In the first year of UNTAET administration, the constituent parties of CNRT basically maintained their separate political identities and new political parties formed outside CNRT, including the Socialist Party of East Timor, the Popular Defense Council of the Democratic Republic of East Timor (CPD-RDTL), and the United Christian Democracy Party.[11]

By midyear 2000, with cross-border militia activity increasing external political pressures, some intimidation in domestic politics emerged.[12] This combination of factors led Gusmão and José Ramos-Horta to resign—until implored to reverse themselves—as president and vice president of CNRT, respectively, at the first CNRT congress since independence in August, citing a need to clear the way for fresh blood, but perhaps also hoping to sharpen awareness of the fragility of the achievement of CNRT to date.[13]

A key task for UNTAET is the establishment of a constitutional framework for East Timorese independence. Many members of the former Indonesian regional assembly who were elected and appointed under military rule fled the country following the independence vote. Without assessing the proposed models for assemblies, it is important to bear in mind the negative lessons of the Palestinian Authority (PA), the executive body headed by Yasir Arafat. In a short time the PA came to disregard the authority of the legislative branch of the state. Legislation was simply ignored, as were legislators' attempts to require that executive agencies limit their actions to domains specified by the legislature.[14]

A second question is the structure of administration. Unfortunately, East Timor's historical legacy in this area, a product of Portuguese authoritarian rule and neglect and of Indonesian bureaucratism and violence, is a dismal one. Here perhaps it will be important to remember some of the successes of the brief period of Fretilin administration in 1974–75, which were marked by a willingness to invent new structures based on a closeness to the people.[15] Whether the democratic potential inherent in that short-lived experience of a guerrilla movement can be resurrected and adapted to peacetime rule is a formidable challenge.

A third question about the self-governing state concerns the role of courts, especially their role in defending the rights of individuals against the power of executive government. In this respect, too, Palestinian experience has been extremely bitter, with judges who were critical of the procedures of the Palestinian Authority either forcibly removed or their decisions ignored. The task for an independent East Timor will be to find a way to make the ideals of the Magna Carta concrete, so that first and foremost citizens feel secure and confident in their everyday lives.

A fourth question relates to the role of women in the new East Timorese state. Timorese custom—which included polygamy and *berlake*, a form of bride price paid to a woman's parents before marriage—and Catholicism both consigned women to a second-class status. The years of struggle against Indonesian aggression and the dislocation resulting from Jakarta's scorched-earth policies both contributed to undermining the subordination of women. Fretilin outlawed polygamy and *berlake*—though changes were slow—and in guerrilla-controlled zones, women experienced new freedoms and responsibilities.[16] There was equality, too, in suffering. Women were among those who fought and died as guerrilla soldiers and many were the victims of gender-specific violence perpetrated by the Indonesian authorities and the militia: rape and other forms of sexual abuse, sexual harassment, forced "marriage," forced recruitment as sex "slaves" or "comfort women," and forced sterilization.[17] Postreferendum violence left an estimated sixty-thousand female-headed households, with husbands or fathers either dead or exiled outside East Timor.[18]

The 1998 Magna Carta explicitly committed CNRT to equality between men

Figure 16.1   Women beating gongs on the way to a water rites ceremony at Venilale. Courtesy: Steve Cox.

and women. On September 28, 1999, Gusmão told a press conference that women held leadership positions in East Timor—for example, they were two of the seven members of CNRT's National Political Commission at the time—and that CNRT aimed to promote gender equity.[19] Grassroots women's groups—Fokupers, Gertak, ET-WAVE, and the Organization of Timorese Women—have addressed such issues as women's employment and domestic violence. Women are three of the eleven Timorese members of the National Consultative Council, one of three on the Transitional Judicial Services Commission, and three of the first ten judges and prosecutors to be appointed in East Timor.[20] It remains to be seen how the new influence and prestige of the Catholic Church in East Timor will affect women's rights, but we note that the Church did not impede a targeted condom distribution campaign in Dili in March 2000.[21] As with other social and political issues, much remains to be done in progressing toward women's equality.

A final core political issue concerns CNRT itself. In her chapter, Sarah Niner has traced the long and difficult history of efforts to transcend the historic splits between Fretilin and the Timorese Democratic Union (UDT) dating back to the mid-1970s.[22] Gusmão's extraordinary personal standing and the political skills of CNRT leadership generated the unity required for victory under conditions of Indonesian repression. However, CNRT has no underlying principle of unity beyond the goal of independence from Indonesian rule. With CNRT leaders coming from different parties, some of which fought each other militarily, and differing in their class backgrounds and experiences, including their positions in traditionally legitimated elite structures, conflicting perspectives and frictions are inevitable. Challenges of the transition to self-government and internal strains within diverse sectors of the movement will transform CNRT. With the emergence of other political parties and groups, UNTAET's task of establishing representative political structures has become more urgent and delicate.

ISSUES OF POLICING AND DEMILITARIZATION

East Timor faces three critical security questions. These are the issues of armed rebellion, revenge, and obstacles to demilitarization after a quarter century of war.

The immediate issue is the threat of renewed violence and intimidation by pro-Indonesian militia forces. In September 2000 militia groups and their Indonesian military masters continued to control most refugee camps in West Timor holding about ninety-thousand East Timorese. Foreign observers estimate that perhaps half of this number wish to return to East Timor, but are being prevented from doing so by militia violence and intimidation.[23] Within East Timor, militia violence was limited and rapidly contained by InterFET and, after February 23, 2000, by UNTAET's peacekeeping force. Indonesian military forces, after an initial period of tolerance, if not outright support for cross-border militia attacks on InterFET soldiers, worked more or less effectively to limit border hostilities.[24] Yet the capacity for militia violence remained real, and since summer 2000, cross-border militia operations have grown rapidly in number and violence, resulting in several armed clashes with U.N. peacekeeping units and the deaths of two U.N. soldiers and an unknown number of militia. Captured militia were carrying equipment used by the Indonesian armed forces (TNI), and in one case a *Kopassus* (Special Forces) identity card, leading UNTAET officials to state that the raids were at least tolerated, if not planned and equipped, by some sections of the TNI in West Timor.[25] Throughout August and early September 2000, violent intimidation of U.N. and other aid workers in the West Timor camps by militia escalated without any serious restriction by the Indonesian armed forces or police. On September 6, three U.N. aid workers were killed by militia forces in Atambua. The remaining U.N. staff in West Timor were evacuated, leaving the refugees unprotected and without support. Militia violence in the camps continued unchecked despite severe condemnations by both the Indonesian president and the Security Council.

The inability of InterFET, and subsequently UNTAET, to resolve the problem of East Timorese refugees held captive in West Timor, reveals the limits of U.N.–sponsored efforts to resolve issues of the Indonesian invasion and violence in East Timor. The situation in West Timor in fact worsened through the year as the effective authority of the Indonesian state disintegrated in the province. The killings of the U.N. aid workers, timed to coincide with President Wahid's September appearance before the United Nations General Assembly, reflected the degree to which at least some powerful factions of the Indonesian army had effectively wrested control of portions of the armed forces from the central Jakarta authorities.

Second, it is inevitable that, after all the suffering flowing from war and colonial occupation, many East Timorese will feel extreme bitterness toward Indonesians in the territory, and more importantly, towards those East Timorese whom they regard as collaborators and perpetrators of crimes of violence. It is well to remember how fierce such feelings can be. After the end of World War II in Europe, some thirty to forty thousand French citizens deemed collaborators with the Nazi occupation (which was only four years in duration, compared to twenty-four years of a bloodier Indonesian occupation) were summarily executed by French resistance forces.[26] The ability to heal the wounds of war and bring an end to the cycle of killing will constitute one of the most difficult challenges for both the transitional administration and its East Timorese successor.

Gusmão and Ramos-Horta have stressed the need to eschew revenge in order both to forge unity and to build a society based on compassion. After the violence and terror that was inflicted on the East Timorese people, and particularly on the proindependence majority, by the Indonesian military and its paid militias, this will be an extraordinarily difficult task, but a crucial one. The first step is to forget the straightforward dichotomy of "collaborator" and "patriot" altogether. In twenty-four years of Indonesian occupation, the families of even the most ardent supporter of independence have had to make accommodations and compromises with Indonesian authority just to survive. Lives are not always lived politically. CNRT's great achievements as a resistance movement included its appeal to unity and its avoidance of terrorism. The challenge for the future will be to maintain this stance against the inevitable frustration of chaotic peace and job shortages, especially as refugees with a militia background, and their families, return home.

The issues of reconciliation are not, of course, limited to healing wounds created by Indonesian violence; equally difficult will be overcoming the legacies of internal conflicts within East Timor. Recent reports indicate that former Fretilin leaders now affiliated with CNRT are beginning to air and apologize for serious abuses by Fretilin against UDT, Apodeti, and its own dissidents during the 1975 civil war and its aftermath.[27] This development, and the broader national discussion of past tensions among Timorese political groups encouraged by the current CNRT leadership, should contribute to the important process of reconciliation that Gusmão and others have called for.

The third security issue that CNRT faces is a product of two decades of war. Will it be possible to overcome the habits of violence and secrecy necessary for survival under alien occupation? And will it be possible for Falintil fighters to make the transition to the demilitarized East Timor that CNRT has envisaged? Even more difficult, will militia fighters—who, whatever their motivations, were effectively the losers in the war for independence—make such a transition?[28] Again, the Palestinian solution of transferring former PLO fighters to the police force of the Palestinian Authority illustrates dimensions of the problem, as police violation of human rights has been widely recognized as one source of popular antagonism towards the PA.

During the initial period of transition, CNRT articulated its goal of a demilitarized East Timor without an army. As cross-border militia activity grew rather than diminished during the first year of UNTAET rule, however, CNRT called for an army for an independent East Timor based on the CNRT military wing, Falantil, which had been in cantonment since the arrival of InterFET. UNTAET broadly supported that position, and accordingly commissioned a study of the new nation's military security needs and capacities from a British consultancy group. Falantil in September 1999 had in fact been a relatively small group, consisting of about one thousand soldiers. U.N. forces in July 2000 amounted to about eight thousand in total. Calls early in the year by Gusmão and others (including the U.S. ambassador to the U.N., Richard Holbrooke) to reduce the number of U.N. peacekeepers gave way after the midyear militia killings to concerns that the rules of engagement under which the U.N. troops operated were unduly restrictive. The shape of a future defense force is not yet clear, but the transition of Falintil forces into an effective security force, with or without participation of former militia, remains a difficult challenge for both UNTAET and CNRT.

JUSTICE AND RECONCILIATION

Another critical issue is the question of responsibility for war crimes and crimes against humanity. In practical terms this involves East Timor, Indonesia, and the United Nations. However, the attitude of CNRT will be crucial. Gusmão's remarkable capacity to take the long view by trying to overcome the traumas of invasion and war will be stretched.

For the Timorese there are two basic sets of issues concerning the question of trauma. The first is whether they choose to face the criminal past through a legal framework of crime and punishment, through trials under law, or whether they opt, as did South Africa after an analogous experience, to deal with trauma through public inquiry predicated on goals of reconciliation. The latter course involves public testimony by victims and public expressions of remorse by the perpetrators of crimes, with the possibility of criminal prosecution for the unrepentant. The model of the South African Truth and Reconciliation Commission would appear consonant with the reparative inclinations of Gusmão and Bishop Carlos Filipe Ximenes Belo. While Gusmão has spoken of his interest in such a commission, however, Belo has stressed the need to balance reconciliation with justice. For Belo, reconciliation with militia members who show remorse is possible, but he has stressed that the international community must stand by its responsibility to try the senior Indonesian officers who orchestrated the terror. The reconciliation approach, while painful and difficult for victims and their families, holds the potential to minimize future divisions while permitting the airing rather than the burying of long suppressed grievances. Above all, it invites the prospect of encouraging citizens to move from anger and grief to face the difficulties of confronting what must be a common future of a people that has been ravaged by colonial rule and protracted war.

But if truth and reconciliation seem appropriate for redressing the crimes of low-level Timorese such as militia members, the question of prosecuting war crimes by high-ranking Indonesian officials is more complicated. Major international players —the United States, China, Britain, Australia, and Secretary-General Kofi Annan—initially called for permitting Indonesia, rather than any international body, to conduct trials of those responsible for the atrocities, with an international tribunal to convene only if Jakarta fails to take adequate action. This position made sense in terms of respecting and supporting Indonesia's moves toward democracy. It ignored, however, the fact that the crimes committed were committed not against Indonesians, but against people that the United Nations has recognized as victims of illegal Indonesian aggression and occupation, as well as against the international community itself, which had organized the

August 30 referendum. In any event, both Indonesia and Security Council members have restricted the time period of their concern only back to January 1999, thus exempting Suharto-era crimes from examination.[29] And, unsurprisingly, neither Jakarta nor any of the members of the council have called for an investigation into state crimes: specifically the providing of military, economic, and diplomatic support for Indonesia's brutal rule in East Timor.

The troubling question remains whether Indonesia's fledgling democracy is capable of mounting a fair investigation of the nation's most powerful military leaders, a formidable challenge to any society, and above all one long dominated by the military. Slow but persistent progress by Indonesian attorney-general Marzuki Darusman toward promised trials of senior military officers received a major setback in August 2000 when the Indonesian People's Consultative Congress amended Article 28 of the Indonesian constitution to ban retroactive prosecution of human rights crimes. Darusman subsequently maintained, somewhat optimistically, that East Timor offenses would be exempted from this provision, and, in any case, the trials could be conducted under international, rather than Indonesian, law. Criticism of the amendment within Indonesia and East Timor and elsewhere was immediate.[30] The head of the U.N. Commission for Human Rights, Mary Robinson, immediately called on the Security Council to establish an international tribunal for East Timor. The simultaneous condemnations of the Indonesian government's failure to halt militia killings and intimidation in West Timor strengthened these calls, but equally drew attention to the declining authority of the Wahid administration and uncertainty about what would take its place should it fall.

Beyond criminal trials, there is the question of pressing financial compensation claims against Jakarta. Aceh was promised compensation by the Habibie administration for criminal acts committed by Indonesian military forces during the New Order period, and East Timorese leaders will have to decide whether they wish to press comparable claims. But Indonesia's financial situation is now much worse than it was a few years ago, so the prospect of significant compensation is much reduced. And the resentment in Indonesia that raising such claims may provoke could well poison whatever limited chances of a new start may exist.

These factors suggest the likelihood that East Timor will seek reconciliation rather than reparations or financial compensation from Indonesia or the powers that supported Indonesian aggression. The harsh reality is that East Timor is likely to get more in aid by throwing itself on the mercy of the rich nations than by pressing reparations claims, however just.

If this view seems likely to prevail within East Timor, there may be other considerations for those outside. (See the chapter in this volume by Richard Falk.) International human rights organizations have long argued that it is essential to establish the precedent that crimes against humanity cannot be committed with impunity.[31] The behavior of the TNI–controlled militia in East Timor was so blatantly horrific that there is a degree of international expectation that responsible

Indonesian officers will be held accountable. Even if an international war crimes tribunal for Indonesia is not in the cards, the demand to bring to trial those guilty of crimes against humanity serves an important educational and political point. And going beyond the positions of most human rights groups and calling for the indictment of officials of the U.S. government that armed and trained the killers, of the Australian government that conspired with Indonesia to deprive East Timor of its right to Timor Gap oil, and of the Japanese government that bankrolled the Indonesian regime—this too might serve to illuminate some issues of responsibility, though the chances of any such indictments are unfortunately nil. Likewise, the call for reparations from those governments that backed Indonesia may be another way to make the point about responsibility, even if the prospect for reparations is no greater than it was in the case of U.S. destruction in Vietnam, Laos, and Cambodia.

LANGUAGE

A key issue before the new government is language, with its implications for identity and educational policy. There are three widely spoken languages in East Timor today—Tetum, Indonesian, and, less broadly, Portuguese. Most East Timorese are necessarily multilingual, and there are substantial cross-overs of vocabulary from one language to another. Benedict Anderson has pointed out that for Indonesian nationalists "at the turn of the century, the language of the colonizer, Dutch, was the language through which it became possible to communicate across the colony and to understand the real condition of the country. It was also the language of access to modernity and the world beyond the colony."[32]

One important effect of a quarter century of Indonesian colonization of East Timor has been to create an Indonesian-speaking and -reading young generation able to reach out to the Indonesian archipelago and beyond. Moreover, since Tetum only recently acquired a written language, and written Tetum was never effectively integrated into formal education, the written language for those within East Timor is effectively Indonesian. The language issue is complicated by the fact that documents of the external resistance leadership were either in Portuguese or English. The firm foundation of widely spoken Indonesian is likely to be sustained by the consequences of proximity and convenience, by its use as a language of business in neighboring areas, and by the availability of a much wider written literature than exists in Tetum, which is only the most widespread among indigenous languages of the East Timorese people. And given that so much of East Timor's human capital is today in the form of young people schooled in Indonesian, dispensing with that language would represent a squandering of a scarce resource.

But Tetum has also become a language of East Timorese nationalism: a nationalism deriving both from its indigenous roots and from its association with membership in the Catholic Church. "[T]he decision of the Catholic hierarchy in East

Timor to use Tetum, not Indonesian, as the language of the Church," Anderson notes, "has had profoundly nationalizing effects. It has raised Tetum from being a local language or lingua franca in parts of East Timor to becoming, for the first time, the language of 'East Timorese' religion and identity."[33] After the Suharto government required that all Indonesians belong to one of a limited number of officially recognized religions in the early 1980s, the size of the Catholic Church in East Timor swelled considerably. As a result, the nationalist implications of the Church's use of Tetum were magnified still further.

The situation linguistically is further complicated by the fact that Portuguese, English, and Indonesian have emerged as critical languages in the East Timorese diaspora. João Mariano Saldanha (this volume) estimate the number of Timorese outside East Timor and Indonesia at twenty to thirty thousand, with the largest concentrations in Australia, Portugal, Macau, and Mozambique.[34]

An important potential resource for staffing the East Timor government and contributing to economic development is the East Timorese living abroad, some of whom have had education as well as job training and experience. Returnees would also likely retain strong links with relatives and associates in their former host countries and some would have access to financial remittances from abroad. In short, these English- and Portuguese-speaking returnees may well have a presence stronger than their numbers would suggest. Furthermore, English will inevitably be bolstered by the long-term presence of a multinational United Nations administration and peacekeeping force and other international agencies, whose dominant language will be English. Within days of a World Bank advisory team entering the country, senior CNRT leaders were criticizing what they saw as a presumption by the Bank and other multilateral agencies that English would be the effective language of administration.[35] In January 2000, a crowd of Timorese job-seekers rioted when they learned that U.N. jobs required some knowledge of English.[36]

The CNRT Magna Carta states that Portuguese will be the official language of an independent East Timor and invokes the country's "Judeo-Christian" identity. In February 2000, CNRT announced that Portuguese would be the official language of independent East Timor. Explaining the decision, Gusmão maintained that East Timor owed its independence to Portugal, or rather, to the cultural identity formed through Portuguese colonization. "If the Portuguese left many years ago, the Dutch would have taken this area and we would have become Indonesia. We have them to thank for our identity."[37] This points to the ambiguities of the Portuguese colonial experience for East Timor. Prior to 1975, education—however limited—combined the Portuguese language and the teachings of the Catholic Church. And after 1975, it was exactly the "Judeo-Christian heritage" of East Timor that was often invoked by resistance forces as the key to identity in the face of Indonesian attempts at forced assimilation. Thus, ironically, the relationship with Portugal—the historic colonial power—helped to create the

East Timorese national identity that was so central to the modern anticolonial struggle against Indonesia.

Portugal's offer to subsidize the entire East Timorese government budget for at least two years, and possibly three, and Portuguese financial contributions illustrate the continuing bonds between the former colonizer and East Timor. But if Portuguese linguistic and cultural nationalism is still alive, particularly among the Portuguese-educated older generation, only time will tell whether the Portuguese state has the will and the resources to compete linguistically and in other ways with Indonesian, Tetum, and English as the language of an independent East Timor. The first congress of the East Timor Student Solidarity Council, the primary organization of college students, in its July 24–27, 2000, meeting, proposed a three- to five-year training period during which four official languages—Tetum, English, Portuguese, and Indonesian—would coexist prior to establishing Tetum as the national and official language.[38]

Gusmão's powerful speeches to crowds in Dili on his return to East Timor in October 1999 after seven years of prison and exile were in Tetum. Two decades of education in Indonesian language in East Timor, the "nationalization" of Tetum through the expanded and invigorated Church, and the development of a rich cultural life in other languages such as Indonesian and English have all changed the medium through which East Timorese identity is articulated. The language issue is thorny and potentially divisive in education, administration, cultural affairs, and economic policy.[39] Indeed, the first editorial in East Timor's first Tetum language newspaper charged that CNRT language policy was "clearly a matter of a tiny minority trying to impose their will on a majority."[40]

Official language aside, there is also the question of the language of instruction in school—at the primary, secondary, and tertiary levels. The "language(s) of government," moreover, need not be the same as the language of the nation. If the language challenge looms large in East Timor, it should be noted that many other postcolonial nations, from India to Nigeria to Mexico to Taiwan, have confronted similarly painful language choices involving the language of the colonizer and multiple indigenous languages. For East Timor, though, there have been *two* colonial languages, and perhaps a third, English, is currently emerging.

LAW

The first regulation promulgated by UNTAET continued to enforce Indonesian laws prevailing in October 1999, until UNTAET issues legislation to the contrary, with the exception of certain unacceptable Indonesian laws such as the antisubversive and national security laws.

From the beginning of post-Indonesian administration, the clash of legal systems will be felt.[41] Even if the most egregious cases of coerced legal settlements under Indonesian colonial law are set aside, will contracts and titles that were written freely under Indonesian law, where there was no coercion involved, be considered valid? Where Indonesian law and colonial Portuguese law differ significantly, which, if either approach, will be followed? If Indonesian law is to be followed as an interim step, then for how long in circumstances where significant tensions between legal systems arise? Will norms from other legal systems, including nonformalized indigenous norms, gain acceptance? These are issues of system and process.

Urgent questions with legal ramifications arise that affect the livelihood of the people of East Timor. What should happen to the substantial property owned by Indonesian political and military elites, such as the Suharto family?[42] What is the status of property and other contracts dating from the Indonesian occupation period where some element of coercion or outright expropriation is demonstrable, even if the coercion was not exercised by the present beneficiaries? One approach would be to restore the preinvasion status quo. In all but the simplest and most blatant cases of theft, however, this might produce a moral and practical quagmire detrimental to economic recovery and contributing to social conflict, leaving, for example, farmers uncertain of the rights to their land, residents unclear regarding the ownership of their homes, and businesses reluctant to invest.[43]

OIL

The most significant legal question facing the new state, certainly in terms of its long-term economic and revenue implications, is also unfortunately among the most urgent: the rewriting of the Timor Gap Zone of Cooperation Treaty. The Timor Gap is the region between Australia and East Timor. The critical issue is the division of the rights to the oil and gas reserves in the seabed.[44]

Before Indonesia's invasion of East Timor in 1975, Portugal and Australia had failed to reach agreement on the position of the seabed boundary. After Jakarta took over the territory, Indonesia and Australia saw an opportunity to conclude a lucrative agreement.

International law has two general ways of dealing with maritime boundaries. Customary practice is to consider various aspects of underwater topography—in particular, the deepest point of a trough. Using this approach, which Australia favored, would place the boundary line close to Indonesia and put most of the seabed within Australia's jurisdiction. But customary practice has been superceded by recent developments in the international law of the sea that instead take the median line—the line equidistant between the two countries—as the boundary. This was the view favored by Indonesia. But though Jakarta had recent international law on its side, its eagerness to legitimate its conquest made it willing to settle for less—and Australia knew this. As Canberra's ambassador to Indonesia secretly advised his government, in a cable that was later leaked, "a treaty on the oil- and gas-rich seabed could be more readily negotiated with Indonesia than with Portugal or independent Portuguese Timor."[45]

The Timor Gap Treaty (TGT), signed by Indonesia and Australia in 1989 after twelve years of negotiation, declared that the resources of the seabed between the median line and the deepest point of the trough—that is, resources located in waters that prevailing international law would have awarded entirely to Indonesia—would be shared equally between the two countries. The terms of the treaty were no abstraction. Oil and gas with a potential gross yield worth many billions of dollars have been discovered so far in the seabed between East Timor and Australia, precisely in the area north of the median line referred to by the treaty as Zone A. Thus, Indonesia, in return for Australia's formal recognition of its annexation of East Timor, negotiated away huge potential revenues. But, of course, Indonesia had no legal right to negotiate for East Timor's resources in the first place, given that its occupation of the territory was illegal and recognized by no nation except Australia. Now that Indonesia has withdrawn from East Timor, the critical question concerns the status of the TGT. If a revised treaty were concluded based on the standard median line principle, the newly independent East Timor would be entitled to all, not half, of the oil and gas revenues from Zone A.

The matter was temporarily resolved when UNTAET and the Australian and Indonesian governments announced an agreement under which Indonesia withdrew from the treaty, UNTAET took its place as a representative of East Timor, with East Timorese revenues to be consigned to a trust fund that would be administered by UNTAET. José Ramos-Horta announced CNRT's acceptance of the agreement, which left the original division of revenues intact to the advantage of Australia, saying that in two years' time the treaty would be reviewed.[46]

The question remains whether CNRT leadership has the capacity to renegotiate the treaty in the face of expected Australian opposition and procrastination. The Australian government has called on the new nation to accept all the provisions of the TGT, simply replacing references to "Indonesia" with "East Timor" where appropriate. In the past, Gusmão and Ramos-Horta have stated that they would "honor the Timor Gap Treaty."[47] Geoffrey McKee, an Australian oil and gas industry consultant, argues that what they really meant was that they would "honor the rights of the Timor Gap Contractors," that is, place no impediment in the path of the investment by production companies, but leave open the right to negotiate with the Australian government over the seabed boundary, and hence the disposition of revenues.[48] Indeed, in November 1999, East Timorese leaders stated that maritime borders between East Timor and Australia would have to be renegotiated.[49] There is, however, what McKee describes as the "uncertainty factor": fundamental renegotiation of the Treaty with Australia could take years, during which period not only might investors be scared off, but East Timor would get no hydrocarbon revenues at all, at a time when it will be desperate for funds. An added complication is that Indonesia may claim some right to the oil resources by arguing that *West* Timor is as close to the Timor Gap as East Timor, and closer than Australia. Australia and the oil companies might prefer to deal with Indonesia than East Timor, effectively leaving the East Timorese out in the cold.[50]

Another oil issue with legal implications concerns the positions of Indonesian contractors under the existing TGT, and would-be Portuguese contractors and their possible East Timorese partners. Indonesian politicians and business representatives have called on the Wahid administration to resist what they regard as effectively unilateral Australian renegotiation of the treaty: "The Australians seem to be determined to dominate the Timor Gap oil field."[51] The fact that some existing Indonesian Timor Gap contractors may have secured their positions through close relations with the Suharto family,[52] and that these positions were in any case gained through Indonesian illegal occupation of East Timor, does not alter the fact that the Australian government is trying to take advantage of the present situation to achieve dominance and maximize profits.[53] In principle, it would be in the interest of an independent East Timor to seek to balance a potentially overweening Australian presence with contractors of different flags.

At midyear 2000, UNTAET announced that it did not regard the Timor Gap Treaty as a legitimate foundation for any long-term agreement between UNTAET (on behalf of the people of East Timor) and Australia. The United Nations never recognized the legality of the treaty, and accordingly, a "successor state" model—whereby an independent East Timor took up the responsibilities and rights of the former colonial power—was not appropriate.[54] Negotiations between UNTAET and Australia were planned for October.

Australian responses were mixed. The opposition Australian Labor Party—under whose government the Timor Gap Treaty had been negotiated and ferociously defended—reversed its position and supported new arrangements whereby the revenues from any joint production zone were split 90:10 with an independent East Timor receiving the lion's share. Liberal Party minister for foreign affairs and trade, Alexander Downer, rejected that position, but was sympathetic to some reallocation of revenues, if only to ensure that the independent state had a sound revenue base. In any case, senior Australian legal officials were anxious to negotiate the matter "between states," rather than see "states lose control" of the whole matter by allowing it into the international judicial arena.[55]

On the East Timorese side as well, strongly differing positions emerged. Senior CNRT oil affairs representative Mari Alkatiri faced substantial criticism for his defense of UNTAET's position at the CNRT congress in August. Alkatiri argued that any agreement UNTAET reached with Australia would be ratified by the legislature following independence, and that CNRT radicals' calls for ejecting the existing investors were not only impossible, but more importantly, inimical to East Timor's interest in a rapid development of a hydrocarbon revenue flow. Above all, Alkatiri argued, Phillips Petroleum, the operator for the Bayu-Undan consortium, had already begun to invest a large part of the more than $1.4 billion needed to bring production online at its full rate of 113,000 barrels a day by early 2004. The argument, Alkatiri concluded, was not with the industry operators, but with Australia.

Clearly there is a good chance that substantial oil revenues will come to an independent East Timor in the next decade. Moreover, the employment provisions of the Timor Gap Treaty provide a path to skilled work for some East Timorese, with sufficient support for training. East Timorese companies, private or public, will potentially profit from association with foreign oil companies. And yet the promise of an oil boom, or even a miniboom, brings its own dangers. Under Indonesian occupation, plenty of East Timorese learned the arts of corruption at the corporate level. There is as yet no East Timorese state competent to directly protect the rights of East Timorese citizens in relation to oil. And oil has a phantasmagorical quality to it, the apparent answer to a people's prayers, which has all too often produced vast personal fortunes but very little real social change benefiting the majority.

THE MISSING AND THE DEAD

The most catastrophic aspect of Indonesian rule was the appalling number of East Timorese deaths. Long before the terror campaign leading up to and after the August 30, 1999, ballot, Indonesian rule had exacted a terrible toll.

Prior to 1999, a figure of two hundred thousand dead as a result of the Indonesian invasion was very widely quoted, in most instances without a source or a specification of the time period during which these deaths were said to have occurred. The figure in fact originated in a 1980 study by the Australian researcher John Waddingham, based on a careful analysis of data from Portuguese, Catholic Church, and Indonesian sources. The essence of Waddingham's analysis, which stressed the great uncertainties inherent in the work, was that given Indonesian population figures of 523,000 East Timorese in June 1979 and the known 1975 population of 663,000, some 133,000 to 170,000 people were unaccounted for, depending on assumptions concerning the accuracy of Portuguese and Indonesian census procedures. Factoring in East Timor's population growth rate of 1.7 percent per annum prior to 1975, the number missing by 1979 could have ranged from 177,000 to 217,000.[56] While Waddingham's analysis was derided at the time by the Indonesian government and pro-Indonesian writers, there has been no serious analysis contradicting or significantly modifying his findings.[57]

Waddingham's analysis, it must be stressed, estimated the numbers unaccounted for and presumed dead for the period from December 1975 to mid-1979. This included the period of the invasion itself, Fretilin's recovery and establishment of effective bases and tactics for guerrilla operations in the following year, and the ferocious Indonesian counterinsurgency campaigns of 1977 to 1979 with U.S. training and aircraft that nearly broke Fretilin as a guerrilla force. Hundreds of thousands of people were driven from their mountain villages to coastal

Figure 16.2   Baguia, 1995. A typical Baguia house on a small family farm. The soil has been tilled awaiting the rain before planting. Courtesy: Ross Bird.

camps, famine and disease were rampant, and the mountains turned into free-fire zones. Against this background, Waddingham's careful analysis was highly plausible, and consistent with refugee accounts. There are no systematic data for East Timorese deaths for the period 1980 to 1999.

As of September 2000, the death toll from the violence following the August 30, 1999, referendum was still unknown. In early November 1999, the InterFET commander had announced that eighty thousand people still remained unaccounted for. Many may have been in the mountains, hiding in West Timor or elsewhere in Indonesia. "There is always speculation about a fourth fate for some of these people," Major General Cosgrove said.[58] Few bodies have been found, but this by no means resolves the issue, for a few days later an InterFET officer, Lieutenant Colonel Nick Welch, stated that "Bodies were taken from here, taken to the sea about 30km, weighted and dumped in the sea."

Plagued by inadequate numbers of forensic staff, InterFET nevertheless spent the months following the vote in searching for the bodies of murdered East Timorese. By July 2000, some 345 bodies had been found, and reports of gravesites suggest well over one thousand dead.[59] Human Rights Watch estimates that about one thousand died in the September 1999 violence.[60] But given the reports of bodies dumped at sea and the possibility that many others may have decayed in East Timor's tropical climate, it seems clear that any final estimate of the numbers killed in September 1999 must await a careful population count. To this toll must be added the hundreds of East Timorese who died of disease and militia terror in refugee camps in West Timor—and continue to do so—a consequence of the violence and displacements following the referendum.[61] And given the considerable margin of error in estimates of the number of refugees in West Timor or elsewhere in Indonesia, at this point it remains impossible to distinguish between the missing and the uncounted.

RECONSTRUCTION AND ECONOMIC DEVELOPMENT

Beyond the killings, the militia rampage of September 1999 caused horrific destruction. The World Bank described the situation *before* the postreferendum devastation:

> East Timor was one of the poorest areas in East Asia. Indonesian Government figures indicate a per capita GDP of under US$395 in 1997. Approximately 50 percent of households are clustered around the poverty line. Key social indicators were at extremely low levels, with life expectancy estimated at 56 years, only 41 percent of the population literate, primary school enrollment at 70 percent and secondary school enrollment at 39 percent. Provision of social and economic infrastructure was also low before the crisis, with only 29 percent of households having access to potable water, and only 22 percent with electricity. Only 49 percent of villages were accessible by paved road before the crisis.[62]

After the September violence, these grim conditions got far worse. Per capita income was estimated to have fallen by half.[63] Almost 700,000 displaced East Timorese were found to "need full food rations for six months."[64] "Up to 50 percent of the homes in Dili and the western part of East Timor" were "damaged or destroyed."[65] In March 2000, there were a total of twenty doctors to care for the entire population of 800,000 people.[66] "With virtually every hospital and clinic destroyed," reported the Australian Broadcasting Corporation that same month, "easily treatable diseases are now going untreated and people are dying for want of simple medicines available in any Australian pharmacy."[67] Half a year after the ballot, 80 percent of the working population was still without visible means of support.[68]

The dramatic effects of the final weeks of Indonesian destructiveness added yet another terrible burden at the end of a long war of resistance. Centuries of Portuguese colonial underdevelopment and extraction were followed by twenty-four years of Indonesian destruction and further siphoning off of East Timor's resources. However, as Saldanha and Da Costa show, both the final years of Portuguese rule (1960–75), which they style "the ethical economy," and the years of "uncertain development" under Indonesian rule (1980–95), had significant developmental impact whose legacy continues.[69] They date the foundations of a modern economy to the last fifteen years of Portuguese control, noting the creation of infrastructure, trade, and financial institutions as well as the promotion of agriculture and tourism, through an injection of state resources. To be sure, many of these fragile gains were destroyed in the initial years of Indonesian onslaught, both in the first months, and then notably in the great famine of 1977 to 1980 that followed a new Indonesian strategy of warfare supported by U.S. counterinsurgency aircraft and other military aid. In addition to the lives lost, livestock was devastated and the agrarian economy destroyed as the Indonesian military cleared the population from the mountains to lowland concentration camps. Over the next decade and a half, however, substantial Indonesian funds were invested in infrastructure, particularly roads, but also in education, health, and agriculture. Indeed, these developmental efforts produced a flow of migrants from Indonesia who secured the most lucrative jobs in both the private and state sector, contributing to widening income inequality. A large share of the annual budget for East Timor—which totalled more than $100 million—either went directly as wages to the bloated Indonesian bureaucracy, or disappeared through channels of corruption large and small.

Saldanha and Da Costa do not shrink from highlighting the daunting economic prospects facing the people of East Timor. They, and Saldanha in his chapter for this volume, nevertheless offer cautiously optimistic prognoses for East Timor's economic prospects. They point particularly to East Timor's resource endowment, oil being the most important, followed by coffee (the traditional dominant export), coconuts and other agricultural products, as well as the potential for tourism. They also look to foreign remittances as potential sources of income and

Figure 16.3   Students on floor of makeshift classroom, Aileu, December 1999. Courtesy: Ross Bird and East Timor Human Rights Centre.

foreign exchange capable in the short run of overcoming dependency and producing a viable economy.

Constâncio Pinto, CNRT representative to the United Nations in an October 22, 1999, interview[70] stressed the importance of Portugal to East Timor's future. Pinto stated that the East Timor currency will be the escudo, a decision that was heavily shaped by Portugal's agreement (as mentioned above) to fund East Timor's budget during the transition period, and one reinforced by the fact that the Portuguese currency is far stronger than the Indonesian currency previously in use. The escudo would also give East Timor access to Western Europe, a useful counterweight to the likely overwhelming U.S. and Japanese economic influence. Contrary to CNRT's original hope, however, UNTAET adopted the U.S. dollar as East Timor's official currency. Although the decision was reportedly taken by the National Consultative Council, CNRT was critical, preferring the Portuguese escudo, and by extension, the euro.[71]

Like all poor countries, East Timor receives economic advice from the world's financial institutions. Some of this advice will no doubt be valuable, but some will certainly be directed to getting East Timor to adopt the neo-liberal model that places the interests of multinational investors above those of one's own people. Indeed, Gusmão has accused the World Bank of at times trying to impose its own views.[72] In the face of their severe socio-economic problems, CNRT leaders will need great vigilance and vision to resist neo-liberal pressures from diverse quarters.

Such issues have emerged quickly. The World Bank preliminary survey team made the sensible point that the new state could not afford to replace the very large numbers of Indonesian civil servants and called for a substantial reduction in the civil service. After ten days in the territory, it proposed a primary emphasis on agricultural recovery, particularly through coffee exports.

> We have an opportunity here to restore the agricultural cycle back to its normal situation if it's acted upon quickly. If the programs for the distribution of seeds and tools do not get underway quickly, then you would be in a situation of aid dependency for a longer period.[73]

One wonders if the whirlwind tour allowed the World Bank team time to observe the extremely widespread loss of one key element in Timor's shattered agricultural economy: buffalo for plowing and hauling, a fact long recognized by both CNRT and independent aid groups. Increasing productivity and the urgent distribution of seeds and tools are desirable goals, and coffee is an important crop and source of foreign exchange, particularly given that in East Timor it is "produced almost entirely by small-holder farmers, employing several thousand people."[74] But a January 2000 report from the United Nation's World Food Program underlines the dangers inherent in an export-oriented strategy: the one place in East Timor with confirmed malnutrition-related illness is the case of Lasaun in Ermera, which is an area historically prone to malnutrition, because of a number of reasons. This goes back to geographic vulnerability. They get cut off in the wet season. They are a community that relies on cash crops as opposed to food crops; their main product is coffee.[75]

Another issue is the apparent sense of superiority among some U.N. officials: "East Timor has 'no leadership class,'" one U.N. official lamented, adding: "How are we in the United Nations going to find five hundred competent people who can come and run the country?" Presumably the multiple skills required to sustain twenty-four years of resistance and survival and the construction of social movements are not among the job descriptions.

In the aftermath of the destructive decolonization of East Timor, the tasks of rehabilitation, infrastructure reconstruction, and economic development are formidable. A critical part of the process is the new village and subdistrict councils that have been forming in each of East Timor's 442 villages since March 2000 as the core of a community empowerment project promoted by the World Bank and by CNRT. These democratically-elected village councils will consist of one man and one woman elected from each hamlet, with a similar gender balance for the subdistrict councils. The councils will administer grants, initially $5,000 to $15,000 rehabilitation grants designated for rebuilding infrastructure from meeting halls to water systems. They are expected to play a leading role in planning, attracting local funding, and other forms of support for subsequent development projects from within the village community.[76]

One important issue will be whether or not CNRT will attempt to build on the initiatives in village-level agricultural cooperatives undertaken by Fretilin in the first year of its brief existence.[77] The importance of this history lies not so much in the question of cooperatives as such as the manner in which village-level economic and social transformation is approached. Given the disastrous consequences of recent decades of war and dislocation, and the range of development advice that CNRT and UNTAET can be expected to receive from the IMF, the World Bank, and other donors and prospective investors, a critical question will be the extent to which economic approaches will be rooted in the indigenous social structures and based on forging close bonds with rural producers that served Fretilin and CNRT so well in the long years of resistance.

CONCLUSION

This review has touched on only the most pressing questions facing East Timor. If the problems are daunting, there are perhaps also strengths. One of the most encouraging aspects of the last phase of the Indonesian period in East Timor's history was the impressive work begun by East Timorese intellectuals and activists, including those in Indonesia and in the wider diaspora. Activists working under excruciatingly difficult conditions inside East Timor have displayed a keen sense of sophistication and commitment to justice and social development. With the coming of independence, these, together with the efforts of the United Nations and foreign nongovernmental organizations (NGOs), promise to provide a critical resource for the new country. Resistance over two decades, sustaining military, political, and cultural opposition in the face of overwhelming power, has honed valuable political skills and the recognition of the importance both of social and economic development in the villages and towns of East Timor and of linkages to supporters in the international community.

Politics is always a matter of inventing the future on the run. There is no perfect plan. But the most extraordinary resource of this small and beautiful country is the remarkable courage and resilience of its people.

NOTES

We are very grateful to Ben Anderson, Russell Goldflam, Geoffrey Gunn, Geoff McKee, and John Waddingham for suggestions and comments on earlier drafts.

1. See Geoffrey C. Gunn in this volume.

2. UNTAET Regulation No. 1999/2, 2 December 1999, <http://www.un.org/peace/etimor/untaetR/etreg2.htm>.

3. Briefing to the Security Council by Mr. Sergio Vieira de Mello, Special Representative of the Secretary General for East Timor, "On the situation in East Timor," New York, 3 February 2000, <http://www.reliefweb.int>, This Web site is for the U.N. Office for the Coordination of Humanitarian Affairs.

4. UNTAET Regulation No. 2000/24, On the Establishment of a National Council, 14 July 2000.

5. *Report of the Secretary-General on the United Nations Transitional Administration in East Timor (for the period 27 January–26 July 2000)*, S/2000/738, United Nations Security Council, 26 July 2000.

6. "Top E. Timor Official Says U.N. Acting Like Dictator," Reuters, 10 November 1999.

7. Paul Daley, "Gusmão Wary of Bank's Policy Push," *Sydney Morning Herald*, 10 November 1999.

8. The full text of CNRT Magna Carta is available at <http://www.easttimor.com/cnrt/cnrt_0025.htm>.

9. For details of the composition of CNRT and its National Political Commission see "East Timor Activists Agree on Statutes for New Council," <http://www.easttimor.com/cnrt/cnrt.htm>.

10. See Yayasan HAK, "From 'Scorched Earth Operation' to 'Humanitarian Operation,' " Dili, [accessed 10 January 2000]. <http://etan.org/news/2000a/fromscor.htm>,

11. In late August 2000 the former pro-Indonesia integration party, Apodeti, was reported to be applying to join the CNRT. *Tempo Interactive*, 23 August 2000.

12. The U.N. secretary general's report in July summarized these trends as follows: "Regrettably, there have been disturbing cases of intimidation against groups and parties

not under the CNRT umbrella. CPD-RDTL, a group that split from Fretilin, has encountered sometimes violent CNRT opposition, especially in the Suai area. In June, unknown assailants vandalized the Dili office of the Student Solidarity Council, one of the strongest proindependence groups in East Timor prior to the popular consultation. In March, death threats were directed against the staff of the Catholic Radio Timor Kmanek to prevent their announcers' speaking about politics on the radio. Ethnic and religious minorities have also been the targets of harassment and intimidation. On 8 June, the Protestant churches in Ermera and Aileu were burned. There were also several attacks on the mosque in Dili, and ethnic Chinese were threatened and harassed." *Report of the Secretary-General on the United Nations Transitional Administration in East Timor (for the period 27 January–26 July 2000)*, S/2000/738, United Nations Security Council, 26 July 2000.

13. Interview with José Ramos-Horta, Radio Australia, Asia-Pacific, 28 August 2000.

14. Edward Said, *Peace and Its Discontents* (New York: Vintage, 1995); Ibrahim Shehadeh, *Abuses of the Palestinian Security Forces (March 1996–June 1996)*, Gaza Center for Rights and Law, July 1996; Mouin Rabbani, "Palestinian Authority, Israeli Rule: From Transitional to Permanent Arrangement," *Middle East Report* 201 (Fall 1996); Yifat Susskind, "Palestinian Political Prisoners," *Middle East Report* 201 (Fall 1996); Amnesty International, *Palestinian Authority Defying the Rule of Law: Political Detainees,* MDE 21/03/99, April 1999; Palestinian Society for the Protection of Human Rights & the Environment, "Judicial Independence in PNA–Controlled Areas (Reality and Ambitions)," 1999, <http://www.lawsociety.org/Reports/Files/Judind.htm>.

15. See Jill Jolliffe, *East Timor: Nationalism and Colonialism* (St. Lucia: University of Queensland Press, 1978); and Helen Hill, "Fretilin: The Origins, Ideologies, and Strategies of a Nationalist Movement in East Timor," (master's thesis, Monash University, 1978).

16. Constâncio Pinto and Matthew Jardine, *East Timor's Unfinished Struggle: Inside the Timorese Resistance* (Boston: South End, 1997), 47.

17. See, for example, East Timor Human Rights Centre, *Violence by the State Against Women in East Timor: A Report to the U.N. Special Rapporteur on Violence Against Women, Including Its Causes and Consequences*, Prepared by Dr. George J. Aditjondro (Newcastle University, Australia), 7 November 1997, Ref: R 7/97; Miranda E. Sissons, *From One Day to Another: Violations of Women's Reproductive and Sexual Rights in East Timor*, East Timor Human Rights Centre, SR 2/97, Melbourne 1997.

18. Charles E. Costello, testimony before the Asia and the Pacific Subcommittee of the House International Relations Committee and the East Asia and Pacific Affairs Subcommittee of the Senate Foreign Relations Committee, 10 February 2000.

19. U.N. Press Briefing, Press Conference on East Timor by Xanana Gusmão and José Ramos-Horta, 28 September 1999.

20. United Nations Transitional Administration in East Timor, Dili, <http://www.reliefweb.int>, [accessed 8 March 2000].

21. U.N. Transitional Administration in East Timor, "UNTAET Humanitarian Pillar Situation Report 04 to 06 Mar 2000," <http://www.reliefweb.int>, [accessed 6 March 2000].

22. See also José Ramos-Horta, *Funu: The Unfinished Saga of East Timor* (Lawrenceville, N.J.: Red Sea Press, 1996), 29–39.

23. U.N. Administrative Committee on Coordination/Sub-Committee on Nutrition (ACC/SCN), 3 March 2000.

24. U.N. peacekeeping forces in western East Timor came under fire four times in twenty-four hours on March 3. U.N. authorities regarded it as "a deliberate and coordinated effort" apparently unimpeded by Indonesian military forces. Associated Press, 3 March 2000.

25. Interpress Service, 7 September 2000.

26. Noam Chomsky and Edward Herman, *After the Cataclysm: Postwar Indochina and the Reconstruction of Imperial Ideology* (Boston: South End Press, 1979), 38–39.

27. Mark Dodd, "Fretilin Admits Its Bloody Past to Ensure East Timor's Future," *Sydney Morning Herald*, 15 May 2000.

28. See the comments by CNRT Representative to the United Nations and North America, Constâncio Pinto: *The Future of East Timor: An Interview with Constâncio Pinto, October 28, 1999*, on Asia Society web site, <http://www.asiaSource.org/news/>, [accessed 3 November 1999]. Pinto does not, unfortunately, address the issue of militia fighters.

29. However, a senior United Nations prosecutor investigating Indonesian war crimes committed in 1999 plans to compile a report on atrocities going back to 1975 in order to prove a pattern of systematic abuses. See Mark Dodd, "War-Crimes Lawyer to Study 1975 Invasion," *Sydney Morning Herald*, 26 August 2000.

30. See, for example, the reactions of Amnesty International and Human Rights Watch: Amnesty International, "Indonesia: Retroactivity Amendment Regressive for Human Rights," Press Release, 18 August 2000, AI Index ASA 21/033/2000—News Service Nr. 159, <http://www.amnesty.org/news/2000/32103300.htm>; and Human Rights Watch, "Indonesia: Lawmakers Let Perpetrators off the Hook," <http://www.hrw.org/hrw/press/2000/08/indo0819.htm>, [accessed 19 August 2000].

31. See, for example, Amnesty International, "East Timor. Demand for Justice," Report—ASA 21/191/99, 28 October 1999, <http://www.amnesty.org/ailib/aipub/1999/ASA/32119199.htm>, [accessed 16 November 1999].

32. Benedict Anderson, "Imagining 'East Timor,' " *Arena Magazine*, April–May 1993, 7.

33. Anderson, "Imagining 'East Timor,' " 7.

34. Cf. João Mariano Saldanha and Helder Da Costa, *Economic Viability of East Timor Revisited: Outlook for the 21st Century*, East Timor Study Group (ETSG) Working Paper 1. This was one of a number of papers at CNRT, Strategic Development Planning Conference, Melbourne, 5–9 April 1999, <http://www.ozemail.com.au/cnrt/confer.html>, [accessed 10 October 1999]. Saldanha and Da Costa's paper is a basic resource for future economic planning.

35. See David Lague, "Portugal's Legacy a Stumbling Block for East Timorese," *The Age*, 5 November 1999.

36. Joanne Collins, "Violence Erupts Among Timorese Job Applicants," Reuters, 15 January 2000.

37. "East Timor Chooses Portuguese As Official Language," Associated Press, 11 February 2000.

38. Media release, First Congress of the East Timor Students Solidarity Council, Dili, 28 July 2000.

39. See Geoffrey C. Gunn, "Language, Literacy and Political Hegemony in East Timor," in *The Politics of Multiculturalism in the Asia/Pacific*, ed. David Myers (Darwin: Northern Territory University Press, n.d.), 117–23.

40. "Shadows," (Editorial) *Lalenok*, Dili, 18–25 January 2000 (editor-in-chief: Virgilio da Silva Guterres), <http://etan.org/et2000a/january/15–21/18etfir.htm>.

41. East Timor International Support Group, discussion paper about planning for an independent East Timor, has a useful brief listing of legal issues. <http:www.com/html/notices4.html>.

42. For a review of property holdings of Indonesian political and military elites and their East Timorese allies, see George Aditjondro, "Unmasking the Interests Behind the Pro-Jakarta Militias," APCET website, <http://www1.qzn.skyinet.net/apcet/views-militia.htm> [accessed 8 November 1999].

43. See, for example, Daniel Cooney, "Land Disputes Disrupt E. Timor," Associated Press, 16 July 2000.

44. The following section draws in part on Australian Government, Department of Industry, Science and Resources, *Submission to the Senate Foreign Affairs, Defense and Trade References Committee Inquiry into East Timor*, 21 June 1999, <http://www.isr.gov.au/resources/timor-gap>, and Geoffrey McKee, "The New Timor Gap: Will Australia Now Break With the Past?" *Inside Indonesia*, No. 62, April–June 2000.

45. Cable of 17 August 1975, in J. R. Walsh and G. J. Munster, *Documents on Australian Defence and Foreign Policy, 1968–1975* (Sydney: Hale & Iremonger, 1980). The Australian government went to court to ban this book.

46. "East Timor to Renegotiate Oil and Gas—Horta," Reuters, 30 January 2000.

47. See, for example, CNRT *Statement on Timor Gap Oil*, 22 July 1998, <http://etan.org/et/1998/july/july14–21/21CNRoil.htm>: "CNRT supports the rights of the existing Timor Gap contractors and those of the Australian Government to jointly develop East Timor's offshore oil reserves in cooperation with the people of East Timor."

48. Phillips Petroleum, however, has indicated its strong preference for the provisions of the Treaty to remain in place: "We need the legal surety of the treaty to remain in place along with its economic and fiscal terms *and we are confident it will remain in place.*" (authors' emphasis) *The Australian*, 27 October 1999, 41.

49. Paul Tait, "East Timor Backs Gas Project but Warns on Treaty," Reuters, Darwin, 10 November 1999.

50. See "East Timor May Be Sidelined in New Timor Sea Discussion," Stratfor, Commentary, 18 February 2000, <http://www.stratfor.com/asia/commentary/0002182346.htm>.

51. Ferdi Tanoni, chairman of the Communication Forum of businessmen from East Nusa Tenggara, East Timor and Australia, "New Govt. Expected to Ratify Timor Gap," *Indonesian Observer*, 29 October 1999; "Indonesia's E Nusa Tenggara to Lobby for Share in E Timor Gap," Antara, 28 February 2000.

52. For suggestions to this effect, see George Aditjondro, "Unmasking the Interests Behind the Pro-Jakarta Militias."

53. Asia Pulse, "Timor Gap Oil Could Be a Source of New Conflict: Analyst," 27 September 1999, APCET website, <http://www1.qzn.skyinet.net/apcet/views-timor-gap.htm>. This is most noticeable in the attitude of the Northern Territory (NT) government, the part of Australia with closest relations with both East Timor and Indonesia. The NT capital of Darwin has been the main Australian base of both the relief efforts and the peacekeeping operations. The extremely conservative Northern Territory government, after many years of completely ignoring the East Timor issue and local East Timorese

refugees, overnight became vociferous not only in support of East Timorese self-determination, but also in its willingness to help with relief efforts. One of the authors (Tanter) observed letters sent directly by the NT government to large numbers of businesses in Darwin and elsewhere in October 1999 urging them to combine sympathy with self-interest and to not "miss their chance" in East Timor. The NT government views Timor Sea oil and gas development as "providing substantial impetus to the Territory economy." The NT government's "vision" involves Darwin as a regional offshore service center; "reasonably priced gas" to power mining and processing activities; value-added oil and gas processing; direct and indirect job creation; and gas supplies for southern Australia. See Northern Territory Government, Department of Mines and Energy, *Major Projects: Timor Sea*, 1 July 1997, <http://www.nt.gov.au/majorprojects/timorsea.shtml>, [accessed November 5, 1999].

54. "Indonesia-Australia Treaty on Timor Resources 'Illegal,' " *Energy Asia,* 24 July 2000, <http:www.energyasia.com>.

55. "Indonesia-Australia Treaty on Timor Resources 'Illegal.' "

56. See John Waddingham, "East Timor: How Many People Missing?" *Timor Information Service*, no. 28 (February 1980); reprinted with further comment in Australia, Senate Standing Committee on Foreign Affairs and Defense, *Inquiry into East Timor, Transcript of Evidence*, 1982, 697–714.

57. Waddingham refuted important criticisms of the 1980 study in his Senate testimony, *Inquiry into East Timor*, 710–14. Note that even Indonesian government figures are horrific: in November 1979, Foreign Minister Mochtar Kusumaatmadja acknowledged 120,000 East Timorese dead since 1975. (John G. Taylor, "East Timor: Contemporary History; A Chronology of the Main Events since 1974," in *East Timor at the Crossroads: The Forging of a Nation*, ed. Peter Carey and G. Carter Bentley [New York: Social Science Research Council/Honolulu: University of Hawaii Press, 1995], 240.)

58. "General Asks for Word on Fate of 80,000," *The Australian*, 4 November 1999.

59. "Report of the Secretary-General on the United Nations Transitional Administration in East Timor (for the period 27 January–26 July 2000)," United Nations, S/2000/738, 26 July 2000, paragraph 47; Carmel Eagan, "Mass Vanishing Remains a Mystery," *The Australian*, 8 January 2000.

60. Human Rights Watch, "East Timor: Serious Obstacles to Justice Remain," New York, 2 September 2000, <http://www.hrw.org/press/2000/09/etimsusp91.htm>.

61. Refugees International, "East Timorese Refugees in Indonesia," 23 February 2000, <http://www.reliefweb.int>; letter from NGOs to President Clinton, 27 January 2000, <http://www.etan.org/news/2000a/01ngo.htm>; "At least 547 Refugees Have Died In Indonesian W Timor: Governor," Associated Press 19 July 2000.

62. East Asia and Pacific Region—The World Bank: Background Paper Prepared for the Information Meeting on East Timor, 29 September 1999, 3. <http://www.worldbank.org/html/extdr/offrep/eap/pdfs/etimor/reconstruction.pdf>.

63. Robert Garran, "World Bank Rounds Up Cash Cows for E Timor," *The Australian*, 1 March 2000.

64. *United Nations InterAgency and NonGovernmental Organization Preliminary Assessment of Needs for Humanitarian Assistance for East Timorese: September 1999—February 2000, October 1999,* <http://www.reliefweb.int>. The assessment reported "almost total crop loss for 490,000 DPs (Displaced Persons) and partial crop loss for a

further 150,000 persons; externally displaced persons have not planted during last harvest and have no food stocks left. If the October/November planting season for maize and rice is successful (i.e. sufficient seeds and rains), most of the displaced persons could be reasonably self-sufficient after the next harvest, in March. However, lack of seeds and lack of land preparation are likely to be major constraints."

65. East Asia and Pacific Region—The World Bank: Background Paper Prepared for the Information Meeting on East Timor, 29 September 1999, 3.

66. "WHO," Agence France-Presse, 7 March 2000.

67. "Disease Emerges as New, Deadlier Threat in East Timor," Australian Broadcasting Corporation Transcript, 7:30 News with Kerry O'Brien, 10 March 2000.

68. Briefing by de Mello (see note 3).

69. Saldanha and Da Costa, *Economic Viability of East Timor Revisited.*

70. Pinto, *The Future of East Timor.*

71. "East Timor: CNRT Drops Euro Plan for Dollar," *Financial Times*, 25 January 2000.

72. Paul Daley, "Gusmão Wary of Bank's Policy Push," *Sydney Morning Herald*, 9 November 1999.

73. "World Bank to Recommend Smaller Govt. Budget For East Timor," *Dow Jones Newswire*, 9 November 1999.

74. Mark Dodd, "Fine Coffee Offers Sweet Smell of Trading Success," *Sydney Morning Herald*, 28 February 2000.

75. Press briefing by Kerren Hedlund of the World Food Program, Dili, U.N. Transitional Administration in East Timor, 28 January 2000, <http://www.reliefweb.int>.

76. UNTAET Regulation No. 2000/13, "On the Establishment of Village and Sub-District Development Councils for the Disbursement of Funds for Development Activities," 10 March 2000, <http://www.un.org/peace/etimor/untaetR/Reg0013E.pdf>. Some leading U.N. officials in East Timor are said to be reluctant to promote the community empowerment project, and CNRT has been frustrated at the slow pace of the project's implementation. See Mark Dodd, "U.N. Staff Battle Over Independence Policy," *Sydney Morning Herald*, 13 March 2000, and Joanna Jolly, "Respect for U.N. Mission Is Falling, Warns Local Adviser," *South China Morning Post*, 15 March 2000.

77. See John Taylor, "The Emergence of a Nationalist Movement in East Timor," in *East Timor at the Crossroads*, 21–41; and Hill, *Fretilin*. Taylor especially stresses Fretilin's success in articulating its political campaigns with indigenous social structures and value systems.

Glossary

ABRI. *Angkatan Bersenjata Republik Indonesia*; Indonesian Armed Forces; a restructuring in early 1999 separated the armed forces (TNI) from the police (*Polri*), both of which had been part of ABRI.

Aitarak. Literally "Thorn"; major militia group organized by Indonesian military to oppose East Timor's independence, primarily active in Dili.

AMS. Agreement on Maintaining Security (Australia-Indonesia).

ANZUS. Australia-New Zealand-United States Security Treaty Organization, signed 1951.

Apodeti. *Associação Popular Democrática Timorense*; Timorese Popular Democratic Association, first called the Association for the Integration of Timor into Indonesia.

ARF. ASEAN Regional Forum.

ASDT. *Associação Social Democrática Timorense*; Timorese Social Democratic Association, forerunner of Fretilin.

ASEAN. Association of Southeast Asian Nations.

babinsa. Bintara pembina desa; TNI noncommissioned officer based in each village.

Bais. Strategic Intelligence Agency; Indonesian military intelligence; formerly BIA.

Bais ABRI. Indonesian military intelligence agency founded by Benny Murdani; later BIA, and then *Bais.*

BIA. Badan Intelijen ABRI; Armed Forces Intelligence Agency; Indonesian military intelligence; formerly *Bais* ABRI, later *Bais.*

Brimob Brigade Mobil; Police Mobile Brigade.

BRTT. *Barisan Rakyat Timor Timur*; East Timor People's Front; prointegration front group in East Timor.

bupati. District head.

CNRM. *Conselho Nacional da Resistência Maubere*; National Council of Maubere Resistance (became CNRT in 1998).

CNRT. *Conselho Nacional da Resistência Timorense*, National Council of Timorese Resistance, the principal proindependence formation in East Timor today.

Core Group. A group consisting of the United States, United Kingdom, Australia, New Zealand, and Japan that informed and guided the United Nation's East Timor policy.

CRRN. *Conselho Revolucionária de Resistência Nacional*; National Council of Revolutionary Resistance; formed 1981, forerunner of CNRM.

273

Dadurus Merah Putih. Red and White Typhoon; militia group active in Maliana subdistrict, Bobonaro district, East Timor.

dandim. District military commander.

Darah Integrasi. Blood of Integration; grouping of anti-independence militias in Ermera district, East Timor.

DEA. U.S. Drug Enforcement Administration.

Deplu. *Departemen luow negeri*; Indonesian Foreign Ministry.

DPA. United Nations Department of Political Affairs.

DPKO. United Nations Department of Peacekeeping Operations.

ETAN. East Timor *Action* Network; U.S. support group.

ETISC. East Timor International Support Center; Australian support group.

Falintil. Forças Armadas de Libertação Nacional de Timor-Leste; Armed Forces for the National Liberation of East Timor; armed wing of Fretilin and then of East Timorese resistance more generally under the command of CNRT.

FPDK. *Forum Persatuan, Demokrasi dan Keadilan*; Forum for Unity, Democracy and Justice; prointegration front group in East Timor.

Fretilin. *Frente Revolucionária do Timor-Leste Independente*; Revolutionary Front for an Independent East Timor; political party formed in 1974, leader in independence struggle.

funu. Tetum for war; used to refer to the historic East Timorese struggle.

GAM. *Gerakan Aceh Merdeka*; Free Aceh Movement.

Golkar. Golongan Karya; ruling party in Indonesia under Suharto and, subsequently, Habibie.

Habibie, B. J. Confidante of President Suharto; President of Indonesia, 1998–99.

Halilintar. Lightning/Thunderbolt; main militia group in Bobonaro district, East Timor, coordinating militia activities in neighboring districts as well.

Hametin Merah Putih. Red and White Vice; militia group active in Bobonaro subdistrict, Bobonaro district, East Timor.

IFET. International Federation for East Timor; formed in 1991 by groups from Europe, Japan, and North America to coordinate international NGO campaigns on behalf of East Timor.

IFET-OP. IFET Observer Project; organized to monitor August 1999 referendum in East Timor.

IMET. International Military Education and Training program; U.S. Pentagon program for training foreign military officers in the United States.

IMF. International Monetary Fund.

InterFET. International Force in East Timor; U.N.–authorized armed force led by Australia dispatched to East Timor in September 1999.

JAM. World Bank–led Joint Assessment Mission to East Timor, November 1999.

JCET. Joint Combined Education and Training program; U.S. program to provide military training for foreign military officers on foreign soil.

KIPER. *Komite Independen Pemantau Pemungutan Suara*; Independent Committee for Direct Ballot Monitoring; a joint Indonesian-East Timorese observer mission.

kodim. Komando Distrik Militer; district military headquarters.

Kopassus. Komando Pasukan Khusus; Special Forces Command, elite Indonesian commando unit.

koramil. Komando Rayon Militer; Military subdistrict command.

korem. Military subarea command.

Kostrad. (Indonesian) Army Strategic Reserve.

KPP-HAM. The (Indonesian) Commission for Human Rights Violations in East Timor, established on September 22, 1999, by the Indonesian National Human Rights Commission, *Komnasham.*

liurai. East Timor's historic village chiefs or district rulers, coopted by both the Portuguese and Indonesian colonial administrations; thus, the *liurai* system is the traditional feudal system.

Mahidi. Dead or Alive for Integration; prointegration militia group centered around Cassa in southern Ainaro district, East Timor.

Maubere. Originally a Mambai word meaning "my brother" that was used by the Portuguese colonial authorities as a derogatory term to mean "poor, ignorant native" and then reclaimed by Fretilin to mean a nationalist. Dropped when CNRT formed because UDT, one of the component organizations, opposed use of the term.

mestiço. People of mixed Sino-Timorese, Afro-Timorese, Goan-Timorese, or Portuguese-Timorese ancestry.

MNF. Multinational force.

MPR. *Majelis Permusyawaratan Rakyat*; Indonesian People's Consultative Assembly (parliament). Sometimes referred to as the Super Parliament because it includes all the members of the DPR (*Dewan Perwakilan Rakyat*; People's Representative Council)—a parliamentary body that sits throughout the year and passes legislation—plus members drawn from elected provincial assemblies as well as some unelected "functional groups" such as the military. The MPR meets to appoint and dismiss the president, alter the constitution, and set "guidelines to state policy."

NCC. National Consultative Commission, established in East Timor by UNTAET, the U.N. Transitional Administration.

NGO. Nongovernmental organization.

PA. Palestinian Authority.

PAM Swakarsa. Pengomanan Swakarsa; Volunteer Community Security; formed in January 1998 from Islamic groups backing Suharto; later the formalized structure for some prointegration militias in East Timor.

PAN. *Partai Amanat Nasional*; National Mandate Party; Indonesian political party, headed by Amien Rais.

PDI-P. *Partai Demokrasi Indonesia-Perjuangan;* Indonesian Democratic Party of Struggle, headed by Megawati Sukarnoputri and formed by her and her supporters to contest the 1999 elections after government ousted her as leader of the *Partai Demokrasi Indonesia* (PDI).

PKB. *Partai Kebangkitan Bangsa*, National Awakening Party, Indonesian party headed by Abdurrahman Wahid.

PKI. *Partai Komunis Indonesia*, Indonesian Communist Party, decimated in 1965–67 massacre.

Polri. Polisi Republik Indonesia; Indonesian Police.

Renetil. Underground organization of East Timorese students in Indonesia.

SGI. *Satgas Intel*; *Satuan Tugas Intellijen*; *Kopassus* intelligence unit

Subianto, Prabowo. Son-in-law of Suharto, former lieutenant general, key military officer in East Timor, member of SGI and *Kopassus.*

Suharto. General who led military coup in 1965; second president of Indonesia, 1967–98.

Sukarno. Leader of Indonesian independence struggle and first president of independent Indonesia, until Suharto coup in 1965–67.

Sukarnoputri, Megawati. Current vice president of Indonesia; daughter of Sukarno; opposition leader, head of PDI-P and the leading vote recipient in the 1999 Indonesian election.

TGT. Timor Gap Zone of Cooperation Treaty, 1989; treaty between Australia and Indonesia allocating oil and gas rights in the waters between Australia and East Timor.

Timor Loro Sae. East Timor; term used by Timorese for independent East Timor; literally, "Timor of the Rising Sun" in Tetum, used widely even preindependence, to contrast with Timor Timur (East Timor in Indonesian).

TNI. *Tentara Nasional Indonesia,* Indonesian National Armed Forces (see ABRI).

Udayana IX. Name of the Indonesian Regional Military Command (number 9) that ran from Bali (where its headquarters are) to East Timor. East Timor is no longer part of this.

UDT. *União Democrática Timorense;* Timorese Democratic Union; moderate East Timorese party, initially favored independence after extended period of autonomy, then led unsuccessful coup in 1975 against Fretilin in support of integration with Indonesia; in 1998 became part of the nationalist movement for independence.

UNAMET. United Nations Assistance Mission in East Timor, the U.N. mission that conducted the August 30, 1999, referendum on independence or integration.

Unetim. *União Nacional de Estudantes Timorense;* National Union of Timorese Students.

UNHCR. United Nations High Commissioner for Refugees.

UNTAET. United Nations Transitional Administration in East Timor; U.N. governing authority for East Timor until independence, authorized by the Security Council.

Wahid, Abdurrahman. President of Indonesia, October 20, 1999–.

About the Contributors

Peter Bartu has worked with the United Nations in Cambodia (1991–93, 1998), the Democratic Republic of the Congo (1998), and East Timor (1999). He speaks Indonesian. Email: pbartu@ozemail.com.au.

Noam Chomsky is Institute Professor of linguistics at the Massachusetts Institute of Technology. He is the author of books on politics and the media, most recently *The New Military Humanism: Lessons from Kosovo* (1999). Email: chomsky@mit.edu.

Richard Falk is Albert G. Milbank Professor of International Law and Practice at Princeton University where he has been on the faculty since 1961. His most recent book is *Predatory Globalization: A Critique* (1999). Email: rfalk@princeton.edu.

Geoffrey C. Gunn teaches in the faculty of economics, Nagasaki University, Japan. His most recent book is *New World Hegemony in the Malay World* (2000). Email: nag-gunn@net.nagasaki-u.ac.jp.

Peter Hayes is co-executive director of the Nautilus Institute for Security and Sustainable Development (Berkeley, California). Professionally active as an environment and energy consultant in developing countries, he also writes widely about security affairs in the Asian-Pacific region. Email: phayes@nautilus.org.

Wade Huntley is program director for Asia-Pacific Security at the Nautilus Institute for Security and Sustainable Development. His areas of expertise include international security, nuclear nonproliferation and arms control, political relations in the Asia-Pacific region, and political theory. Email: huntley@nautilus.org.

Arnold S. Kohen is author of *From the Place of the Dead: The Epic Struggles of Bishop Belo of East Timor* (1999). Email: askohen@aol.com.

Allan Nairn, who was badly beaten while reporting the Santa Cruz massacre in Dili, East Timor, in 1991, is an award-winning correspondent for *The Nation*. He is the author of *Our Kind of Guys: The United States and the Indonesian Military* (1999).

Sarah Niner is completing her doctoral dissertation on the life of Xanana Gusmão at Latrobe University in Melbourne, Australia. She is editor of *To Resist is to Win: The Autobiography and Selected Writings of Xanana Gusmão* (2000). Her interest in East Timor stems from a visit there in 1991. Email: S.Niner@latrobe.edu.au.

Constâncio Pinto was head of the East Timorese underground movement until 1992, when he was forced to flee the country. He now serves as the CNRT representative to the United States and Canada. Email: constancio@igc.org.

Geoffrey Robinson is professor of Southeast Asian history at UCLA and author of *The Dark Side of Paradise: Political Violence in Bali* (1995). Email: robinson @history.ucla.edu.

João Mariano Saldanha is executive director of the East Timor Study Group (ETSG) and a Ph.D. candidate in political economy, Graduate School of International Relations and Pacific Studies, University of California, San Diego. Email: jsaldanha@aol.com or jsaldanh@ucsd.edu.

Charles Scheiner is national coordinator of the East Timor *Action* Network (ETAN) in the United States and represents the International Federation for East Timor (IFET) at the United Nations in New York. He was International Coordinator for the IFET Observer Project and was an accredited observer in East Timor for two weeks before and one week after the referendum. Email: charlie@ etan.org.

Mark Selden teaches sociology and history at Binghamton University and is regional and comparative editor of the *Bulletin of Concerned Asian Scholars*. His recent books include *China in Revolution: The Yenan Way Revisited*, *Censoring History: Citizenship and Memory in Japan, Germany, and the United States* (with Laura Hein), and *Chinese Society: Change, Conflict, and Resistance* (with Elizabeth Perry). Email: ms44@cornell.edu.

Stephen R. Shalom teaches political science at William Paterson University in New Jersey and is a co-editor of the *Bulletin of Concerned Asian Scholars*. Among his books are *The Philippines Reader* (co-edited with Daniel B. Schirmer) and *Imperial Alibis: Rationalizing U.S. Intervention after the Cold War*. Email: shaloms@wpunj.edu.

Richard Tanter teaches politics and sociology at Kyoto Seika University. His main areas of current research are Indonesian military politics and the role of intelligence organizations and contemporary Japanese nationalism. With Ken Young he edited *The Politics of Middle Class Indonesia.* Email: richard@kyoto-seika.ac.jp.

Gerry van Klinken teaches Asian studies at Griffith University (Brisbane, Australia). He edits the quarterly *Inside Indonesia.* Email: editor@insideindone sia.org.

Helene van Klinken is an Indonesian language teacher who has lived and worked in Indonesia and East Timor.

Timorese poets **Elizabete Lim Gomes, Emanuel Braz**, and **Fernando Pires** were all born in East Timor. They all were forced to leave their homeland at various stages of their lives and have since been living abroad. They are currently writers, arts organizers, and performers in Melbourne's East Timorese community. Their work has a strong emphasis on healing and empowering the community. All three writers have been working in Puckapunyal where more than eight hundred East Timorese who fled the latest violence have been accommodated.